WHO KILLED LYNNE HARPER?

WHO KILLED LYNNE HARPER?

By Bill Trent with Steven Truscott

OPTIMUM PUBLISHING COMPANY LIMITED

Montreal · Toronto

Published by Optimum Publishing Company Limited, Montreal

Legal deposit-4th trimester 1979
Bibliothèque nationale du Québec

Design: Suzanne Vincent Poirier

For information contact:
Optimum Publishing Company Limited
245 rue St-Jacques
Montreal, Quebec
H2Y 1M6
Michael S. Baxendale, Director

ISBN 0-88890-115-1

Printed and bound in Canada

ACKNOWLEDGMENT

I am indebted to the National Parole Board which, in 1969, granted me permission to conduct extensive and exclusive interviews with Steven Truscott. The interviews provided the basis of a first book, entitled *The Steven Truscott Story,* and led eventually to this present work. I am grateful for the co-operation of a number of individuals. In particular, I am grateful to Kingston Penitentiary psychiatrist Dr. George Scott and Mr. E.B. Jolliffe, Q.C. for their kind consideration and understanding in the crucial pre-publication period. I should also like to thank my publishers Optimum Publishing Company, and their editor Jill Schichter, whose insistence on detail and elaboration has done much to provide a new clarity and understanding of a complex subject.

INTRODUCTION

This is the twentieth anniversary of one of the most widely-discussed murder cases in the history of Canada.

The victim was Lynne Harper, twelve-year-old daughter of Flying Officer Leslie Harper, raped and murdered in deep woods just beyond what was then a Royal Canadian Air Force station at Clinton in Ontario's Huron County, in 1959.

Charged, convicted and sentenced to hang for that murder was a fourteen-year-old classmate named Steven Murray Truscott, son of the late Warrant Officer Dan Truscott.

Steven Truscott, who has been proclaiming his innocence ever since the terrible June night of the murder, spent four months in a death cell, fully expecting the hangman to put the noose around his neck. His sentence finally was commuted to life and he served ten years behind bars.

This year marks the tenth anniversary of his release on parole.

Steven Truscott is thirty-four now, and looking at him today, you'd have to say he has a lot going for him. In fact, a lot of people might envy him. He has a good job, a wife who loves him, two adoring children and a wide circle of friends (who know nothing, mind you, of the horrors he went through.)

How much more would a man want?

Well, Steven wants one more thing – and he wants it so badly, it hurts. He wants the world to know he is innocent.

In fact, if there is one thing that Steven Truscott cherishes above all else this anniversary year, it's the hope that someday soon he will be exonerated.

And that is really what this book is all about.

Some people may not like finding reference to themselves in the pages of this book. In fact, I suspect that some people are not going to like this book at all.

But if I have trodden on some important toes, or tweaked the tails of some special sacred cows, I can only say I have done so in the hope of bringing justice to an individual who has spent twenty years of his life without it.

The killing of Lynne Harper is a bizarre story in which there are far more questions than answers. Some of the incidents recorded here will baffle you, I am sure. Some may even frighten you, as they did me.

The case officially is closed. Steven has served his time in prison. Yet still people come forward with information and accusations. Some of them do so though fearing for their lives. I believe the serious reader has to end up asking this one very pertinent question:

If Steven Truscott was really guilty, why did all these people come forward? And why do they continue to do so in 1979, twenty years after the crime?

The answer to that, of course, has to be that Steven Truscott is *not* guilty.

This book has three distinct sections. It is, in fact, three books in one. The first deals with the public outcry and subsequent investigations of the murder. The second is Steven's own sad, personal story, and the third contains the majority and minority reports of the Supreme Court. To assure a fuller understanding of the complexities of the story, a system of cross-references has been introduced.

The names of several people in this book have been changed to protect their identity. These fictitious names are: Hank Peterson, Mrs. Nichols and Luc Gagnon.

Every writer hopes his book will make good reading. But I have a more important hope. I hope it will lead to the killer, or killers, of Lynne Harper, and the exoneration of Steven Truscott.

I believe it may well do just that.

Bill Trent
October 1979

CONTENTS

BOOK ONE

Who Killed Lynne Harper?

BOOK TWO

BOOK THREE

BOOK I

Who Killed Lynne Harper?

TUESDAY, JUNE 9, 1959

Tuesday, June 9, 1959, had been a sweltering hot day on the Royal Canadian Air Force station at Clinton, Ontario, and Lynne Harper, twelve-year-old daughter of Flying Officer Leslie Harper and his wife Shirley, having just gulped down her supper, asked her parents to take her to the pool. They refused and an argument ensued. Annoyed, she walked out of the house shortly after six o'clock without telling anyone where she was going.

She walked to nearby A.V.M. Hugh Campbell School and there on the grounds she joined in a scavenger hunt with some Brownies. Some time later, spotting a fourteen-year-old classmate named Steven Murray Truscott, sitting on his bicycle, she wandered over to chat. After a brief conversation, she got on the crossbar of his bicycle and the two cycled off down the county road toward the main highway.

When Lynne failed to return home that night, Leslie Harper was worried. But he surmised that she had decided to stay over with friends, perhaps as a way of punishing her parents because they had refused to take her swimming. When she didn't show up the next morning, however, he was frantic. He went about the base making inquiries, stopping finally at the Truscott house. There his worst fears were realized.

Steven Truscott reported that he had seen Lynne the previous evening. She had asked him to drive her to the highway, he said. He had taken her there, then cycled back to the bridge that spans the little Bayfield River, about a quarter of a mile away. From that point, he had seen a car pull over to the shoulder and he had

13

watched Lynne get into it. The car had been headed east toward Seaforth.

Harper lost no time. He called the Ontario Provincial Police and officers from the Goderich detachment soon were on the scene. Some time later, the air force organized a massive search of the area.

The following afternoon, Thursday, June 11, Lynne's maggot-infested body was discovered in a hollow in a wooded area known as Lawson's Bush, a second growth of ash, elm, maple and basswood owned by a farmer named Bob Lawson.

She had been raped and strangled with her own blouse.

Police questioned a great many people on the base, among them a dozen or more of the boys at A.V.M. Hugh Campbell School, but it was on Steven Truscott that the full focus of the investigation was to fall.

As far as the police could see, he was the last *known* person to have seen her alive.

The year 1959 had been a good one for the Truscotts – up until then.

Steven, highly popular among the pupils and much respected by his teachers, had reached a new level of achievement. He had been named Hugh Campbell's best all-around athlete and a trophy was to be presented to him. His father, Dan Truscott, a warrant officer, had also earned a special honor. In recognition of his work among young people, he had been voted Clinton station's Man of the Year.

Leslie Harper's daughter and Dan Truscott's son were classmates, but as officers seldom fraternized with other ranks, so also their children tended to lead separate existences. Lynne and Steven were acquaintances rather than friends. In fact, they seldom had anything to do with one another.

It was one of those strange quirks of fate that had placed Steven in the company of a girl with whom he hardly ever associated – on the very night of her murder. But that now-famous bicycle ride was destined to become the cornerstone on which one of the most controversial cases in the annals of Canadian crime would be constructed.

The police had nothing to go on – nothing, that is, but the knowledge that Steven had taken Lynne for a ride on his bicycle.

But the investigation they launched was to develop into a veritable modern-day Inquisition, a real-life nightmare from which Steven has never fully recovered.

It began in the back seat of an Ontario Provincial Police car, after he had been called out of class on the afternoon of the day after the murder, some twenty-four hours before Lynne's body was found.

Steven told a story he would repeat countless times without variation. He had driven Lynne to the highway, then cycled back to the bridge. From that point, he looked back to the highway and saw Lynne get into what looked like a gray-colored car. It was a 1959 Chevrolet, which he could identify at a distance by its big fins and tail-lights in the shape of cat's eyes. He had also caught a glimpse of something yellow, or orange, at the rear of the car, a licence plate perhaps, or a bumper sticker.

The police listened and then told him to return to class. Later the same afternoon, they were back, wanting him to go over the story again. This time, Dan Truscott was in the car.

Steven recalled that Lynne had mentioned wanting to visit the ponies. They were owned by a man who lived in a little white house on the highway, he said.

The police wanted to retrace the route of the bicycle ride and Steven directed them. They started near the school, where Steven had picked up the girl, drove down the county road past Lawson's Bush, across the Bayfield River bridge and came to a stop at Highway 8. Steven pointed to the shoulder where the car had pulled in for Lynne. Driving back along the county road, they stopped at the river. Standing on the bridge, they watched the traffic on the highway.

Again, they asked about the car. Was he *sure* it was a 1959 Chevrolet? Steven was sure. But how *could* he be, from that distance? Because he *knew* cars, he explained. Knew their lines, their special features. Most of the boys did.

A policeman would state later that it was not possible to identify the make of car from that distance. (See Supreme Court

15

Report, pages 229-230)

Later, I proved the fallacy of the policeman's statement for myself. I stood on the bridge and watched the traffic on the highway. I could see the cars plainly. Had I possessed Steven's knowledge, I certainly could have identified them.

When had he left home? What time had he met Lynne? When had he returned home?

He had left the house between 7:00 and 7:15 p.m., he remembered. He had met Lynne fifteen or twenty minutes later. He was back home, according to his mother, between 8:25 and 8:30.

Then they asked him to tell the whole story over again. From the beginning.

At home that night, Dorothy Truscott listened to her son's account of the police interview. She was worried. What had they expected him to say that he hadn't already said? Steven shrugged. Many of the boys had been questioned, he explained.

The next morning, Steven arrived at school to find the police car parked outside again. Once again, they called him out of class. This time they wanted to know who had seen him with Lynne.

Arnold (Butch) George, his school chum, had seen them, he said. He had waved from the bank of the Bayfield River as they crossed the bridge. Douglas Oats, who had been digging for turtles, had seen them, too. And Gordon Logan, and Richard Gellatly, and... (See Supreme Court Report, pages 218-9, 304-5)

Then Steven remembered an old car had passed them as they cycled toward the highway. It had two occupants, a man and a woman. It bore licence plate number 981-666, he remembered, although he wasn't sure that the first three digits were actually in that order.

When Steven got home from school that day, he heard the news from his parents. Lynne's body had been found. Shocked and saddened, the Truscotts sat down to a silent supper.

After the meal, Steven paid one of his frequent visits to his farmer friend, Bob Lawson. As he walked back home, a police car pulled up alongside him.

"Truscott," the driver called out. "Get in."

The police took him to the R.C.A.F. guardhouse and there

16

they kept him for what Steven still remembers as "seven terrible hours."

Inspector Harold Graham, of Toronto, (now Commissioner of the Ontario Police) had taken charge of the investigation and the questions came in rapid-fire procession.

Steven, frightened for the first time and trembling, recounted the story of his ride to the highway, to Graham and the two officers who had picked him up.

Had Lynne asked for a ride, or had Steven suggested it to her, one of the officers asked? Did he often give rides to girls, another inquired? Had he taken someone to Lawson's Bush before? Was Lynne familiar with that wooded area?

The questions went on and on.

The police had disbelieved Steven's story practically from the start and now they believed they had further information to indicate he was lying.

They had traced licence number 981-666 to someone named Thompson, in Brampton, Ontario who said he had been nowhere near Clinton on the night of the murder. Transposing the first three digits, they had then produced the following registration information: licence number 189-666 belonged to one Vasil, of Toronto; 198-666, to one Mika, of Scarborough; 819-666 to McLaren, of Drumbo; 918-666, to a Miss Wilkins, of Kitchener. None of those cars had been in the area.

The final transposed number checked was 891-666, registered to a Mr. Pigun (also spelled Pigeon in certain sections of the transcript), then on the R.C.A.F. station at Clinton. Pigun, or Pigeon, said he had not been on the county road at the time. (See Supreme Court Report, pages 276-7, 296-8, 308-9)

The licence number given by Steven then had no relevance. Yet later, at the trial, presiding judge Mr. Justice R. I. Ferguson would confuse the issue in his charge to the jury by mentioning the licence number in connection with Steven's story of the car that had stopped for Lynne. Steven had never said he had *read* the plate on the car at the highway. He had simply seen a *color*. The licence number he mentioned had belonged to the vehicle that overtook him on the county road. It was one of many bungled pieces of information that damaged his credibility. (See Supreme Court Report, pages 229-30)

While the police questioned Steven, Dan Truscott was searching the base frantically for him. It was not like Steven to be away for long periods. About eleven o'clock, after checking with several neighbors, Dan went to the guardhouse. There he found the boy.

Inspector Graham introduced himself to Dan and promptly informed him that he believed his son had killed Lynne Harper.

By now, the police were in possession of a highly damning autopsy report from district pathologist Dr. John Llewellyn Penistan, of Stratford. That report placed Lynne's time of death at between 7:00 p.m. and 7:45 p.m., or roughly around the time Steven had driven the girl down the county road. It was a time estimate that would be disputed at length by medical experts in the days to come. (See Supreme Court Report, pages 233 - 242 , 247- 263)

Steven asked his father to take him home. He was exhausted. But Graham wasn't finished. He wanted a medical examination of the boy.

Steven was taken into an anteroom where two doctors examined him: J.A. Addison, a Clinton general practitioner, and David Hall Brooks, the station medical officer. They found lesions on his penis and made a quick assumption: they could have been the result of forced penetration of a young undeveloped female.

Dr. Brooks would make it clear later at the trial, that the sores indicated a "very inexpert attempt at penetration." It was a statement that would be criticized later by Supreme Court Justice Emmett Hall. The doctor, the Justice would say, was "testifying as an expert as to a matter that was not in his special knowledge." (See Supreme Court Report, pages 243-4, 278-9, 301-2)

The doctors, however, didn't restrict themselves to the medical examination. For more than an hour, they fired questions at him, Dr. Addison taking extensive longhand notes that later would be produced in court.

The questions produced no new information, of course, because Steven had only one story to tell – the story he had told all along. What other story could he tell? He was telling the truth.

At one point, the doctors left Steven alone in the anteroom while they discussed their findings with the police in the main area of the guardhouse. Then, after a short talk, Dr. Addison said he was going back to see if he could "get a story out of that boy."

It was another bizarre aspect of the investigation. The doctors were playing detective.

The medical examination, however, was all the evidence the police needed. When they confronted Steven again, it was to tell him that his entire story had been a lie.

There had been no bicycle ride to the highway – and no mystery cars. He had, they said, taken Lynne into Lawson's Bush and there raped and killed her.

It had been a flagrant denial of human rights. Steven had been held without charge until the middle of the night. His parents had never been notified. (It was by chance that his father had found him.) He had never been advised (nor was Dan) that he was entitled to counsel. He had been called a liar. He had been browbeaten until he was exhausted, not only by the police but by the doctors.

It would have been a heavy interrogation for a hardened criminal. For a fourteen-year-old boy, it had been an inquisition without parallel.

Three months later, Steven Truscott went to trial in Goderich with the full assurance of his counsel, Frank Donnelly (later appointed a judge), that no jury would ever convict him on the flimsy, highly circumstantial evidence the police had gathered against him.

Frank Donnelly was proved wrong – but then, he hadn't counted on the open hostility of the Huron County jurors who heard the case.

Toronto writer Isabel LeBourdais interviewed eleven of the jurors (the twelfth refused to be involved) after the trial for her book, *The Trial of Steven Truscott,* with some astounding results.

These are some of the verbatim excerpts from those interviews:

"I knew the boy was guilty right from the start but he was so young and it was so sad, and I kept hoping that somehow they would prove he didn't do it, but they couldn't because, of course, he did."

"I knew by the third day no one was going to prove that young monster innocent. If we'd a had to stay there all winter to convict that fiend, I'd a stayed."

"The boy is an animal capable of anything, isn't afraid of a thing. Sat there looking as though what he'd done meant nothing to him. No emotions. He needs a psycho."

"Of course everyone knew about the police case before the trial. Terrible thing, but the police knew he was guilty. It was so obvious."

These were some of the twelve Huron County men, tried and true, who judged Steven Truscott – and thus the conclusion was inevitable.

On September 30, 1959, Steven heard the ominous words of Mr. Justice Ferguson:

"The sentence of this court upon you is that you be taken from here to the place from whence you came and there be kept in close confinement until Tuesday, the 8th day of December, 1959, and upon that day and date you be taken to the place of execution, and that you there be hanged by the neck until you are dead, and may the Lord have mercy on your soul."

The date of execution subsequently was postponed and in January, 1960, the death sentence was commuted to one of life imprisonment.

THE PEOPLE REACT

The case, however, was not destined to end there. In 1966, as a result of a widespread public outcry for an investigation of alleged irregularities and legal discrepancies in the conduct of the trial, it was referred by the Governor-General-in-Council to the Supreme Court of Canada.

Eight judges subsequently signed a majority report upholding the conduct of the lower court as fair and legal. One dissenting judge wrote a minority report claiming the accused had been denied his fundamental rights in law and suggesting a new trial should be ordered.

The Supreme Court, by majority decision, thus confirmed Steven Truscott's guilt, presumably for all time.

Steven, released from Collins Bay Penitentiary in Kingston on October 21, 1969, at age twenty-four, after serving ten years, is now living under an assumed name in a place he wants to be known simply as *somewhere in Canada.* He is married to a girl who believed in his innocence strongly enough to circulate petitions for the Supreme Court hearing in 1966, and is the father of two, a girl of eight (at this writing), and a boy of four.

The Truscotts are getting along well enough, thank you, they say, despite their enforced anonymity, which they guard jealously, and a deep, though seldom surfacing resentment on the part of Steven that he is on life-long parole for a crime he didn't commit.

Steven has been proclaiming his innocence since the day of his arrest. At age fourteen, however, he was too young to understand the many legal implications of his trial, the contradictions in evidence which, as dissenting Supreme Court Justice Hall would point out later, should have acquitted him, and the web of character assassination the Crown succeeded in building around him, often with little or no explanation to the jury from the Bench. All he knew when he was finally convicted and sent to a death cell was that he was innocent, that he had *not* killed Lynne Harper.

Over the years, he has managed to retain a certain optimism about his eventual exoneration, this in spite of the fact that all of his proclamations to the police and the country's legal machine have fallen on truly stone-deaf ears. He still cherishes the hope that someday his name will be cleared. It is, in fact, his *dearest* hope. He admits, however, that sometimes the optimism is replaced by fears that time is against him, that being able to uncover new evidence so many years after the fact may well nigh be impossible.

"In all the world today," he says, "only two people know for sure that I'm innocent. One of them is me. The other is the killer."

I don't believe that.

Since Steven's release from penitentiary, I have come across considerable evidence to suggest that several people know he is innocent.

A plumber I met in Kitchener, for example, was certain Steven had had nothing to do with Lynne Harper's murder.

A woman in Clinton was also sure. She said the real killer was the subject of open discussion in her town, along with the reason he was never caught.

Two nurses called radio stations on separate occasions to say they knew Steven was not guilty.

There have been persistent reports over the years that Lynne Harper had been seen in Seaforth, a town about ten miles from Clinton, long after the time of her death, as estimated by Dr. Penistan. If this is so, then why has no one come forward with positive information?

The reason probably is fear – fear of getting *involved* in a murder case.

The driver of the car that stopped for Lynne on the highway

may, or may not, have been her murderer. Suppose then that he was *not* the killer. Suppose he was someone from the Clinton-Seaforth area who knew Lynne and who had simply done her the favor of picking her up. Why, if he were innocent, would he have withheld this information? It may be that he was frightened – frightened that he, and not Steven, might have become the last *known* person to have seen Lynne alive.

I have often been asked the obvious question, "Is Truscott *really* innocent?" My answer is a definite *yes*. Invariably then, there is a second question, "What makes you so sure?"

It would be easy to follow the thinking of all the thousands of Canadians who became Steven Truscott supporters. Easy to pick at the flimsy fabric woven around this airman's son during his trial. There were, after all, so many errors, omissions and contradictions in the proceedings, so many great gray areas, so many unexplained situations.

But I base my case for Steven's innocence on something else. Something quite unscientific, yet quite valid if you believe in the business of human relations.

With the approval of the National Parole Board, I went to work with Steven soon after his release. The editors of *Weekend Magazine* had agreed with me that his own personal story was strong magazine material and Canadian publisher Michael S. Baxendale felt it was also a good book project. Steven was enthused. After all, it would be the first time he would be able to tell his story in his own way.

I rented an apartment and, for several months, we lived together. Day in and day out, we worked on the story of his life from the time of his arrest. Some days I questioned him until we both had to give up in exhaustion.

With the possible exception of members of his family, I have spent more time with Steven Truscott than anybody in this country. The psychiatrists and psychologists saw him regularly in prison – but they saw him for a half-hour or an hour. I *lived* with him – ate with him, watched hockey games with him, saw movies with him and, in interviews, lived his life over again with him.

On two occasions, I even took him back to the scene of the

crime to re-trace his movements on the night of the murder. We drove from his old house on the air base to the schoolyard where he had picked up Lynne Harper, and from there to the highway where he had taken her on his bicycle. We then drove back to the bridge from which he had seen her get into a car.

If Steven Truscott was guilty, could he have gone back to Clinton with me twice to retrace his movements? I don't think so. Especially, I don't think he could have faked four months or more of intensive interviewing.

If Steven Truscott is innocent as I believe he is, then Lynne Harper's murderer has yet to be found.

I had hoped that publication of *The Steven Trucott Story* in 1971 might lead to the killer. It didn't. However, from the mass of information gathered since then, have come clues that may very well result in the murderer being found.

The phenomenon of the Truscott case is the widespread, active support it has generated over the years among concerned individuals, the majority of whom have had no personal connection whatever with any of the principals.

In fact, a kind of cult has grown up around Steven Truscott, composed of people who have devoted a great deal of time and energy – and, in some cases, considerable sums of money – in various unrelated efforts at establishing his innocence.

The legal machinery has long since ground to a halt but for these people, the story of Lynne Harper's rape and murder is very much an unsolved case. Steven Truscott, they steadfastly maintain, did *not* kill the girl.

But if Steven didn't kill her, then who did?

Was it a yet-unidentified youngster in a post-rape panic? (There were many teenagers on the station and in the civilian community.)

The murder scene would seem to rule out that possibility. Searchers who found the body noted that Lynne's shoes and socks, her hair band and her shorts lay in a neat pile beside her. The zipper on the shorts was in a closed position. None of this suggests the act of a frightened young boy.

Was it a psychotic adult driven by an urge to rape and kill?

One of the many unsolved riddles of the case concerned Lynne Harper's blouse. A 10-inch square had been cut out of it – and has never been found. Is it possible that a sex-perverted individual kept it to satisfy a fetish? Some observers think this may be the answer.

Was it a gang rape and murder?

Some investigators think so. Dr. Penistan's report gave credence to this theory. In Lynne Harper's upper vagina, Dr. Penistan said he found "tremendous quantities" of acid phosphates, an indication that she may well have been raped more than once, perhaps even several times. New evidence, contained in this book, supports this theory.

As a journalist, I am aware that a sensational murder case – and the Truscott case is now well-ensconced in the judicial history books as a *cause célèbre* – will bring all kinds of crackpots out of the woodwork. There are strange people who try to gain notoriety, or establish some kind of identity, by intimating they have inside knowledge of a crime. Some have even given in to that strange psychological urge to confess to a crime they didn't commit.

I was able to identify, and discount, these people in the Truscott affair – and there were quite a few. Others could not be discounted. The plumber, for instance. If he was fabricating a story, why would a friend warn him that he could be killed for what he was saying?

The incident happened in Kitchener during a promotional tour I was making with John Ross, a marketing executive of the Simon and Schuster of Canada publishing house. I had been interviewed about the Truscott case on the local television station and had fielded questions from callers, and that night in the Holiday Inn, John and I reviewed the events of the day over drinks. Later, walking through the lobby, we ran into a man protesting loudly that Steven Truscott hadn't murdered Lynne Harper and that he knew who had.

The woman with him told him he had had too much to drink and to keep quiet. When he persisted, she hustled him out into the parking lot. John followed them out and tried to persuade the couple to go to his room. They refused.

The next day, we related the incident to a *Kitchener Record* reporter. Later, we read this news story in the paper:

"A man who may be able to help defenders of Steven Truscott prove his innocence may live right here in Kitchener..."

"The man who identified himself only as a plumber and local resident said that Truscott was a 'patsy,' convicted for a murder he did not commit... The man said the town (Clinton) knew all along of Truscott's innocence."

Considering this worth following up, we talked to people at the Holiday Inn bar. They knew the man but not his name. "You can bet after he hears that news report on the radio, he ain't goin' show up at no bar," one customer quipped. The story was already on the air.

Somebody finally did come back with his name and John telephoned him. John, who boasted he could sell anything, sold the plumber the story that he was an architect planning to build a house for a Montreal businessman who was going to settle in Kitchener. That was me. John said he needed advice on plumbing fixtures. The plumber bought the story and showed up in John's room soon after.

Hank Peterson turned out to be a slight, nervous man and the friend who came with him seemed even more nervous. John talked plumbing but the two men kept watching me. They may have seen me on television but at one point, Hank said, "It's about Truscott, ain't it?" We agreed it was.

Peterson wanted to leave but John said he owed it to Steven to help clear his name. "You said last night Truscott didn't kill the girl," I ventured. He was silent. John and I kept firing questions at him. We wanted an answer: if Steven hadn't killed the girl, who had?

Hank began talking about a *gang bang.* More than one person had been involved, he thought. Perhaps three or four.

His friend, visibly agitated, got up out of his chair. "Let's get outta here," he urged.

"You've got to help that kid," John said, referring to Steven. "He doesn't want to spend the rest of his life in hiding."

"I don't know any more," Peterson said.

"Who took part in the *gang bang?*" I asked.

"I don't know." he hesitated. "But there are people who do."

"Shut up," his friend cut in. "Don't say any more. You can get yourself killed for saying things like that."

"Come on," I said. "Things like that don't happen in Kitchener."

"Yeah?" the man snapped. "Don't kid yourself. You can get a guy knocked off for a few bucks."

Peterson headed for the door, stopped and said, "There's a guy who knows."

"For Chrissake," his friend pleaded.

"Find a guy named Frenchie."

"Frenchie who?" John wanted to know.

"I dunno. They just called him Frenchie. He used to be around the base. A lotta people knew him."

Our efforts to find Frenchie through contacts in the Truscott case failed to turn up any clues. The interview with Peterson, however, was not the only strange thing that happened.

The next day, I was a guest on the Dick Berryman Show on CFPL-TV in London and facetiously I said I thought the real killer of Lynne Harper was in the area and, if so, I'd like to talk to him.

The lines were thrown open to the outside audience and a few minutes later, a woman who identified herself as a nurse went on the air.

"Steven Truscott is innocent," she said. "It was an adult on the base who killed her."

When the search for Lynne Harper's body was organized on the second day after her disappearance, she went on, this individual was able to suggest where the search should be made. He was able to do this, she added, because he *knew* where the body was.

"Careful," the interviewer cut in. "Libel."

The woman said no more. She hung up.

John emerged from the studio stunned. Coming so soon after the "plumber" adventure, the nurse's message had taken on a scary significance. Had she planned to *name* someone, John wondered?

There had been much conjecturing among Truscott supporters as to why the search centered initially on the woods. The only information in the possession of police prior to discovery of the body was Steven's story that he had taken the girl to the highway and that she had gotten into a car headed in the direction of Seaforth. Why then had they not begun their search beyond the base? Why had they not sought out clues in Seaforth? More significantly, why had they begun the search in Lawson's Bush, where Lynne's body lay? These questions have never been answered.

We tried to trace the nurse after the show but there had been so many calls to the studio that no record had been kept of them. (A similar incident occurred some four years later when a Toronto radio station aired an interview with Steven. Another woman, who also identified herself as a nurse, called the studio to say Steven was innocent. There was no record of that call either.)

For John Ross, however, there was more to come.

We were chatting in the kitchen of his former London home soon after the promotion tour when he decided to make a telephone call to a friend. After some good-natured chit-chat, John said that he and I were busy looking into the Truscott case. Suddenly the grin that had been on his face disappeared.

"Well, listen now," he mumbled. Moments later, he said, "Sure but...yeah, I read you...but wait a minute, I don't understand... ."

When John hung up, he was grim, his face an off-white. His wife, Muriel, brought coffee. "What's up?" she asked. "You look as if you've seen a ghost."

"That was..." he paused in mid-sentence, remembering I was there, "...an old friend. His name doesn't matter. He's an important man, knows everybody, everybody knows him. And do you know what he just said to me? He said, 'John, if you don't leave this thing alone, I'm going to go over there personally and shoot you.' "

It had been a figure of speech but it had left him shaken. The case had taken on undertones he couldn't understand. For that matter, neither could I.

I prodded John several times after this conversation but he would say nothing about it. Was John's friend shielding someone? It's possible, though I have nothing to substantiate this. If he was protecting someone, it certainly wouldn't be the killer. So, who could it be? And why?

I have no explanation for that telephone conversation. I have put it down as another one of the mysteries surrounding the Truscott affair.

On my desk at *Weekend Magazine,* where I then worked as a staff writer, was a pile of letters from readers all over Canada, and even from some in the United States. It took several secretaries to sort them out. An open-line show I did, via conference line hookup from my office for Dan Fisher's CKCO broadcast out of Kitchener, brought dozens of calls and a new avalanche of letters. Many of the correspondents were university and high school students using the case as a basis for school projects.

* * *

The case had fired the imagination – and indignation – of the country in the 1960's when Isabel LeBourdais published her book and now, in the 70's, the fires were alight once more, fanned in part by ghastly stories of rape and murder that rolled off the presses of Ontario newspapers. There were so many stories of sexual attacks at one point, that many area women refused to go out alone.

The oft-expressed complaint that people don't want to get involved didn't hold here. People were concerned. They wanted to help. They believed in Steven's innocence. One woman sent me a copy of a news story datelined London, February 1, 1972, which read in part: "Police are searching for a 1957-model Meteor in connection with a 1966 rape and murder at Aylmer. Wrecking yards in the Kitchener-Waterloo area have been checked without success."

My correspondent added this note: "The case seems so identical to Steven's in 1959. Do you think there could be some connection in any way? If I can be of service, please don't hesitate as I am for Steven all the way. He's innocent."

The case was one of the area's most sensational. It concerned a twenty-year-old girl named Georgia Jackson, a dairy bar waitress whose partly-clad, sexually-molested body had been found a few miles outside Aylmer. The woman who wrote me was correct in her observation of similarities.

Like Lynne, Georgia Jackson had been seen getting into a car. The vehicle, like the one in the Truscott case, had been a Chevrolet, and it was gray. Like Lynne, she had been raped and her body found in a woodlot.

Police brought the case to a close, six years after the murder, with the arrest of a one-time railroad worker named David Bodemer, father of five and son-in-law of Jehovah Witness preacher Albert Crooker who, in a chilling rain back in March, 1966, had prayed at the graveside of Georgia Jackson. Bodemer was sentenced to life imprisonment.

No connection between the murders of Lynne and Georgia was ever suggested. Bodemer, twenty-six at the time of his conviction, would have been thirteen at the time of Lynne's murder – a year younger than Steven.

Another letter came from a Kitchener woman who remembered having read some years earlier about a flying officer from the Clinton base who had been accused of killing a nurse in London in September 1959, less than three months after the murder of Lynne Harper.

"I wondered if this man was ever questioned to find out where he was at the time of Lynne Harper's death," she wrote. "It seems highly coincidental that two individuals, both associated with the air force base at Clinton, would commit murder within a three-month period."

Highly coincidental it was.

Arthur Langford Cranstoun, a West Indian in training at Clinton, charged with the murder of Ruth Buckley, a nurse at London's Westminster Hospital, however, was declared not guilty by a Supreme Court jury. Freed, he returned to the station to complete his training.

In what must have seemed irony of the first order to supporters of Steven Truscott, Mr. Justice R. A. Danis directed the jury in the Cranstoun case to bring in a verdict of acquittal because the only evidence adduced by the Crown was circumstantial.

"The law of the land requires that before you can find the accused guilty, you must be sure," the presiding judge said. "There must be no room for doubt. The evidence adduced is as consistent with the innocence of the accused as with the guilt and I direct you to bring in a verdict of acquittal."

While Mr. Justice Danis was saying these words, fourteen-year-old Steven Truscott sat in a death cell, fully expecting the hangman.

The mail kept pouring in.

"Had you ever any cause to think of...in connection with Lynne Harper?" another Londoner wrote. (The deletion of the name is mine.) "He taught school at that time. He was in court ('69 I think) for assaulting a woman in her car and was acquitted because Crown evidence was not properly conclusive. If you are interested, you can add these facts: Georgia Jackson was baby-sitter for his child before her murder. Jackie English was seen talking to him the night she disappeared, before her murder, and the subsequent finding of her belongings near where the Jackson girl was found."

The Jackie English case was another of the London area's grisly murders. Her nude body was found floating face down in shallow Big Otter creek about ten miles northeast of Tillsonburg in October of 1969. She had been the victim, police said, of a vicious beating.

Her killer is still at large.

Jacqueline Louise English, a pretty fifteen-year-old, was a part-time worker at the Treasure Island Metropolitan Store on London's southern outskirts. She sometimes worked late and, since she was a long way from a bus stop, she often accepted rides. Then one night, she was walking along toward Wellington Road, presumably to hitch a ride home, and she disappeared.

Could the killer of the English girl also be the killer of Lynne Harper? The police have never made that assumption, but the possibility exists.

Steven, his wife, and I met frequently to discuss the questions posed in letters from my correspondents. I'd ask them if they knew someone named so-and-so, if they were aware of such-and-such an occurrence, if they had heard this or that comment. Somewhere, I thought, there must be a positive clue.

Steven himself never accused anyone, but the possibilities, he admitted, were numerous. Lynne had told him on the night of the murder that she was going to see a man who lived in a little white house on the highway and who owned ponies. The police spoke to that man and he stated Lynne had not called on him.

But supposing Lynne had made up the story of wanting to go to see the ponies? Supposing she had made arrangements to meet someone at the intersection of the county road and the highway? Supposing again she had just hitched a ride to the town of Seaforth to meet someone *there*?

Suppositions were plentiful, facts few. But there were those on the base who claimed Lynne, though only twelve, had dated some of the enlisted personnel. Had she, on that fateful night, made such a date? The answer to that question became unnecessary to the police with Steven's conviction.

And then there was the strange case of Dr. David Hall Brooks, the base medical officer whom Steven accused of being *vindictive*. In one of my early interviews with Steven, he said, "I have the same impression, after all these years, that he was bent on doing whatever he could to have me found guilty. Persecution complex? I wonder. From the beginning he had taken an active part in proceedings. He was an eager member of the search party who, after a mere glance at the body, pinpointed the crime as the work of an 'amateur teenager.' "

Steven's observations about Dr. Brooks were shared by a number of private citizens, some of whom went so far as to play detective and arrange interviews with him in the hope of uncovering new evidence. It would come as a surprise to the doctor that a magazine writer who once visited him was, in actual fact, not a writer at all but a Truscott supporter wanting to question him about the murder.

* * *

In the files of a Toronto investigation firm are confidential reports on a prominent figure on the Clinton air base who, after the trial of Truscott, left the area for a job in the Maritimes where subsequently he was alleged to have made indecent advances to women and to have indulged in certain sexual perversions. I cite the case as an example of how far some of the independent investigations went.

The report might have been discounted from the start, except for the reliability of its source. The information came from a woman lawyer who was upset over the allegations of a close friend (also a woman) concerning the sexual conduct of the man in question. This friend, who had worked with him in New Brunswick, said that he was eventually fired from his job without being given a reason.

The lawyer admitted her information was all hearsay and she refused to divulge the name of her friend. However, she was taken seriously by the investigator. "In my opinion," he wrote to the client who had requested the investigation, "this lady is a responsible, sensible person, and the information supplied is accurately reported as she received it."

It was some time later that the "Shady Lady" of Clinton came on the scene. She used this pen name, instead of her real name, in her correspondence. Actually, she should have called herself *Frightened Lady* because if ever a woman ran scared, it was this one.

Her letter arrived with a London postmark. Inside was another letter, addressed to Steven. My letter said in part, "I believe I have information vital to Steven Truscott." She gave no name, just a box number in Clinton.

The letter to Steven, which he turned over to me, read in part:

"Dear Steven Truscott:

"Did you know that the real killer of Lynne is quite openly discussed around Clinton now and the reasons why he was not caught? If you wish more information, write to the above box in Clinton. In case you say, 'Why now?', it is only because I am fairly new to Clinton and just heard it today.

"I also wish to remain unknown, not for myself but because of my children who would be the victims of any publicity right now.

I also respect and well understand your wish to remain unknown in your new life, and I trust you to appreciate my concern.

"I will reveal *only to you* (her underline) what I know but I honestly believe the information I received to be correct because it makes sense. It also came from someone who is in an excellent position to be informed and who is one of the few people in life I respect."

Steven wrote a letter saying he would like to hear from her and I mailed it. A few days later, I received another letter from the woman, mailed from another town. She was afraid to send a letter from Clinton, she said, in case someone might link her with the Truscott case. "It is difficult to get to another city so I let someone else mail the last letter," she wrote. "Without any explanation, I got a real dirty look. It is hard to find someone you can trust enough, so I wouldn't tell anyone the truth."

Shady Lady wrote several letters, always expressing fear and always mailed from another area. She didn't want to put her information down in writing for fear the letter might be intercepted. She wanted to *talk* to Steven. I offered to visit her but she declined. A visit by me would put everyone in Clinton on the alert. (Everyone in town, she said, had read *The Steven Truscott Story.*) Besides, it was *Steven* to whom she wanted to speak.

Finally, a telephone conversation was arranged, on the understanding that I would not divulge what arrangements had been made for that call. Steven's wife spoke for him. What information, she asked, did the woman have that would help Steven? The woman hesitated. She was afraid to talk, she said. How could she be sure no one else was listening? Steven's wife persisted.

In a line that might have come right out of a movie murder mystery, the woman said she wanted to speak to Steven in person and that she would like to meet him on a county road near Clinton at night, when no one likely would be around to see them. Steven's wife cupped her hand over the mouthpiece and told Steven. He shook his head. She then told the woman Steven would consider the matter and that was the end of the conversation.

We discussed the matter at length after that call and decided it would be ill-advised for Steven to keep an appointment with an

34

anonymous woman on a lonely country road at night. He was, after all, still on parole and subject to surveillance.

We waited a couple of weeks to see if she would make further contact. She didn't. Then I wrote her a letter, telling her we were anxious not to let the matter end there. She didn't answer.

Had someone found out about the telephone call? If she had indeed replied to my letter, had someone intercepted it? In either case, she might have found herself in a very awkward position in Clinton. In fact, judging by her letters, always expressing fear, she may have been in a *dangerous* situation. Perhaps then, she may have been warned by someone that she had gone far enough.

Some people might be tempted to dismiss the story of Shady Lady as the work of a crank. I don't think it was. I believed she knew something and I still do. The aura of implied danger that surrounded her was consistent with the general pattern of fear, warnings and admonitions that have become the hallmarks of the Steven Truscott case.

The man in Kitchener who warned the plumber he could be killed for relaying information about Lynne Harper's death – was he a crank? No, I am certain he was not. The two nurses who called a television and radio station – were they, too, crackpots? No, I am sure they were not.

The simple fact, undeniable in my estimation, is that Steven Truscott is innocent. He did *not* kill Lynne Harper.

The real killer of Lynne Harper is still at large. He has eluded detection for twenty years and likely assumes he is safe. But *is* he safe?

Steven Truscott's supporters have been gathering pieces of the puzzle of Lynne Harper's murder for many years.

But those pieces are beginning to come together, haphazardly from different sources, and an eventual solution can no longer be regarded as impossible.

There is an artist in Montreal, named Betty Galbraith-Cornell, with a message on tape that adds a new dimension to the story. The voice is that of a woman in Seaforth, now deceased, who said she heard that on the night of the murder, Lynne Harper had been seen in that town.

Here it is necessary to do some backtracking.

Police disbelief in the story of Steven Truscott's ride to the highway with Lynne Harper was supported, in their eyes, by the autopsy report of Dr. Penistan, setting time of death precisely within the period of time Steven had been with her. That report was to spark one of the major controversies of the trial.

Dr. Penistan stated that death had occurred sometime between 5:45 p.m. and 7:45 p.m. More specifically, he estimated that it had happened between 7 p.m. and 7:45 p.m. He based his conclusion on the fact that the girl had finished eating supper at 5:45 and that she still had about a pint of food in her stomach when he performed the autopsy. A stomach, he explained, normally emptied itself in two hours. Since there was still food in the stomach then, death must have occurred less than two hours after the meal. To allow for possible variations, however, he granted that death may have occurred as late at 7:45. (See Supreme Court Report, page 233)

The controversy arose out of the testimony of Dr. Berkley Brown, a specialist in internal medicine on the staff of the University of Western Ontario, London. He challenged Dr. Penistan's conclusion.

Dr. Brown testified that it takes between three and a half and four hours for a stomach to empty. On the basis of this, death must have occurred one and a half to two hours later than the time set by Dr. Penistan. (See Supreme Court Report, pages 235-242)

Dr. Brown's estimate of time clearly would have exonerated Steven since it had been proven that he had returned home from his bicycle ride at precisely 8:25 p.m. (His parents had requested that he be home not later than 8:30 so that he could baby-sit with his younger brother and sister.)

It was this specific controversy which led Supreme Court Justice Hall to comment some years later (in his dissenting minority report) that presiding judge Mr. Justice Ferguson had misdirected the jury.

"The jury," he wrote, "should have been told that as between Dr. Penistan and Dr. Brown, if the evidence of Dr. Brown left a reasonable doubt in their minds as to the time of death, they must acquit." (See Supreme Court Report, page 300)

The jury elected, however, to accept Dr. Penistan's evidence and disregard the testimony of Dr. Brown. And Steven was doomed.

The court ruled Steven Truscott guilty and the files were stored away in cabinets to collect dust. But on the base, rumors were circulating. Apparently not everyone was convinced the correct verdict had been reached.

One story that went the rounds was that Lynne had been seen getting into a doctor's car.

What doctor? What car?

Steven's parents questioned several people about this – to no avail. They had heard the story but didn't know where it had originated.

In the Mess one night, the Truscotts heard someone say that Lynne had been seen in Seaforth on the night of her death. Again they were unable to pin down the source of the report.

All of which brings me back to Betty Galbraith-Cornell, a quiet, unassuming woman whose talents as an artist have won her considerable public acclaim. She had been deeply moved by Steven's story after reading Isabel LeBourdais' book and, like the author of that book, she was also anxious to follow up the story of the mystery car.

If it could be proven that Lynne Harper had been in Seaforth on the night of her murder, she reasoned, then Steven Truscott had to be innocent. Her death then would *have* to have occurred beyond the time set by Dr. Penistan and well past the time Steven arrived home.

When Betty took off for Seaforth one summer's day, it was with her sketch books. No one, she thought, would be suspicious of an artist wanting to capture the quiet, pastoral beauty of the Seaforth area. It was the first of several trips she made to the region and several of the canvases she painted of it now hang in her living room, mute reminders of the tragedy that prompted them.

Betty became friendly with a number of Seaforth residents,

among them old Mrs. Nichols, a kindly lady whom she visited in her home. The initial conversation revolved around the beauties of the countryside. Mrs. Nichols supposed it *was* nice country but when one had lived in a place as long as she had, one tended to forget such things, she said.

When Betty got around to talking about the murder, Mrs. Nichols became cautious. She really didn't know anything, she said. Betty persisted. Well, she had *heard* things, the old lady admitted. She had heard that people had seen Lynne in Seaforth on the night of the killing. She didn't identify the people, referring to them only as *they*.

They had talked about seeing Lynne come out of a restaurant adjoining the Queen's Hotel, where *they* said she had had a "little lunch." (*Lunch* in that community is a term used for a meal or snack taken at any time of the day.)

This would have been long after the time at which Dr. Penistan testified Lynne had died.

Mrs. Nichols didn't know it but on a table near her was a tape recorder. It was picking up her words. Betty had thought to pack the machine along with her sketch books.

Betty talked to several other people in Seaforth, none of whom could, or would, comment. But one man aroused her interest. He was Mrs. Nichol's son-in-law, a man of Francophone origin named Luc Gagnon who once had been a civilian driver on the air base and who now lived in Seaforth. Betty questioned him about Lynne Harper without learning anything, Gagnon stating simply that he knew nothing about the case.

Back in Montreal, Betty mulled over her interviews. Her chat with Gagnon bothered her. Call it woman's intuition or whatever, she thought Gagnon *knew* something. On impulse, she sent private detectives to talk to him. They reported later that they had spoken to him and that he had reiterated his statement to her – that he knew nothing about the case.

Considerably out of pocket because of investigational expenses, Betty let the matter drop.

Much later, another citizen-investigator learned that when Gagnon worked on the base, he had been called *Frenchie* by friends.

Was he the *Frenchie* the Kitchener plumber claimed could tell the real story of Lynne Harper's murder? Since Gagnon claims he knows nothing about the case, the question remains unanswered.

BREAKTHROUGH?

Many strange leads have come out of the Truscott investigations, but none that cried out for official action more than the one that went into Kingston Penitentiary files in 1967 as The Case of the Three Painters.

It is a case that carried a documented accusation of murder against one, the self-confessed implication of a second and possible involvement of a third individual, all of whom were inmates of the penitentiary at the time.

It could have brought and still could bring the real killer, or killers, of Lynne Harper to justice – and exonerate Steven Truscott.

But the Ontario Attorney-General's Department, with full knowledge of the facts, has taken no action.

One of the trio has since died. He is believed to have been murdered somewhere in the West. But the other two, known to be the principals in the story, are, in penitentiary parlance, *on the street,* meaning they are free.

They could be found.

They should be found – and questioned. Even after twelve years.

The Attorney-General's Department, however, has demonstrated no inclination to open an investigation. The file, as far as the department is concerned, is closed.

The bizarre case of The Three Painters had its beginnings in the early summer of 1967, eight years to the month after Lynne Harper's murder and a few weeks after the Supreme Court had handed down its judgment, upholding Steven Truscott's 1959 conviction.

Behind the towering limestone walls of Kingston Penitentiary, radios were blaring out news of Canada's centennial celebrations and that great extravaganza, Expo '67, in Montreal. But in the recreation areas of K.P. and in the exercise yard, inmates were talking about something much closer to them.

They were talking about Ronny X, who had been involved in a shoot-out with police during an aborted bank holdup and about his brother, Russ, and a friend named Roy. (It was Roy who was later murdered.)

Ronny and Russ specialized in bank robberies and normally would have been classed among the elite of the penitentiary population. But Ronny had a problem that robbed him of his elitist status. He was a *diddler* – someone who engages in sexual play with young children – and inmates have a notorious dislike for diddlers. In fact, every institution, Kingston Penitentiary among them, has its horror stories of how inmates have meted out punishment to child molesters.

Ronny had another, more serious, problem, though. He couldn't take the prison environment. He couldn't adjust to being locked up behind bars. People who knew him said he sometimes "went wild."

And then there was this recollection of a murder.

Ronny's life in prison was a series of psychological ups and downs and during his despondent periods, his mind would dwell on this murder.

Ronny's mistake was that he kept talking about this killing. That kind of thing gets around in a penal institution.

It was not long before fellow inmates began putting the pieces together. The murder had occured seven or eight years earlier. The victim had been a little girl. Ronny and Russ had been involved, perhaps Roy, too.

Then one day, the prison grapevine, that illusive, clandestine and ironically reliable communications network that collects and disseminates all manner of inmate news, without identifying its sources, carried a startling piece of information.

The information was that Ronny, Russ and Roy had been working as painters in 1959 and that on the day of the Harper murder, they had been painting light standards at service stations in the Seaforth area, just ten miles from Clinton.

No one knew where the information on the prison telegraph had originated, but clearly, fellow inmates were linking Ronny the diddler, brother Russ, and friend Roy with the killing of Lynne Harper.

Whether or not the telegraph message was intended as punishment for a diddler, no one knows, but it led to one of the most thorough investigations in the whole of the Truscott file, conducted by people with the most impeccable credentials, whose wish for strict anonymity I agreed to respect.

It was an investigation that was to put the murder of Lynne Harper in an entirely new light.

It began with in-penitentiary interviews with Ronny, taped and later transcribed. The excerpts from the transcript which follow are rambling and often repetitious but excessive trimming has been avoided in order to maintain the mood of the sessions.

Interviewer: "How are you feeling?"

Ronny: "Not too bad."

I: "Have you felt worried or disturbed?"

R: "Worried is right."

I: "What about?"

R: "This murder."

I: "What about this murder?"

R: "We were involved in it."

I: "Who is we?"

R: "My brother and me."

I: "When was this murder?"

R: "About six or seven years ago." The Harper murder had occurred eight years earlier.)

I: "How were you involved?"

Ronny doesn't answer.

The interviewer tries to put Ronny at ease. He tells him he has nothing to worry about as far as he himself is concerned.

I: "Nothing can happen to you. Do you understand? What I want you to do is tell me as closely as you can the actual facts as far as you can remember. Anything you can remember...would be helpful and there is no point in you trying to protect anybody. Do you understand what I've said?"

R: "Yeah."

I: "Now, tell me about the murder. Can you remember where it happened?

Ronny says it took place in the country, on a small slope of land. He recalls he was with his brother, Russ. He was on a painting job but he doesn't remember whether he was on his way to it, or returning from it.

The interviewer asks him to describe the victim. Ronny hesitates.

I: "Are you able to remember what she had on?"

R: "I thought...I don't know what the heck it was...I don't know what it was she had on...I know I was involved in this bloody thing."

I: "Pardon?"

R: "I know that I was involved in this bloody thing."

Ronny says Russ got out of the car at one point to relieve himself. When he returned, he had spots all over his pants. The thought disturbs him and he remains silent for a few moments.

I: "What are you thinking about?"

R: "What a position I'm in."

I: "What position are you in?"

R: "Who's going to take the hanging?"

I: "Who is going to take the hanging? Not you but we better find out who is. This is your chance. So, what have you got to say?"

R: "Say? Help – that's all I've got to say."

Ronny recalls that when he was released from Kingston Penitentiary on a previous conviction in 1957, two years before the Harper murder, he went into the house repair business with Russ, working for a "big shot" with a real estate business in Toronto's Danforth area. He identifies him simply as a man named Johnny, the "boss of the real estate." He remembers Johnny had a big car and that he was always combing his hair back and standing "like as if he were a real big shot."

Ronny refers to gambling connections. He says that he and

Russ worked for a dry cleaning firm whose owner operated a gambling joint in Toronto's east end for years. Russ, he says, was the *card man* (dealer) in the gambling house.

The interviewer brings the conversation around to the Harper murder.

I: "Can you remember anything more about the girl...how old she was?"

R: "Like...like thirteen, or twelve."

I: "Has this anything to do with the Truscott affair, Ronny?"

R: "Jesus Christ, now I'm all banged up."

I: "You mean you are confused?"

R: "Confused is right."

The interviewer asks Ronny for the name of the girl. Ronny says he doesn't know.

I: "Is this connected with the Truscott case?"

R: "Yes, it is...I keep going back on Russ."

I: "Why?"

R: "I was thinking about my mother."

I: "What about your mother?"

R: "Not sure whether it was after..."

I: "After...?"

R: "She gave me my pants...not sure if it was because I had just thrown them down and got other pants..."

I: "Yeah..."

R: "She came up to me and she had the pants like this (demonstrates) and she said, 'There is a spot on them.' "

I: "A spot?"

R: "A spot that concerned..."

I: "That concerned what?"

R: "My mother told me that...that a girl was killed...was on the radio or something...she heard it on the radio or some bloody thing."

I: "What was she asking you?"

R: "She came up with one of her names...of what you call it... that she had spotted on my pants."

I: "You mean to do with sexual intercourse?"

R: "She called it..."

44

I: "Called it *come?*"

R: "Something like that..."

Ronny admits under questioning that he was involved but he says he himself didn't kill or rape the victim.

I: "You're upset. Why?"

R: "Put in a position like this."

I: "But you say you didn't do it."

R: "I just think somebody's going to hang for this."

I: "They don't hang anybody anymore."

R: "This happened...I don't know. Jesus Christ, how long ago? Five years ago? Seven years ago?"

I: "All right. Your mother comes up to you with the pants. She says there's a spot on them and she says she has heard over the radio that a girl has been killed. What did you say?"

R: "This thing is..."

I: "What did you say – 'Oh, Ma, I didn't do it.' Ronny, you aren't telling me what you know."

R: "The majority of it I am."

I: "Ronny, what keeps you from answering?"

R: "Maybe I just don't want to."

I: "Are you afraid to? Come on, Ronny, you have said you were there."

R: "Yeah."

I: "Who did it, Ronny?"

R: "I guess I forgot."

I: "Who washed Russ's pants?"

R: "Himself."

I: "He washed them himself? That's what your mother said, eh? Why was he washing his own pants?"

R: "I think it was the stuff that was on them."

I: "So, who murdered the girl? (Pause) Who murdered the girl?"

R: "It was my brother."

Ronny had made a blunt accusation of murder against his brother. As for himself, he would only say that, because of the spot on his pants, he knew he, too, was involved.

Two weeks later, Ronny was called for another interview. This time he named the murdered girl.

The transcript reads in part:

I: "What did you say the kid's name was?"

R: "Linda. Linda Harper." (The interviewer didn't question the first name)

I: "How old was she?"

R: "About thirteen or fourteen."

I: "Who murdered her?"

R: "We did..."

I: "Well, was it you?"

R: "No, it wasn't."

I: "Well, who was it?"

R: "Like I've been saying all the time – Russ. I'd like to go out and punch his teeth in for what it has caused me."

I: "A moment ago (before the taped interview) you said something about 'bloody scissors.' "

R: "I got it in my mind that scissors are involved in this bloody murder...like when I was in the car...not sure if it was after it happened that I used this bloody thing to...when you put this other thing across...clop it off or something like this, this bloody thing..."

I: "You mean to strain the paint?"

R: "Yeah. You buy this stuff, put it across the can...and pour the paint...can't get the name...some kind of cloth."

(Had the "bloody scissors" been the instrument used to cut a swatch from Lynne Harper's blouse? The question was not asked).

I: "You say you didn't do this (the murder)? You didn't kill anybody?"

R: "No, I never done that. It's put me in a bloody thing... where it's between Russ and me. Like I walked up to him and punched him in the mouth, or beat him up. They will say, 'Here is the man.' "

I: "Why will they say that?"

R: "Why? Because I beat him up, they will say, 'This man is the violent one and I guess he is capable of killing someone for the fun of it, or something.' I've never ever done that before."

46

I: "Would Russ do that? Would Russ kill somebody for fun?"

R: "He is violent...like if you walk up to him and slap him in the mouth. This is what I was going to do. Then I thought, if I do this, then it's going to give him the right to punch me out and they'll blame me for this thing. It's got me now. I don't know what to do."

The interviewer asks Ronny if he saw the girl murdered. Ronny says he was in the car when Russ came back.

R: "Russ was...like my brother came back, he had that stuff on his front...He said, 'There's a kid up there that's got hurt.' I said, 'Well, where?'... It never dawned on me that a bloody murder like this had happened."

The interviewer asks Ronny if he knows who was blamed for the murder.

R: "Oh, that kid, Truscott...it's a miracle it didn't drive him insane. I feel sorry for the kid."

I: "When you knew he was blamed, why didn't you do something?"

R: "I'm not a bloody idiot. It just came on me that there was violence involved...it never dawned on me that bloody Russ was capable of doing it."

Ronny tells of bad dreams in which he goes to the scene of the murder and picks up the body of the girl and then grabs Russ by the neck.

I: "Did Steven Truscott kill the girl?"

R: "No. Either that or I'm going out of my mind."

I: "You know that?"

R: "Not Truscott. I know he didn't."

The next time Ronny is called for interview, he is presented with a sheet of paper marked, *Statement of Information.* The interviewer asks him to read it aloud.

R: "I, Ronald –, an inmate at Kingston Penitentiary, voluntarily make the following statement: 'In the interest...' "

He stops reading. The interviewer picks up from where he left off.

I: "...'in the interest of my health and to obtain peace of mind, wish to inform the authorities of my certain knowledge of a crime committed in 1959. While in the company of my brother, Russell, a young girl, aged twelve or thirteen, was murdered and raped. The victim was Lynne Harper, of Clinton, Ontario. The offence occurred in the country, a short distance off a main highway, a few miles from a small town approximately 150 miles from Toronto. I believe my brother committed this crime."

Ronny doesn't want to make a statement. The interviewer reminds him that he had confirmed the content of the formal statement earlier.

R: "Well, I could have been making a few things up, you know."

I: "Well, only catch is that you made up the facts."

R: "I guess I did."

I: "And the only way you could have known the facts was to have been there."

R: "Well, it was just kind of a..."

I: "A kind of fantasy?"

R: "Yeah."

I: "Not so fantastic when what you said has been borne out. That's not so funny, eh? You don't think that's so funny, do you?"

The interviewer reminds Ronny that someone else (Truscott) is suffering for the crime. Ronny becomes very distressed.

I: "What are you shook up about?"

R: "I don't know. I'm shook up all the time."

I: "Well, you disappoint me."

R: "I'm terribly sorry." (He laughs.)

I: "I bet. When we were trying to help you."

R: "Thanks a lot, anyways."

I: "I thought you wanted to live."

R: "Doesn't matter anymore."

I: "Why?"

R: "I got to die sometime."

I: "Maybe Russ doesn't want to, though."

R: "I don't want to die, he don't want to die, so what."

I: "So I guess he'll say you did it."

R: "Could be."

I: "Do you think he will?"

R: "Probably."

During one of the interrogation sessions, Ronny talked about making a hasty departure for Toronto on the night in question. Russ was at the wheel, he said, and he drove at high speed all the way, ignoring the little warning light on the dashboard that indicated the oil was running low. On a Toronto street, the vehicle finally broke down. It was later repaired at a garage.

"The day you burned the engine out, had you come a long ways?" the interviewer asked. "In a hell of a hurry?"

"We had been to so many places," Ronny answered. "Places I never even heard of. Towns I never heard of."

"Listen carefully now," the interviewer went on. "Was that the same day as the girl was killed?"

"It must have been the same day," Ronny replied.

Did Russ murder Lynne Harper? Was Ronny an accomplice? Was there a third man at the murder scene? After all, this was the case of The *Three* Painters. If so, would this fit the gang rape theory suggested by the Kitchener plumber?

The investigators, against the background of their yards of professional experience, believed Ronny had been telling the truth.

They believed that Russ had murdered Lynne Harper – and that Ronny may have participated in the killing. They could not determine whether a third person was implicated.

They believed this strongly enough to carry their investigation beyond the walls of the penitentiary.

The interview they arranged with Ronny's father and the woman companion with whom he lived in Toronto produced little in the way of incriminating evidence. However, it did produce some personal insights into the lives of both Ronny and Russ.

The investigators' note pads contained these notes:

"Ron is described as having an awful disposition."

"He was headstrong ('bull-headed'), entertained marked prejudices vs. police and generally hated society and the world."

"He never would do what he was told, and this was so before his head injury."

Ronny was not given to drinking, his father said, but during recent periods on the street, he "drank to excess" and was "kind of wild."

He would "talk big" and talked Russ into their last bank job. Prior to this, Russ had been the boss and had called the action.

The father saw Russ in a different light. He was quiet and not so bull-headed. On the other hand, he tended to be "sneaky." It was difficult to know what he was thinking. He had "steadied down" for a time but then he and Ronny had become involved in some kind of "activity."

Both the father and his companion agreed that the brothers had been very close all through their lives. The fact that Ronny now wanted to attack his brother, they thought, could only be attributed to Ronny having gone insane.

Later, the investigators tried to locate the garage that had removed and repaired the car Ronny and Russ had abandoned on a Toronto street. The search was futile. None of the garage people contacted had any record of it.

Mystery Car Number 3 had now gone into the Lynne Harper file.

Late in 1967, the investigators prepared a report with a scenario that might have led to a solution of the Lynne Harper murder.

It *might* have – had it been followed up.

The scenario they constructed was this:

Lynne Harper *did* get into a car at the highway, just as Steven Truscott had reported. The occupants of that car may have been her murderers. More likely, however, she met her killers in Seaforth. Her assailants raped and murdered her somewhere between Seaforth and Clinton. The killing may have taken place in the car, or outside of it. Looking for a place to dispose of the body, they drove up the county road toward the base. Seeing Lawson's Bush, they decided this would be a safe place. They dragged the body in, then got back into the car and raced off for Toronto. (See Supreme Court Report, pages 232, 256-260)

Did the investigators really believe this is what had happened?

They did.

Clearly, that scenario, circumstantial though it was, demanded a full investigation by the Attorney-General's Department.

But nobody acted upon it.

And until now, the case of The Three Painters has remained a secret file.

* * *

It has been twenty years since Lynne Harper hitched a ride to her death in a mystery car on Ontario Highway Number 8. Is there any hope now that, at this late date, her killer, or killers, can be brought to justice?

The answer is *yes*. Crimes have been solved twenty, twenty-five and even thirty years after their commission.

But those who administer justice must be prepared to investigate every new shred of information that comes to their attention and must not be allowed to sweep it under the official carpet.

There is an understandable reluctance about opening up old cases – and old wounds. The difficulties involved in tracking down evidence and questioning people so long after the fact are enormous.

But the problems in this case go beyond mere *difficulty*. They have also been the elements of a personal tragedy and the cause of one of the great travesties of Canadian justice.

The fact of the matter is that the trial of Steven Truscott, labelled categorically by Justice Emmett Hall as "invalid" and a "bad trial," has been an embarrassment to governments for twenty years.

Steven Truscott's own account of his interview inside the penitentiary with a high official in the government of the late former Prime Minister Lester B. Pearson in 1966, underlines the fact that the case, no longer strictly a provincial matter, had reached the federal level. (See Steven's Story, page 170-1)

In what certainly had to be a most unorthodox procedure, Steven says he was offered a "deal." Would he accept a parole in lieu of a hearing before the Supreme Court? Had he accepted the parole at that time, the case may well have been forgotten. Instead, he declined. (See Steven's Story, page 151).

He wanted a parole – but, even more, he wanted an opportunity to prove his innocence.

The Supreme Court hearing, with its eight-to-one decision upholding Steven Truscott's conviction, might have been expected to bring debate, speculation – and perhaps even embarrassment – to an end. But it did no such thing.

To begin with, a prominent Toronto lawyer let it be known among friends that, almost to the very end, the nine-judge Supreme Court panel had been in a five-four split – and not an eight-to-one position. Five had been in favor of upholding the lower court's conviction and four had been against.

Then, on the day before judgment was to be rendered, the lawyer said, three of the judges who had been against upholding the conviction, changed their minds. The result: eight judges approving the lower court's conduct, one (Emmett Hall) dissenting.

Why did the learned justices change their minds?

The lawyer in question either didn't know – or thought he had told his friends enough. In any event, there was no explanation.

Justice closed the books on the murder of Lynne Harper with the judgment of the Supreme Court. But those who believed the case would simply fade away were wrong.

The tragic case of Lynne Harper is as vivid in people's minds today as it was that hot summer of 1959.

The Harpers have suffered untold anguish over the long years – but so, too, have the Truscotts. All of them. Steven, his parents, his brothers and sister – and now his wife.

For Steven in particular, it has been twenty years of heartbreak. The ten years he spent behind bars are lost to him. He can never get them back. And since his release in 1969, he has been living an anonymous existence, answering to an assumed name, residing and working in a place that can't be identified, all the time knowing that, in the eyes of the law, he is a convicted murderer.

His wife has been living under that same dark, insidious cloud of uncertainty and anxiety for nearly ten years, ever since she married him, and she goes to sleep at night wondering how they are going to handle the problem of their two children when they grow up.

Do the Truscotts invent a story for them to cover all those terrible years since 1959?

Or do they tell them the truth – that their father is an innocent man whose name has never been cleared?

The Truscotts must not be allowed to go on carrying that terrible burden – and certainly they must never be forced to pass it on to their children.

For twenty years, the killing of Lynne Harper has been a self-perpetuating horror story, one that has spawned and nurtured a veritable army of strange, shadowy figures, crackpot tipsters, frightened informers and tragedy-seekers.

People of all shapes, sizes and mentalities have gravitated to it as they would to a traffic accident.

And the horror goes on unabated.

Feel the terror as Steven's wife relates the story of a telephone conversation that took place as recently as March, 1979.

The conversation was with a man who gave a name she didn't recognize. He said he had solved the murder of Lynne Harper. Two men had killed her. He knew who they were and planned to name them.

"He seemed to know so much about the crime, the area, the people involved," she said. "He went into all kinds of details. He talked intimately about the murder itself. He said Lynne had been raped standing up. I wondered how he would know all this. Suddenly, a cold shudder went through me. I thought, 'Suppose I was actually talking to the killer.' "

Twenty years of horror *cannot* go on.

The murderer(s) *must* be brought to justice.

The record on the killing of Lynne Harper *must*, finally, be set straight.

BOOK II

Steven's Story

CHAPTER I

Flying Officer Leslie Harper was visibly shaken when my father introduced him to us. His twelve-year-old daughter Lynne had gone out after supper the night before and hadn't returned home.

"Mr. Harper has been talking to people on the base," Dad said, adressing all of us.

Mom sat at the kitchen table with my younger brother and sister, Bill and Barb. I stood beside them with my older brother, Ken. None of us had ever met Mr. Harper. This wasn't surprising since he was a flying officer and my father was a warrant officer and officers seldom fraternized with non-commissioned ranks. As for Lynne, she was in my class but she didn't belong to my circle of friends and I only had a passing acquaintance with her.

Mr. Harper wanted to know if any of us had seen his daughter. He spoke first to Ken, who shook his head, and then to me.

"I saw her," I said. "I gave her a lift on my bicycle."

"Oh, my God," he said, taking a deep breath. It seemed at this point that any news was good news. "Try to remember. *When* did you see her and *where* did you take her?"

"I met her near the school after supper," I explained. "She asked me to take her down the county road to Highway 8."

Mr. Harper was excited and nodded his head at almost every word. "Did you take her?"

I told him I had. I had left her there and cycled back to the little bridge over the Bayfield River, about a quarter of a mile away. From there, I could see her standing at the side of the highway. Then a car came along, heading toward Seaforth. It pulled in at a sharp angle to the county road and Lynne got in.

"Oh, my God," he said again. It was as though his worst fears had been realized.

Mr. Harper left the house with Dad. Ken and I collected our school books and a few minutes later, Mom walked us to the door. Ken went out first. He put his hand to his forehead and pretended he was fainting.

"Wow, it's hot," he said.

"It can't be any hotter than in the house," I said. I realized my mistake as soon as I got outside. The sun was literally melting the asphalt.

I joined Ken in his fainting act but Mom paid no attention. "I hope nothing's happened to that little girl," she said.

* * *

I spent that morning in class, trying to absorb Lord Durham's report on Canada, and wishing to heck he'd stayed in England where he belonged. I didn't like Canadian history anyhow. I found it terribly dull, and I could never spell any of the French names. I didn't mind American history so much, and I'd read quite a lot about the war between the states.

With exams so close, we were given a study period right after lunch. But I wasn't an enthusiastic student, and as I sat at my desk flipping the pages of my history text the sounds and scents of summer drifted through the open window to distract me. In the humid 90° heat, I imagined myself floating in the Bayfield River, or lying quietly in the June sunshine, on the bank of the stream, watching the clouds scud across the sky.

I spent so much time in class day-dreaming, that I could assume a studious pose the moment a teacher glanced my way. Maitland Edgar, however, was a favorite with most of the fellows, and he overlooked our minor lapses. He taught physical education as well as history, and coached us in baseball, football, soccer and hockey. He had been quite an athlete during his college years, so I guess there was a bit of hero worship on our part.

Just before the end of the period, the principal came into our classroom. He leaned furtively on Mr. Edgar's desk, chatted with him earnestly for a few moments, then turned to one of the pupils and asked him to accompany him out of the room. In a few minutes, he returned with the boy and asked another to go out.

Systematically, he worked his way up and down the aisles until finally he stopped at Arnold George's desk. Butch, as we knew him, sat behind me and was one of my best friends. The heat seemed to have left him wilted and, as he left his desk, he looked at me and shrugged lazily.

By that time, the boys who hadn't been summoned were curious but Mr. Edgar, usually lax in such matters, discouraged discussion. When two boys started whispering, he put his index finger to his lips and shook his head vigorously.

When finally the principal returned with Butch, he gestured to me to follow him. We went out of the room and along the hall to the front door. Outside an Ontario Provincial Police car was parked at the curb. We crossed the lawn to it and were motioned into the back seat.

"This is Steven Truscott," the principal said, glancing at me to confirm his introduction.

The two policemen in the front seat turned to face me. They were big and beefy and barely nodded. The one behind the wheel did the talking. The other just stared at me.

"Did you see Lynne Harper last night?" the driver asked.

I repeated the story that I had told Mr. Harper earlier, about meeting his daughter near the school and driving her down to Highway 8 on the crossbar of my bicycle. Then I remembered something. Lynne had mentioned that she might visit a man who kept ponies and who lived in a "little white house on the highway."

The officers listened to my recital without comment, then sent me back to my classroom.

As I sat down at my desk, Butch stuck his pencil in my back. "What did they ask you?"

"They wanted to know if I had any information about Lynne Harper," I replied.

"Same here," he said. He started to say something else, but Mr. Edgar glanced up from his papers and Butch hastily concentrated on his textbook.

Later that afternoon the principal again called me out. For a second time, I followed him to the patrol car. This time my father was in the back seat.

"Over here, Steve," he called through the open window.

I climbed in beside my father, and as the car started up, Dad explained that the officers wanted me to show them exactly where I had left Lynne Harper.

We travelled along the county road, passing the O'Brien house and barn on the left, and then Lawson's Bush, a second-growth stand of ash, elm, maple and basswood, on the right. Bob Lawson was a young, good-natured farmer, and often I went to his place, to play or to give him a hand with small chores.

We passed a grain field, then the car slowed as we went over the Canadian National tracks. We drove over the little bridge that spans the Bayfield River, and stopped a quarter of a mile farther on, where the county road joins Highway 8. Had we turned left here we would have been headed for Clinton. A right turn would have taken us to Seaforth. There was a STOP sign at the end of the county road, and this was where I had left Lynne.

We then drove back to the bridge and I showed them where I had been standing when I saw Lynne get into the car. It had come from the direction of Clinton and was headed toward Seaforth.

"Any idea what kind of a car it was?" Again the questioning came from the driver. The other man just stared at me.

"It was a 1959 Chevrolet," I replied without hesitation.

"How can you be sure it was a '59 Chev?"

"It had large tail-lights in the shape of cat's eyes and big fins on the back."

"You couldn't be mistaken? It couldn't have been another make of car?"

I said I was certain. I said also that I had seen a flash of orange or yellow at the rear of the car as it pulled away. I might have seen the license, I said, or perhaps it had been a bumper sticker. I couldn't be sure.

Identifying the make of a car was an easy matter in 1959. Cars look more or less alike now but in those days there were marked differences and the kids could tell one from the other from great distances.

Most of my friends could look down the road and say, "There goes a Chevy," or, "There's an Olds." They knew the Fords, the Chryslers and the Caddies. There was nothing unusual about that.

The officers, having no further questions, drove me back to school and I said goodbye to my father. I returned to class to find Mr. Edgar busy with some papers. I went to my desk and was about to sit down when the bell rang. The school day was over. I picked up my books and headed out.

That night, Dad told Mom about our trip to the highway in the police car. I said that most of the boys in my class had been called out for questioning. But my parents had other things on their minds and we didn't dwell on the matter of Lynne Harper.

Ken switched on the television and we all settled down for an evening of quiet viewing. It was about 9:30 when I heard my mother's voice. She was shaking me and saying, "Steve, Steve... Go to bed, you're tired." I must indeed have been tired because I had fallen asleep in the chair.

* * *

The Provincial Police car was already at the school when I arrived next morning. It had become something of a fixture. The same officers continued questioning the pupils and I heard later they had ended up interrogating almost all the boys in school.

Shortly before noon, I was summoned once more to the car and again the man behind the wheel asked the questions. He wanted me to repeat the whole story right from the beginning:

Where had I seen Lynne? What had she asked me? Where had I taken her? Was I certain about the hitch-hike car?

I went into all the details again:

I had met her near the school. She said she was on her way to see the ponies. She wanted a lift to the highway and I gave it to her. A few minutes later, I saw her get into a car – a '59 Chev. That was the last time I saw her.

The constant recital was beginning to bore me. But now there were other questions as well:

What time had I left home that evening? The exact time, now.

How much later was it when I picked up Lynne? Did anyone see me with her? What time did I arrive home that night?

Two nights ago. That was a long time back. But oh yes, I remembered.

I arrived home about 5:30. Supper was late and Mom asked me to go to the store for coffee. I would have to hurry because it closed at six. When I returned, the meal was ready. Between 7:00 and 7:15, I went to the side of the house and got my bicycle. Mom called out to me to be sure to be back by 8:30 because she and Dad were going out and wanted me to baby-sit with Bill and Barb.

I rode to the school where I met a group of Brownies. After, I followed the county road to the bridge, stopping briefly here and there. I went back to the school then, where I met Lynne. We chatted a while about... Well, who remembers what we talked about? She was in a chatty mood and did most of the talking.

Then she said she wanted to go to the little white house down the highway to see the ponies and asked if I would take her to the intersection. I agreed and we pushed the bicycle between us across the school grounds to the county road. There I got on the seat and she mounted the crossbar and we took off. The time? Probably between 7:30 and 7:45.

I took her to the highway, turned around and rode slowly back toward the school. At the bridge I paused to watch the kids swimming and, from that vantage point, I saw Lynne get into the car. I rode on, stopping at the football field for a few minutes. There, some boys were playing a noisy game of touch rugby.

Near the swings in the play area, I met my brother Ken and he reminded me that I had to sit with the youngsters that night. I told him not to worry, that I was conscientious about these things.

At 8:25, or just after, I was back at the house.

My parents went out and Bill and Barb went to bed about nine o'clock, leaving me slumped sleepily in front of the television set.

Who had seen me with Lynne and then later alone?

Well, Butch George for one. He had been on the bank of the Bayfield River and had waved as we crossed the bridge, heading for the highway.

And Douglas Oats, who had been digging for turtles, but was on the bridge as we went by. And Gordon Logan on the big rock in the river. He saw us heading for the highway and saw me return alone. Both times he waved.

There was also Richard Gellatly who was on his way back to the base from the river when we passed. And, of course, Ken, who had seen me minutes after my return from the highway, at the swings.

The questions continued until beyond lunch hour and when I finally got home, my mother was upset. She couldn't understand why the police persisted with their interrogation of me.

"What do they expect you to say that you haven't already said?" she asked in exasperation.

* * *

It was particularly quiet in class that hot, sticky afternoon. We had all seen the airmen marching out from the station and we knew they had been organized into a search party.

Mr. Edgar made no mention of the matter, nor did any of us. But every so often, someone glanced at the vacant desk. We knew the searchers were looking for Lynne Harper and I think we all felt she would not be found alive.

At the county road the searchers separated into two groups. One was ordered to explore the O'Brien farm and adjacent properties, the other the Lawson farm and bush lot.

Bob Lawson's lot covered about twenty acres at the north end of his property and, adjacent to it, was a large field, partially separated from the woods by a rough road usually referred to as a *tractor trail*.

The searchers fanned out, and in the bush, about thirty yards from the trail, they came upon the body of Lynne Harper. It lay in a shallow depression in the earth, swollen and grotesque, maggots already infesting the eyes and nose.

I learned of the discovery of Lynne's nearly-naked body when I got home from school. Dad had got the details from people on the station and was telling Mom the story. I don't think he realized that I could hear him from the other room.

Lynne had been raped, then strangled with her own blouse.

Our supper was a quiet one. Mom, obviously upset by the news, hardly spoke, while Dad tried to fill in the lengthy silences with talk of fishing and baseball. None of us had really known Lynne but we all felt the impact of her murder.

This was my first encounter with sudden – and violent – death and I found it difficult to identify my deeper feelings.

There was an all-pervading sense of horror, of course, but underlying it there was curiosity, too. How did such things happen? Who could commit such a terrible crime?

On air force bases, as in any small community, there is always a certain amount of gossip, often malicious. I had heard that she had dated some of the enlisted personnel. It was possible, I supposed, that one of these men had killed her. But I didn't like to think that somebody I knew, or saw around the base every day, could murder a little girl. Rather, I preferred to think in terms of a stranger, perhaps whoever had been in the car I had seen stop for Lynne.

I forced myself to stop conjecturing, I put the crime out of my mind for the moment, as only a healthy child can turn his back on tragedy, and I wandered over to Bob Lawson's place.

Bob was usually a happy, talkative kind of guy, but this night he was quiet and sombre. He didn't mention Lynne but I could tell he had been pretty shaken by the whole thing.

About 9:00 p.m. I decided to head for home.

I crossed the road in front of Bob's farm and before I'd gone a dozen yards back toward the base, a Provincial Police car pulled up alongside me.

"Hey, Truscott."

I recognized the driver. He was the officer who had questioned me.

"Truscott, get into the car."

I didn't argue. I climbed into the back and slouched down on the seat. The tone of his voice frightened me.

CHAPTER II

No one spoke. I had become accustomed to the surly silences of his partner, but I half-expected the usual questions from the driver. When these were not forthcoming, my uneasiness increased.

I wanted to ask where we were going, but the broad backs before me didn't encourage communication. We were heading toward the base, so perhaps the officers intended going to my house to pick up my father, as they had once before.

Instead, the car turned in the direction of the R.C.A.F. station proper, and soon we drew up before the guardhouse, a squat, unimaginative structure that looked like every service building I had ever seen.

The car jerked to a stop. As he opened his door, the driver indicated with a barely perceptible nod that I should accompany him and his partner. I scrambled out of the back seat and followed them.

Inside, the driver spoke briefly to the airman at the reception desk, and he in turn pointed to an open door on the left. Still without speaking, the officers motioned me to precede them into the room, where another curt gesture instructed me to sit down on a wooden chair.

I had no idea why I had been brought to the guardhouse. Surely there would be no more questions. I had told over and over, all that I knew of Lynne Harper. I had been over my own movements a dozen times. What more could I tell about the events of the night of Lynne's disappearance?

Once I tried to speak, but my throat was dry and I managed

only to utter an almost inaudible croaking sound. Suddenly I was frightened.

Only once before had I been more afraid. It was in Edmonton and I was nine years old.

I had to pass a park on my way to school and one day I was chased by a huge German shepherd, a vicious brute of a dog that bounded from behind some bushes and was almost on top of me before I moved. I was terrified. I hurled my school bag at him and he fell on it as if it were alive.

In the time that it took the dog to tear the bag to shreds, I managed to climb onto a swing in the playground section of the park and there I stayed, straddling the bar from which the seat hung. The dog, hurling himself upward, snapped his jaws within inches of my feet.

Sitting on the edge of that hard chair in the guardhouse, I remembered the feel of the cold steel bar of the swing through my thin trousers. I recalled how I had tried to draw up my legs, but I had been afraid of losing my balance.

Finally a man, obviously the dog's owner, had appeared. He had grasped the animal by the collar and attached a heavy chain that dangled from his wrist. I had climbed down from my perch and leaned against the upright bar of the swing. I had trembled from head to foot.

I glanced at the officers who sat at a table in the center of the room. They stared back at me impassively, one of them drumming his fingers impatiently on the edge of the table. This was the first sign of emotion I had detected in either of the men. They might have been robots for all the feeling they had displayed since we met.

Despairingly, I thought, no one is going to rescue me from this menace. I felt my teeth begin to chatter, and I wrapped my arms about myself to stop the trembling. I longed for – and dreaded – the end of that night.

* * *

As the minutes passed, I began to realize that the police were waiting for something – or someone. They steadfastly maintained their silence but occasionally one or the other shifted his gaze from me to the door. At last it opened.

The officers hoisted their huge bulks out of the captain's chairs they'd been wedged into, as a man and a woman entered the room.

The woman, who was thin-lipped and wore glasses, walked directly to the table without a word to the officers or a glance at me. She seated herself in one of the chairs recently vacated and produced a shorthand notebook and several pencils from a large, shabby brown purse which she placed on the floor beside her chair. I had seen enough TV to guess she was a police stenographer. I wondered what she expected to record.

The man was big, bigger than either of the officers, and solid as a wall. He towered above me when he walked over to my corner and introduced himself. I had begun to feel like Gulliver in Brobdingnag.

"I'm Inspector Harold Graham, from Ontario Provincial Police Headquarters in Toronto," the newcomer told me.

I said nothing. For a few moments we stared at each other, and I had the small satisfaction of seeing him look away first. Not exactly a victory.

Graham wasted no time on preamble.

"You say that you met Lynne Harper near the school, and that she asked you to give her a ride to the highway...," he began. He was obviously familiar with my account of that evening.

My throat was still dry, and I spoke with difficulty.

"Yes, sir," I said. Then I repeated what I had told the officers so often. I mentioned the ponies, the names of people we had passed on the bridge, and the car that had stopped for Lynne. The recital no longer bored me. I was careful not to omit any details, because with the arrival of Inspector Graham the entire incident had assumed immense proportions in my mind. It was evident these men felt I was withholding information, and I searched my memory painstakingly for some fact, however insignificant I might have regarded it, that I had overlooked or simply forgotten. There was nothing.

"Let's have some times on this little jaunt of yours," the Inspector suggested. The police stenographer paused expectantly.

As I had done with the other officers that morning, I carefully timed my movements from the moment that I'd left our house on Quebec Road, just before 7:00 p.m. until I returned at 8:25.

In my mind I saw my evening's activities set out as a sort of railway schedule:

7:00 – Quebec Road
7:15 – schoolyard
7:30 – county road
7:45 – Highway 8
7:55 – bridge
8:05 – schoolyard
8:25 – Quebec Road

How was I so certain of the time?

I'd glanced at my watch occasionally, and besides, I'd ridden down to the highway so often that I knew almost to the second how long a return trip would take, and I had stopped only a moment on the bridge. I was positive of the hour that I had arrived home because my mother and father left at 8:30, approximately five minutes after my return.

"Okay," Graham said, "now let's run through it again, from the beginning."

"I've told you everything," I insisted, my voice cracking. I longed now for a drink of water.

One of the other officers took over the questioning, this time with minor variations. Had Lynne really suggested that I drive her, or was it my idea? What was I wearing that evening? Did I often give girls rides on my bicycle?

It went on interminably. The three policemen towered over me, firing question after question.

"Start from the beginning," someone would say, and I would obey. But the more I persisted in repeating my original story, the more insistent my inquisitors became that this was not a true account of what had happened that night.

Some time during the interrogation Dr. David Brooks, the station medical officer, came into the room. He spoke briefly to one of the policemen before sitting in the vacant chair across from the police stenographer. He ignored my presence completely at first. Then several times he stared at me oddly, as if he were trying to make up his mind about something.

The police, on the other hand, obviously had their minds already made up. They were convinced that I was lying.

Once more, Graham took over the questioning. I was familiar with Lawson's Bush, was I not, he wanted to know?

I didn't deny it. I had played there often, as had most of the kids on the base. Bob never minded our hanging around, so long as we didn't damage anything. But what did this prove? That I was familiar with the area? So were dozens of others.

Graham was persistent. What did Lynne do in her spare time? Did she frequent the Lawson property?

I hardly knew the girl, I kept trying to tell them. We were classmates but she was not among my friends. What she did outside school (and inside it, too, for that matter) had never interested me.

"Until perhaps two nights ago, Truscott?" Graham snarled.

I wished desperately that I had had other information so that I might have satisfied these men – but there was none. I had told them the simple truth and it had not sufficed.

At one point I considered appealing to Dr. Brooks. Being with the air force, he could perhaps intercede for me, help convince the police I was not lying. But one glance at the medical officer discouraged me. He was smiling thinly and I had the impression he was enjoying the inquisition.

I can close my eyes now and picture the room and its occupants. I can remember the words that were spoken that night. Yet I cannot recall what I felt when Inspector Graham accused me of raping and murdering Lynne Harper.

I was fourteen and very tired. Had I been older, less bewildered, I might have realized where the persistent questioning was leading. As it was, I was totally unprepared for the final shock.

My mind heard the words – but refused to react.

* * *

When I failed to go home that night, my father conducted a

hasty search of the base and general neighborhood. Not finding me, he made inquiries and was finally told that I was at the guardhouse.

When he arrived at 11:00 p.m., I had been in custody for almost five hours. During that time, the police had made no effort to contact my parents.

The moment I saw my father, my mind was filled with thoughts of escape. I wanted to yell, "Take me home, Dad. Please tell them to let me go home."

Graham cut me off before I could say anything. Turning to my father, he said bluntly that he believed I had killed Lynne Harper.

"Good God," my father said and his face was white with shock.

I was allowed only a moment alone with my father. He attempted to comfort me, to reassure me that everything would be fine, that a terrible mistake had been made, and that it would be rectified. But he was as confused as I over the night's happenings and he was terribly angry at the highhanded methods of the Ontario Provincial Police.

At that time neither of us was aware of the complete illegality of the proceedings, but small good it would have done if we had been. Every right afforded the worst offender in the country had been denied me; I had been held for hours incommunicado and without charge; I had not been advised of my rights in the situation and no counsel had been present, nor had I been told that I might summon such aid.

I asked my father if my mother knew where I was, but before he could answer one of the police officers returned and hustled me out of the room and into an adjoining, smaller cubicle. The door closed firmly behind me and I was alone. Only an indistinguishable murmur reached me from the room beyond, where my father was conferring with the inspector from Toronto.

I don't know how long I sat in that room, but I must have dozed off several times before the door finally opened and my father came in with Inspector Graham. Dad's face was ashen.

"Steve," he said, "the police want you to have a medical examination."

My throat was dry. I tried to swallow and couldn't.

"A doctor will come in and look you over," Inspector Graham announced.

"Why do I have to have a medical examination?" I whispered, hoping my father would object.

"We don't have any choice, Steve," he replied.

I dreaded this new ordeal. How embarrassing – no, degrading, – right there in the guardhouse.

In the hallway, Inspector Graham was talking to the men who had brought me to the guardhouse. I couldn't hear what they were saying but they must have been discussing what doctor to summon because one of them walked toward a telephone in the reception area.

"Don't worry, it's going to be all right," Dad told me.

"You bet," I answered, standing close beside him.

* * *

Dr. J. A. Addison was a general practitioner in Clinton and he must have had a rough day, because when he walked into the guardhouse, he looked pretty scruffy to me. He put his medical bag on a chair and spoke briefly to my father.

"I'm going to stay with you, Steve," Dad said.

Dr. Addison told me to strip and I did. Then he proceeded to go over every inch of my skin. He literally examined me from head to toe and he wanted an explanation for every scratch.

He found a scratch on my arm and I explained I had received it playing football. He found a bruise on my knee and I told him I had fallen off my bicycle. Then he saw a scratch on my penis and I said I had caught it in the zipper of my pants. He made no observations. After he had looked me over thoroughly, he told me to dress. He then went into the next room where the police were waiting.

A few minutes later, Inspector Graham came in. He stood in front of me and pronounced the words slowly. I guess he wanted to be sure I heard things right the first time.

"You will be taken to Goderich," he said. "There you will be charged with the murder of Lynne Harper."

I didn't say anything. My throat tightened and I felt my stomach muscles contract.

Inspector Graham spoke to my father in the doorway. I could hear Dad's voice rising. Graham was shaking his head violently. Whatever Dad's protest, he lost the battle. The Inspector shrugged and walked away.

Dad walked back to where I was standing with one of the officers and gave me a friendly punch on the arm.

"I'm going home now," he said. "Your mother will be frantic with worry."

He paused as he went out the door, and winked.

"This will never stick," he assured me. "You'll be back home by morning."

A moment later the officer escorted me out to the waiting squad car. The same driver was behind the wheel. The tires squealed as he took off from the curb. There was no traffic on the highway, and when we reached Goderich I didn't see a single car or pedestrian. By that time it must have been almost 2:00 a.m.

"I think this is it," the driver said.

We had stopped in front of an ordinary-looking house set back from the street, its small patch of lawn bisected by a cement walk. A light shone over the front door, so I guess we were expected. The neighboring houses were in darkness.

A rather plain-looking woman dressed in a faded housecoat answered the officer's knock. Her hair was untidy and she gave every appearance of having been roused from a sound sleep. She was the local justice of the peace.

We were shown into a small living room to the right of the entrance hall and the officers gestured for me to sit down. Gratefully, I sank into a huge armchair.

The justice of the peace sat at a small desk in the corner of the room, and I noticed in the glow from the desk lamp that she was older than I had first thought. Late fifties, maybe. There was no sympathy in the brief glance she gave me before she conversed in low tones with the officers.

Finally, she began:

"Steven Murray Truscott," I heard her say, "on or about June 9, 1959..."

She was reading my indictment and trying to stifle a yawn. She was tired, and I could sympathize. I ached with weariness.

"...did unlawfully murder one Lynne Harper..."

My eyes closed and I forced them open. I thought, at least I should stay awake to hear myself charged with murder.

The J. P. read the charge through and signed the paper, which she handed to one of the officers. It had all taken less than fifteen minutes.

The officer who had taken the initiative from the beginning of my questioning motioned for me to get up. For a moment I hesitated. I wanted to say, "Let me stay here. Let me sleep. I won't run away. Please. Just let me rest for a little while."

Instead, I dragged myself out of the chair and stumbled out of the room ahead of the police. The woman had already disappeared. Probably she was preparing for bed once more. I wondered if she considered charging a fourteen-year-old boy with murder all in a night's work?

I walked back to the car and crawled into the back seat. But I was no longer alone. The officer who had been sitting beside the driver now climbed in with me. They could take no chances, now that I had been formally charged.

* * *

The Goderich courthouse stands alone in the center of the town, an island isolated from other buildings by four intersecting streets, on the opposite side of which are the Bedford Hotel, a Woolworth store, a men's clothing establishment, a drug store and a bakery.

This unimpressive nondescript gray structure, belonging to an unidentifiable architectural period, was our destination that night. The officers escorted me through the front door and down two flights of stairs, where we met a small, bespectacled old man, who accepted wordlessly the papers handed him by one of them.

"Come with me," he said, and I followed him into a small room containing a table and chair and a bed.

"You'll sleep here tonight," the little man told me. Then he was gone, locking the door behind him.

I was alone.

CHAPTER III

My mother used to say that childhood was the most precious and beautiful time of life.

"You'll look back on these years and wish that you could live them over again," she'd smile.

How could she know that most of my growing-up years would be snatched away from me, that the pleasant memories of childhood would be eclipsed by months of terror and years of despair?

How could anyone foresee that, still a child, I would one day stand before a fat, aging Juvenile Court judge named Dudley Holmes, and hear myself arraigned on a charge of murder?

Judge Holmes was the typical bored, disgruntled civil servant, whose prototype one encounters so often in post offices and other government establishments. Throughout the proceedings he didn't even bother to look at me, and he might have been presiding over a traffic case for all the interest that he showed.

But my parents, smiling encouragement, never took their eyes from me, and this eased the situation somewhat.

The police considered me a juvenile delinquent within the meaning of the Juvenile Delinquents Act because I was under the age of sixteen. The Crown Prosecutor, however, thought that I should be tried in adult rather than juvenile court.

Glenn Hays, Q.C. and the judge discussed the matter at some length, without reaching a decision. Finally, Judge Holmes decided to take the matter under advisement and remanded me.

Minutes later I was in a police car, bound for a place that I shall remember in terrifying detail for the rest of my life.

* * *

Sometimes still, when I lie sleepless, or when I awake suddenly in the night, it looms before me, that great stone wall on Gloucester Terrace, with the towering archway and the immense wooden door with the number 50 prominently displayed. This is the county jail in Goderich, built in 1841 of Huron County stone. Here, in this fortress-type prison, the wrongdoers of Huron County have been incarcerated for more than a hundred years, in true mid-nineteenth century tradition.

One of my escorting officers put his shoulder to the door and it opened with a protesting squeak. I entered a long dark stone corridor that was well over 100 feet in length. Our footsteps echoed loudly, amusing the officers. One coughed and the other laughed and suddenly the place was alive with sound. It was eerie and I felt a shiver go through me.

There was a small, heavy door with a peephole at the end of the corridor and one of the policemen banged on it with his fist. A face appeared at the hole and the door opened, admitting us into a cramped reception area with a spiral staircase in the center.

The officers handed a paper to the guard on duty, then they left, with neither a word nor a backward glance for me.

The guard led me up the stairway and into a tiny room with thick stone walls. The jail was clean but that was the best one could say for it.

"Take off your clothes," he ordered.

I undressed and stood naked and trembling in the center of the room. This was my first experience with fanning, or frisking. I wanted to cry but my fourteen-year-old pride denied any outward display of emotion.

My eyes burned and I bit my lower lip when the guard barked, "Put up your arms. Over your head."

I raised them and he stared into my armpits. The act revolted me and I clenched my fists.

"Bend over and touch your toes," he said.

I obeyed, fighting tears. He crouched behind me and inspected my anus. This was standard procedure at all institutions, since prisoners had been known to conceal various items on their bodies.

"All right," he said, assured now that I wasn't hiding anything, "go take a shower."

I stood under the lukewarm water for a few minutes and returned to the room. Another guard was waiting for me with a spray can and he shot de-lousing powder all over me. I was still damp from the shower and the stuff clung to my skin in places. The smell nauseated me.

Someone threw pants, a shirt and some heavy socks on a chair and dropped an old pair of shoes on the floor.

"Get dressed," he said.

The pants were big and uncomfortable. The shoes were too big and they looked dirty as well. I wondered how many men had worn these clothes before me and the thought depressed me.

The guards didn't believe in wasting words. In fact if they could avoid talking to me at all, they did so. When I finished dressing, one of them indicated the door with his thumb. They didn't have to shout or push me around. Outside the room, another guard used his thumb to order me down the stairs, where I was fingerprinted.

A guard then led me to an empty cell block, where I was assigned the center cell. The door was locked and he left the block, locking another door behind him. A sharp click, then complete silence.

The cell was eight feet long and four feet wide. It had a steel frame bed and a chamber pot. There was room for nothing else. I stood on the bed and my head almost touched the ceiling. Through a tiny window I could see into the jail yard, encircled by the high stone wall. I slumped down on the bed and ran my hand over the mattress. It was paper-thin and the only blanket was folded into a pillow at the head of the bed.

I tried to make myself believe that the whole thing was unreal. If I succeeded in believing that I was dreaming, I decided, then it would all really *be* a dream. I concentrated so intensely I became dizzy.

I got up to pace and realized there was no room to walk.

Stretching my arms, I could touch both walls. I was afraid I would panic.

There was a coldness in my belly that seemed to radiate throughout my body. I sat down on the bed again, folded my arms around my knees and drew them close against my chest. I huddled there like a frightened animal.

At supper time a guard unlocked my cell, showed me to a small anteroom at the end of the corridor, and there at a table I sat down to eat.

Afterward I had a few minutes to walk around. I noticed that at the other end of the corridor there was a wash basin and toilet and a guard said I would be allowed to use this instead of the pot in my cell. No one had thought to enclose the facilities. When you relieved yourself, it was in the open corridor, in full view of the guards in the reception area and, of course, in front of any inmate who was in the block. As it happened, I was the only inmate.

After my walk, they locked me in again. The sound of the key disturbed me more this time than it had earlier. I guess it was the thought of being trapped with night approaching.

Cells are often referred to as cages by inmates, but the hole I occupied in Goderich was so cramped that it really did resemble a cage. All it needed was a swing hanging from the ceiling.

As darkness came on, I stood on the bed again and looked out the window. The yard was dark now but I could still see a faint glimmer of light above the wall.

It was a hot sticky night and I thought about the Bayfield River. At this hour I might be riding back from a swim. Slowly, so as not to get overheated.

Later, I looked through the window again. The light was very faint and I thought of home. This was my second night away. Bill and Barb would be in bed now. Ken would be studying. Mom and Dad would be – it hurt to think of home. In many ways though, my imprisonment would be harder on my family than on me.

I lay on the bed. The block was quiet, except for the fluttering of a moth, beating itself against the iron mesh around a bare light bulb in the corridor ceiling.

I was too tense to sleep and I was afraid the feeling of panic might return. I had to put my thoughts beyond the walls. I couldn't allow myself to dwell on my present situation.

There in the dark I sought out my most pleasant memories. They weren't really hard to find. They were all out on the west coast where I had spent so many holidays. And they all centered around Pop. I really loved that man.

Pop was my grandfather on my mother's side and we had a lot in common. We both liked hunting and fishing and the outdoor life in general. Ken and I sometimes spent our entire summer vacations with Pop and Granny.

Pop had a beautiful fishing boat he used for trawling and often we spent several days in Burrard Inlet, catching lobster, crab and salmon. Usually Pop ran the boat himself and cooked most of the meals. On the way up the inlet we'd eat pork and beans, or spaghetti. Landlubber food. But once we got into good fishing waters, it was different. We'd get a supply of crab, or sometimes oysters, and cook them right on the boat. We would have fish for lunch and again for supper. Out there on the water with the mountains on either side, a man could sure work up an appetite.

In the evening, Pop would tell us stories. He spun the usual tall yarns of the fisherman, even though fishing was really just a hobby with him. His real job was foreman of a pile-driving outfit and he worked on dams and projects of that sort. He was a happy-go-lucky kind of man who always saw the bright side of the world and all of his tales reflected this philosophy.

At one time Pop had had a tugboat, which he used to move the booms down to the lumber mills. One of the best vacations I ever had was the summer I worked with him on that boat.

Working the waterways to the mills could be pretty exciting and even an experienced man like my grandfather could get into trouble now and then.

On one occasion, for example, we were behind a boom, trying to direct it away from shore when the tide went out. I guess Pop had miscalculated somewhere. Anyway we were left stranded a short distance out with the boat imbedded in the mud. That might have bothered some people but not Pop. He told me to go into the cabin and sleep while he stayed on deck and watched for the tide to return. I couldn't understand why it was necessary for him to watch for the tide but I didn't question him.

Granny was a different kind of person altogether. She preferred the city to the wilderness and didn't really enjoy roughing it on boats or anywhere else. Occasionally, however, she went fishing with us and she was always a good enough sport to at least pretend she was having a great time. And she could sure fix a fine fish fry.

Pop never knew it but he helped get me through that first terrible night in the County Jail. He was a kind of symbol, I guess. He belonged to the sea and the woods and was guided by the honest, uncomplicated ways of nature. To me, he probably represented freedom.

Whatever it was, I fell asleep that night, imagining myself lying on my back on the deck of his boat. It was rising and falling with the great swells of Burrard Inlet and my face was wet with the cold salt spray.

CHAPTER IV

The tiny wire-enclosed room was regulation. I stood inside and talked through the screen to my mother and father on the outside. They were there when I arrived and they smiled and said hello, and if I hadn't known them so well, I might have been fooled by their calm, cheerful exteriors.

"I'm very proud of you," Mom said, showing me a statuette. "I asked them if you could have it – but it's against regulations."

It was the A.V.M. Hugh Campbell School sports trophy, awarded me for my showing in the annual field day the previous fall. I had taken part in almost all the events, including the 100-yard dash and the 220, 440 and 880 running events, the high jump, the broad jump and the pole vault. By the end of the day, I had captured the senior boys' championship.

"If I'm good in sports, it's because of him." I was talking to Mom and nodding in Dad's direction. This pleased him but it was only the truth. He had played hockey at one time and taught Ken and me all we knew about the game. There was a rink beside our house in Clinton, which we flooded ourselves, and every evening Dad would come out and show us some fancy stickhandling.

Dad was an active man, interested in all sports. He was a hockey coach in winter, a baseball manager in the summer, and between times supervised target practice for the youngsters on the base. He liked being involved with young people and in recognition of his efforts was named Man of the Year for 1959.

This was no small honor. It was a title bestowed annually upon the serviceman deemed to have contributed most to the air force community for that particular period, and Dad was justifiably proud of the distinction.

I was extremely happy about winning the trophy, particularly since two years earlier Ken had captured the senior championship of the school.

"Now there are two champions in the family," Mom said.

Visits were of half-hour duration, so there was little time to discuss my situation. "Ken and Bill and Barb send their love," she said. She paused. "We'll tell them you're looking just fine."

"Goodbye, Champ," said my father.

* * *

In my cell block, I was segregated from the rest of the prisoners, who occupied another wing. Governor Bell told me one day that I was to remain in segregation but gave no reason. I suspected it was because of my age.

With no one to talk to, the days were long. But being alone had its compensations. For one thing, I could walk the corridor almost at will and, whenever the other inmates weren't using it, I was allowed into the yard.

Occasionally one of the guards brought me jigsaw puzzles, which I spread out on the anteroom table. I became so expert at this that there was little challenge – until I came up against Niagara Falls. There was so much water in this particular picture that every piece looked like every other. It was so frustrating that for a time I actually forgot my predicament.

The guard also brought me a pack of cards and I spent hours playing a variety of solitaires. How I longed for a good game of gin rummy!

I was grateful for the puzzles and the cards, but the guard who provided them was the one who had frisked me upon my arrival, and I had to overcome a natural resentment before I allowed myself to really appreciate his friendly overtures.

The other guards were completely indifferent but this man tried, insofar as he was able, to make things easier. And he called me "Steve," reminding me that I still had a Christian name. The others addressed me as "Truscott," or simply, "You!"

I never knew his name but he coached a girls' baseball team, and he had a formidable knowledge of hockey as well. We discussed endlessly the comparative merits of our favorite teams, what players should be traded, and to whom, and whether or not the NHL should expand. No one overhearing us, I am certain, would have suspected the relationship – that of accused murderer and jailer.

At one time I'd been a great racing car enthusiast – Barney Oldfield and Jimmy Snyder were boyhood heroes – and I never missed the Indianapolis 500 or the Daytona 500 on T.V. I thought that sometime I'd like to build my own racing car, and when I mentioned my ambition to the guard, he said that he'd had the same idea when he was younger. Our relationship, then, was simply that of two sports enthusiasts.

* * *

One day Governor Bell came to my cell with an invitation to watch a baseball game on television in his home. For a prisoner, this was indeed an honor and I accepted eagerly.

It was an appealing prospect, leaving my cell for even a commonplace event, and it was once more brought home to me how circumscribed my life had become. But the depression I felt was momentary and I counted the minutes until noon.

After lunch, the governor came for me and we walked to his home where we watched the game together. I remember the Orioles won but I don't recall the opposing team.

I was despondent when he returned me to my cell. It had been disconcerting. I had ventured briefly into the outside world of everyday people and things only to realize that I no longer belonged, that I could not count myself a part of that world.

* * *

During the last two weeks of June, I made three more appearances before Juvenile Court Judge Holmes and now I had counsel. My parents had retained J. Frank Donnelly, Q.C., of Goderich, to defend me.

Donnelly, who immediately after my trial was appointed to the High Court Division of the Supreme Court of Ontario, had been introduced to my parents as one of Huron County's most prominent legal minds, a description that said little for the other lawyers of the area, as I see it now. I guess he tried hard enough but in a completely lacklustre performance, he even lost the first skirmish in Juvenile Court.

Glenn Hays, the Crown Prosecutor, insisted that I be tried in an ordinary – that is, an adult – court. And Frank Donnelly maintained that the case should be heard in Juvenile Court.

Whether or not a juvenile should be tried as an adult is left to the discretion of the court, when the act concerned is an indictable offense under the Criminal Code and the person involved is fourteen years of age or older. Section 9 of the Juvenile Delinquents Act states further that no juvenile shall be tried in the ordinary courts *unless the court is of the opinion that the good of the child and the interest of the community demand it.*

Hays, however, managed to convince the court that the interest of the community demanded that I be tried as an adult and on June 30, 1959, Judge Holmes remanded me for preliminary hearing on July 13 in Magistrate's Court.

I have no clear recollection of Frank Donnelly, beyond his ineptitude as a lawyer, and even that was not brought home to me until months later. In fact, it was only after years in prison that I came to the full realization of what had happened to me. From my arrest until my conviction I was the center of a series of events, the true significance of which was lost on a fourteen-year-old.

Vaguely, I remember Donnelly as a balding man in his mid-fifties. He was not an impressive figure, and when he first visited me in my cell at Goderich his promise that my release from jail was but a matter of time failed to inspire confidence. From the beginning, I had a child's instinctive distrust of him.

The first question he asked me was, naturally, had I killed Lynne Harper. When I said that I had not, he proceeded to discuss the statement I had given the police. I gave the same answers to the same questions. What time did I leave the house? Where did I first see Lynne? What time did we leave the school? Who saw us on the road? Could I remember anything more about the car that had stopped at the highway?

WHO KILLED LYNNE HARPER?

Donnelly appeared satisfied with my answers, and a day or two later made his first move. He applied to the High Court of Ontario for leave to appeal the decision of Judge Holmes.

Permission to appeal was denied. This I learned from my mother, a short time after Donnelly had assured me that it was all a formality, that I was not to worry!

Leave to appeal, I was told, could be granted only if it were deemed essential to the public interest or for *the due administration of justice.* These were only words with no meaning for me at the time, beyond the fact that I understood I would remain in jail, whatever.

* * *

One day, two police officers visited me. Using a tape, one measured my height and the length of my legs and arms, while the other gave me a comb and told me to run it through my hair. Strands were then removed from between the teeth of the comb and placed carefully in an envelope.

I was unaware of the fact at the time, but marks had been found in the ground not far from Lynne's feet, possibly made by the shoes of her killer.

When the searchers discovered Lynne's remains, there were three or four branches from nearby trees, lying diagonally across the body but in no way concealing it. They had been broken off hardwood saplings, at a height of some seven feet from the ground. (At that time, I was barely five feet tall). In addition, a small sampling of hair had been discovered near the body.

I knew that it wasn't *my* hair and doubtless lab reports revealed this fact to the police. But the evidence of the hair was never introduced into court, perhaps for the reason that, rather than strengthen the Crown's case, it would help establish my innocence.

* * *

Mom listened to my account of the officers' visit, and shook her head sadly. Where was it all leading?

That morning, my father had received another blow. The

R.C.A.F. had transferred him to Ottawa, ordering him to report there by July 15. Normally, a person on transfer was given two months' notice, but he was given a week! This meant that he would have to travel 500 miles to visit me.

Poor Dad. He wouldn't even be permitted to finish his term as Man of the Year. Mom was terribly upset and couldn't understand the situation at all. The commanding officer at the base had awarded Dad his title – and now, with no explanation, my father was sent to Ottawa. Since there had been no mention of transfer prior to my arrest, it all seemed more than coincidental.

I wanted to comfort my mother, but what could I say? What do you say to someone you love, when her son has been accused of a murder he didn't commit and her entire way of life is abruptly terminated? And always, there was that wire screen between us.

Suddenly the visit was over and we separated, each with a sense of frustration. I felt responsible for my family's predicament, yet was helpless to resolve the situation. My mother would now have to cope with a great deal on her own.

On her next visit, Mom told me that Dad had purchased a secondhand trailer before leaving for Ottawa, and had moved it to a lot on the outskirts of Goderich. Ken and Bill and Barb would be sharing it with her.

"A trailer?" I asked increduously.

"That's right," she smiled happily. "Now at least the children and I can be close to you."

CHAPTER V

Butch George and I were not just classmates. We raised the flag at school together in the morning and lowered it at night. We liked and disliked the same teachers. We played sports together. In every sense of the word, we were buddies.

Now at my preliminary hearing in the Goderich Courthouse, I could hardly believe my ears. A police officer was on the witness stand, quoting incredible things from statements allegedly made by my friend.

How could he have lied like that? Why would he deliberately try to incriminate me?

The policeman said Butch had made three statements. In the first, he had said that he had been at the river on the night of the murder and that he had seen me cross the bridge with Lynne and return a few minutes later alone. In the second, he said that he had been swimming on the evening in question but had not noticed me on the bridge.

The really damning statement was the third, in which he stated that he had not seen me at the bridge but that at some point in the evening I had asked him a favor. My supposed request was that if the police questioned him, he was to say he had seen me cross the bridge and then return to it.

The three statements were, of course, in conflict and my lawyer pointed this out, though not too forcefully.

Then followed the testimony of Gordon Logan, another class-mate, who had also been at the river. He had seen me cross the bridge with Lynne on the bar of my bicycle, then come back alone, stop on the bridge for a couple of minutes and proceed toward the station.

Richard Gellatly testified that he had been returning from the river and had seen me heading toward Highway 8 with Lynne on my bicycle.

I listened half-heartedly to the evidence of Dr. John Llewellyn Penistan, the district pathologist, who said the time of death had been somewhere between 7:15 and 7:45 p.m. Later, Dr. Brooks and Dr. Addison took the stand.

The proceedings were dreary and every once in a while Dudley Holmes, who had first considered my case as a Juvenile Court judge and was now presiding over my hearing as a magistrate, became impatient with counsel. Two or three times he even told them to make their points quickly because he wanted to get the session over with. I didn't know it at the time but he was a sick man and he died a few months later.

Then the Crown called what it considered its key witness, a thirteen-year-old girl named Jocelyne Goddette who was also in my class, and her testimony really infuriated me.

She testified that early on the day of the murder, I had made a date with her to look for newborn calves in Lawson's Bush. She said further that between 5:30 and 6:00 that day, I had gone to her house to collect her but, not having had supper, she was unable to accompany me.

She was saying that I wanted to go to the very place where they found Lynne Harper. And at the time she placed me at her house, I was actually buying coffee for my mother.

How could she lie like that? *Why* would she? I was asking the same questions I had asked about Butch George.

The court recessed after her testimony and, in anger, I flung open the door of the prisoner's box. My action attracted the attention of the magistrate and he called my lawyer to the Bench.

Donnelly came to me after and said, "Judge Holmes wants you to cool down."

"That was a lie," I snapped. "That girl lied. I did *not* go to her house."

"Just take it easy," he repeated.

The preliminary hearing ended without my knowing the outcome and I was returned to my cell. Two days later Mom came to see me. She didn't have to say anything; I could tell from her face that the news was bad.

Magistrate Holmes, by the authority given him under section 460 of the Canadian Criminal Code, had ruled that I should be committed to trial at the Fall Assizes.

"Mr. Donnelly says that no judge or jury would ever convict anyone on evidence as flimsy as that at your preliminary hearing," my mother assured me. I wanted to believe her.

* * *

I seldom show my feelings.

"You're like your mother," my father used to say whenever I was sick or hurt and didn't want to cry.

And it was true. We both took a kind of pride in not letting others know how we really felt.

But strife manifests itself in other ways, and after the preliminary hearing I began to have headaches, which sometimes lasted for hours. One of the guards said that they were from tension, and he gave me pills a couple of times, but they didn't help.

It was almost two months between the preliminary hearing and the opening of the trial. All day, day after day, I sat huddled in my cell, walked in the yard or played solitaire in the anteroom.

The evenings were the hardest to bear. Gradually the yard darkened, and as I watched the last vestige of light disappear from the sky above the wall, I drifted into a restless sleep, a sleep filled with dreams of home.

Every day was the same. I got up at 8:00 a.m., washed in the corridor basin, ate breakfast in the anteroom, sat in my cell until lunch, played cards in the afternoon and returned to my cell after supper.

But one day there was a surprising diversion. I was in the yard when I heard a voice call softly, "Hey, Steve!"

I looked up. There, perched in a big tree whose branches rose above and overhung the twenty-foot-wall, was my brother Ken. So thick were the leaves at that time of year, he was barely visible.

"How did *you* get up there?" I asked, incredulous.

"It was easy," he answered. Poor Ken. He had a terrible fear of heights. He got dizzy just standing on a table. "But it's a long way down."

He had nothing special to report. Mom and the kids were fine and life in the trailer had turned out to be a lot of fun. They were hooked up for electricity and water and it was almost like living at home. Well, no, not quite.

"I wish we were back out West," he said at one point.

"Vancouver?" I asked.

"Yeah. Or Edmonton."

We both liked the West which we considered so much friendlier than Ontario. We had found Clinton a cold place. People didn't make friends there the way they did in Alberta and British Columbia.

"That was a pretty good paper route, huh?"

Ken was reminiscing about the Edmonton base. With 400 families, it had been quite an undertaking. We used bicycles in summer and toboggans in winter. Ken and I had been taught that money didn't grow on trees and that if you wanted it, you went out and earned it. Reared on this philosophy, we were go-getters and when we weren't delivering papers, we were cutting lawns or shovelling driveways.

"Do you want anything?" Ken asked.

"I'd like my bike," I laughed. "Now figure out how to get it to me."

It was a strange conversation between two boys. There was Ken high up in a tree, and here was I, down below in a jail yard. I was, of course, glad to see my brother again but there was an air of fantasy about the whole episode.

"I'll try to get back in a couple of days," he said as he started down the tree. "Keep watching the branches."

He made good his promise and two days later he was calling again from the tree. This time, however, our meeting was short-lived. We chatted for two or three minutes, then suddenly he waved, called a hasty goodbye and clambered down through the branches.

My mother explained his sudden departure next visiting day.

89

Some old busybody living across the road from the jail had seen him climbing the tree and had called the police. Fortunately, Ken spotted the squad car before it reached the jail and he got away safely.

CHAPTER VI

Summer passed and the leaves began to turn and on September 16, 1959 I went on trial for my life.

From the time of my arrest in June, until Mr. Justice R. I. Ferguson ordered me escorted to the prisoner's box, a sort of numbness, a sense of unreality, had sustained me. Even the preliminary hearing had had little significance. But suddenly, gazing across the crowded courtroom, I knew at last that this was no nightmare from which I would awaken. The black-robed judge, the lawyers, the guards – these people were real. This was not happening to someone else, a stranger. *I* was on trial!

Most people live out their lives without ever seeing the inside of a courtroom. But for me, at fourteen, that dingy room was almost as familiar as the lobby of the local movie house. I felt that I knew every warped floorboard and every crack in the dingy gray ceiling. I had even counted the buttons on the uniforms of the guards.

But of many aspects of the trial itself, I have only the vaguest recollection. Perhaps my mind succeeded in wiping out the memory of much of that travesty, or maybe it is simply buried beneath the ten years of injustice, fear and frustration that followed.

No one, not even my lawyer, had told me what to expect. I knew nothing of courtroom procedure, but what kid does? Aside from the spectacular – and usually inaccurate, I have discovered – murder trials which are produced for the television audience, and the novels of Erle Stanley Gardner, the average teenager is unfamiliar with the machinery of justice.

My parents could do little to prepare me for the ordeal of a murder trial, for they were as ill-informed on procedure as was I. Looking back, the thought persists that everyone involved, legally, was intent upon making the experience as harrowing as possible for us.

The first morning of the trial was devoted to the selection of a jury. I learned later that my mother had suggested to my lawyer, Mr. Donnelly, that perhaps he should try to include some women among the jurors. I don't know how he reacted to this suggestion. I know only that when the final selection was made, it was an all-male jury that was empaneled.

The jurors were not an impressive group. The majority of them were farmers from several sections of the county, and there was a barber and a grocer from Seaforth, a couple of factory workers, a garage mechanic, a dairyman, a hardware salesman and the operator of a bowling alley.

I doubt that, taken together, their knowledge of trial procedure was any greater than mine. I do know that when each declared himself to be unbiased he wasn't fooling anyone.

Over the years, writers and commentators have observed that had I gone on trial in Toronto, or any large Canadian city, it is almost a foregone conclusion that I would have been acquitted. I think this is so. I could feel the antipathy of that small-town jury, moved not by sympathy for Lynne but hatred for me.

I recall one juror in particular, who stared at me constantly and whenever I returned his stare, he averted his glance. I later learned that this man told everyone:

"Whenever I looked at him, that boy stared right back. He didn't even have the decency to lower his eyes!"

It was always the same story. Whenever some action on my part might have been construed as a sign of innocence, it was interpreted as an indication of guilt. Had I *not* stared back, I would have been accused of being unable to look him in the eye!

The same sort of remark was made about my behavior the day following the murder. I did extremely well in an exam that day, thus I was pictured as callous and cold-blooded, with no conscience! It never occurred to my accusers that perhaps this was a sign of my innocence – that I did well because nothing was troubling me.

Prior to the actual proceedings, the prosecution ordered an impressive number of exhibits to be brought into the courtroom. They included several tree branches, withered and brown; the shoes supposedly worn by Lynne when she was killed; a number of lab containers and a stack of photographs. By contrast, I noted that the defense table was naked of exhibits. Only a few papers and law books were visible.

The significance of the branches escaped me until I remembered that when they found Lynne, her body had been covered with several boughs which had been ripped from ash trees in the area. I recalled, too, the day that two police officers had measured the length of my arms, to establish whether or not I could have torn them off – seven feet from the ground.

Sometimes when I looked at those branches and realized they had covered a dead body, I forgot the hopelessness of my own situation in contemplation of what Lynne must have endured. She had been only a casual acquaintance, but the manner of her death filled me with horror. It meant little that it had been a sexual crime. I thought only of how frightened she must have been of her attacker and I wondered if she had known she was going to die.

Inevitably, this line of thought went full circle and I returned once more to my own predicament. My grandfather used to say, with reference to some minor wrong-doing, "Well, boy, they can't hang you for that."

I wondered now. Could they hang me for a murder I hadn't committed?

* * *

The trial lasted two weeks, and as one day followed another, I began to lose track of time, a common condition among prisoners. It is the sameness of the days that eats away at you. My day started with a guard waking me. Then I washed and pecked at cold porridge or soggy toast and gulped weak tea. After this, I put on the blue suit and white shirt my mother had bought for me at a store across from the courthouse.

When I was finally forced to discard that suit in favor of an ill-fitting one provided by the government, I remembered that during my trial it had been a sort of talisman.

Throughout the summer of 1959, my mother walked the several blocks to the courthouse every day. Sometimes my brothers and sister were with her and they waited outside while she spent a half-hour or so with me. Other times, she came alone. But always she was cheerful and confident, and on the day she brought the suit to me, I recall that she was particularly optimistic.

"I know it's going to be all right," she said.

Then she gave me the suit and shirts and told me how important it was that I be properly dressed.

"I want everyone in the courtroom..." She paused for a long moment. "I want them to see what a fine boy you are."

It was all so futile. I could have sat in the prisoner's box with wings and halo and still not have convinced that jury that I was not the devil himself.

Still, I treasured the suit. It was a link with normalcy, a part of a world from which I'd been suddenly alienated. I even convinced myself that it was *lucky,* and each night I laid out the trousers and folded the jacket carefully on the floor beside my cot.

Although the trial was an ordeal, I was always impatient for the arrival, at 8:30, of the two police officers who escorted me to the courthouse. Anything was preferable to the confines of that cell, and in the beginning, I had not abandoned hope of gaining my freedom.

As the trial progressed, however, my adolescent optimism began to fade. It became evident even to me that from the moment Mr. Justice Ferguson instructed the guard to "place the prisoner in the box" each day, until court adjourned at four in the afternoon, the whole thing was a mere formality. Later, of course, I realized that it had been a complete farce from the start.

On several occasions, when His Lordship addressed the jury, it seemed to me he implied that witnesses for the defense were not to be relied upon as truthful, whereas those of the prosecution were beyond reproach.

At the preliminary hearing I had been incensed at the lies of Jocelyne Goddette, and astonished by the conflicting testimony of Arnold (Butch) George, as read by a police officer. Now, I listened increduously as Butch himself related a conversation I had allegedly had with him the night of Lynne's murder.

The testimony of some other witnesses might be forgotten the moment I heard it, but because I had always considered Butch one of my best friends, what he told the court remained with me. In a sense, this was his *fourth* statement concerning that night, because at the preliminary hearing he'd made no mention of any cow and calf.

Under oath, he told the Crown Attorney that he had visited me at my home that night about 8:45, and told me he'd heard that I'd been in Lawson's Bush with Lynne. According to him, I then denied this, saying, rather, that we'd been looking for a cow and calf at the *side* of the bush. Further, I was supposed to have asked him why he was so interested in what Lynne and I had done that night, to which he replied: "Skip it. Let's play ball."

I was amazed. In the first place, Butch George had, to my knowledge, been nowhere near my home that night. Secondly, it seemed to me that his sudden interest in cows and calves had been suggested by the trumped-up story of Jocelyne Goddette.

Since I knew *I* had told the truth concerning that night, it was obvious to me the statements of Butch and Jocelyne had been a conspiracy of lies. It was not so apparent to the Crown, nor to my own counsel who failed to discredit the testimony.

At the time, my reaction to Butch's perfidy was shock and outrage. But later in penitentiary, I would be able to read about my case and be almost objective about it. In fact, sometimes it was as though I were reading about someone else.

Those first months following my arrest, I was naturally completely preoccupied with the hideous predicament in which I found myself. It would be years before I would really begin to wonder about things and try to explain the strange developments in my case. So much was incomprehensible.

I remembered a picture I'd seen – *The Witches of Salem,* I think it was – in which a group of young girls lied about a woman in the village, saying that she was a witch, and before long half the town was accusing the rest of the inhabitants of black magic. In the beginning, though, the children had lied simply for the excitement of it and the attention it attracted.

Perhaps this had been the motive behind Jocelyne's testimony. She may have craved the limelight and was too stupid to realize the terrible thing she was doing. It was difficult to believe this of Butch, yet what other explanation could there be? At one stage, I theorized that he and Jocelyne had been paid to lie. But by whom? That didn't make sense. Nothing about anything made sense, really.

A number of theories about what actually did happen to Lynne have been put forth by writers, police, lawyers, even detective story addicts. But so many questions remain unanswered, are perhaps unanswerable.

Although I couldn't put it into words at the time of the trial, the thought was always there – the feeling that so much was unexplained. Yet no one, including my own lawyer, thought this strange.

One of the aspects of the case that puzzled me a great deal concerned the search party that found Lynne's body. In the first place, who organized and directed it, and why was Lawson's Bush the first area searched?

Even if I had lied about the car at the highway, which I hadn't, it was only logical to assume that the police would first investigate the possibility that Lynne was miles away.

It's amazing when one realizes that, with the exception of the schoolchildren, not a soul was questioned *extensively* about Lynne's disappearance. From the moment that I revealed having given her a lift to the highway, I became the chief – and only – suspect. It's almost as if someone – someone with influence and authority – wanted it that way.

This sort of theorizing I have kept mostly to myself. It wouldn't have done for anyone to think that I was developing a persecution complex!

But other possibilities have also crowded my thoughts.

Perhaps Lynne's encounter at the highway had been prearranged. She told *me* she planned to visit a man who kept ponies, but this might have been a spur-of-the-moment tale. It's possible that she thought her parents might be looking for her, especially since she had argued with them just prior to leaving home. Perhaps she didn't want them to know that she had accepted a date with someone.

It is just possible that her date may also have been her murderer.

CHAPTER VII

As the trial wore on, it became evident even to me that we were losing ground.

The medical testimony, concerned primarily with establishing the cause and time of Lynne's death, seemed especially damaging, although I'd have needed an interpreter to understand what was being said. It wasn't so much the words of the witnesses but rather their attitude.

Doctor Brooks appeared almost vindictive, and I have the same impression, after all these years, that he was bent on doing whatever he could to have me found guilty. Persecution complex? I wonder. From the beginning, he had taken an active part in the proceedings.

Brooks was an eager and willing member of the search party, who reportedly had, after a mere glance at the body, pinpointed the crime as the work of "an amateur teenager." Later, when I had been picked up and taken to the guardhouse, he was present for most of the questioning, and he assisted Dr. Addison in his examination of me. This fact he emphasized at the trial, and he seemed, from the words he chose in testifying, eager for a conviction. (See Supreme Court Report, pages 233-4, 242-3, 301-2)

By contrast, the testimony of Dr. Penistan, district pathologist, while nonetheless damning, was unbiased. (See Supreme Court Report, pages 232-233, 235-242, 299-300)

The Crown had based its entire case on the time of Lynne's death, which Dr. Penistan had established as "between seven o'clock and a quarter to eight." And I had admitted being with Lynne part of that time!

Later, Dr. Berkeley Brown, testifying for the defense, set the time of death at more than an hour later, which made sense to me, because I *knew* that she hadn't died when Penistan said. (See Supreme Court Report, pages 234, 236-7, 242-4)

But the jury didn't seem too interested in testimony other than the Crown's.

Damaging as the medical testimony was, I could accept that the pathologist was honestly in error. The police witness, however, who testified to being unable to distinguish one make of car from another on the highway while standing on the bridge, angered me. This was an outright accusation that I had been lying about what I'd seen.

Under cross-examination, the officer admitted that no cars had stopped at the intersection while he was on the bridge, that he had watched only vehicles speeding along the highway at 50 m.p.h., and that had a car stopped , he wouldn't have known its make or model because he was unfamiliar with cars!

Further, Mr. Donnelly secured the admission that it had been ten or fifteen years since the policeman had had his eyes examined. Still, I was annoyed.

I was even more annoyed at the treatment afforded my mother on the stand. She was cross-examined endlessly by Hays, and every second remark of the Crown Attorney contained an implication that she was lying.

This was the one time throughout the trial that I really struggled to keep my composure, because I wanted nothing so much in the world at that particular moment as to leave the prisoner's box and take a swing at the arrogant Mr. Glenn Hays, Q.C.

* * *

At the outset of the trial, Mr. Justice Ferguson referred to section 427 (now 441) of the criminal code under which proceedings against an accused under sixteen years of age must be conducted *without publicity.* This meant that newspapermen were not barred from the courtroom but that they could print nothing until a verdict had been returned.

Every day, reporters sat in court and mixed with the spectators in the hall after each session. I suppose that this was when they received the impressions recorded after the trial. One reporter referred to me as a "cool customer," and another, as "clever and devious."

Doubtless the fact that I resorted to neither tears nor hysterics established the "cool" description, but I was unaware that there were ground rules for court behavior, other than the obvious one, the breach of which meant a charge of contempt. I had no idea that one's general mien was of such major significance.

As to "clever and devious," had I intended to rape and murder Lynne Harper, would I not, rather, have been stupid beyond belief, to drive my victim, minutes prior to killing her, past innumerable witnesses? This fact occurred to no one, not even to my counsel.

The reporters, however, were only doing their job. The spectators were a different species. Every day at the noon recess and again in the afternoon, they crowded about outside the courthouse when I was being escorted back to the jail.

"There he is!" someone would exclaim, pointing, and all eyes would turn to stare avidly at the sex fiend of Huron County.

Sometimes I caught the words "monster" or "bastard" as the guards hustled me into a waiting car, and I wanted to turn and stare down my attackers, not appear to be running away.

In retrospect, the aversion I felt to being a public spectacle remains. But there is another, different kind of anger I feel when I speculate on the murder.

I wonder, did the real killer of Lynne Harper sit each day in that courtroom, awaiting a verdict that would set him at ease for all time? Then did he mingle with the spectators outside the court, enjoying my humiliation?

* * *

The verdict, when it came, was almost anticlimactic.

The parade of Crown witnesses; the valiant efforts of Gordon Logan and Allen and Douglas Oats, testifying for the defense, to collaborate my declaration of innocence; the outright denunciation of their testimony as lies, by Mr. Hays; and finally, the judge's partisan charge to the jury, are all a matter of record in the case of Regina vs Truscott.

What is not on record is my dismay at the treatment of Logan and the Oats boys. Because until he is in a similar situation, no one can imagine the frustration another feels when he *knows* something to be so, yet all around him are convinced that it is otherwise. Gordon, Allen and Douglas were telling the truth. *I* had told the truth. All for nothing.

I tried to take heart from Mr. Donnelly's assurance that no jury could possibly find me guilty, but when those twelve men retired to decide my fate, there was a crawling sensation in my stomach, and my hands were damp.

I awaited the jury's decision in a small anteroom off the main courtroom. The officer who escorted me there and remained with me was a young O.P.P. officer, recently arrived in Canada from Ireland. I found his accent and manner of speaking strangely comforting, and when it was time for him to take me back, I almost believed him when he said that everything would be all right. Still, a small, nagging fear remained.

I was ordered into the prisoner's box and told to stand while the jury filed back into the courtroom. It was then 10:55 p.m. They had been out since 8:38 p.m.

I listened impassively to the words of the foreman:

"We find the defendant guilty as charged, with a plea for mercy."

Mercy.

The judge then proclaimed:

"...The sentence of this court upon you is that you be taken from here to the place from whence you came and there be kept in close confinement until Tuesday, the 8th day of December, 1959, and upon that day and date you be taken to the place of execution, and that you there be hanged by the neck until you are dead, and may the Lord have mercy on your soul."

* * *

And so I was taken to the place from whence I came. Back to the County Jail in Goderich.

My tiny cubicle was now a death cell, from which I was permitted to emerge only once a week in order to bathe, and I was under constant surveillance by a guard.

I longed to walk in the corridor, and I begged the jail governor to allow me into the yard. But prisoners under sentence of death were not allowed out of cells.

How to describe the agony of those weeks of waiting.

To me, the miracle is that I was able to survive them and still retain my sanity. I use the word *miracle* because how else could a human being endure such torment.

My parents spoke encouragingly of appeals, but how does one manage to keep a condemned person's hopes alive when he is constantly immersed in thoughts of death?

I was sentenced to be executed and not once during those early weeks did I doubt that it would be carried out. Commutation was not a wholesale process in those days.

Something in my body mechanism kept me from going berserk but that same something made me painfully aware that days that had once seemed endless had somehow passed with alarming speed.

The death cell is a destructive place, robbing its occupant of all dignity, and at that time, abandoning him all too frequently to the ultimate humiliation of the scaffold.

I had been filled with despair for some time but as my execution drew near, I felt the horror of fear – the fear of approaching death.

And into my frightened, bewildered world one day he came, a soft-spoken air force chaplain with a message: repent and be saved.

I had been taught respect, even a certain awe, for the clergy. Thus I sat there silently while my visitor spoke of God's forgiveness and of His Commandment, *Thou shalt not kill.* Then I realized that what the chaplain was really saying was that God's forgiveness was contingent upon a full confession. He was forgetting that the Sixth Commandment might well be applied to the State that had ordered my execution.

Looking back, I wish that I'd had the temerity to shout:

"Tell God to save His forgiveness for the jury, and for the real killer of Lynne Harper. And there is another Commandment that says, 'Thou shalt not bear false witness against thy neighbor.' "

But I said nothing, until at last, shaking his head sadly and raising his eyes slightly toward heaven, the chaplain left.

* * *

October became November, and one morning I awoke to the sound of hammering outside my cell.

My nerves were raw, my imagination over-stimulated by fear and I saw in my mind a picture of the gallows, as pictured in my English history text.

They were building a scaffold!

The hammering went on all morning and I winced with every blow. Yet, it couldn't be. It was too soon. They wouldn't build a scaffold and leave it there for weeks. Or would they?

I stood on my bed and peered through the window but could see nothing. Finally my favorite guard reported for duty and I asked him what was going on outside.

"They're repairing a house across the road," he said casually.

I didn't tell him why I had asked. Weak with relief, I sank down on the edge of my bed and buried my face in my hands.

CHAPTER VIII

A late November wind howled across Lake Huron. It cut like a knife through Goderich and descended upon the county jail, whistling through the cracks in the ancient stonework and filling the corridor of my cell block with weird, wailing sounds.

I fell asleep just before daylight, clutching my thin blanket to me against the cold and cursing the wind that wailed like a banshee. When I woke, there was snow on the ground. It was the first of the season and once would have filled me with joy.

* * *

It was played by many children under different names but I called it the *if and then game.* The mechanics of the game were the same all over – just the stakes were different in my case.

In this instance, I had decided that if by the end of November any leaves remained on the tree branch overhanging the yard outside my cell window, then I would not be hanged in December.

Thus, each morning I forced myself to examine the branch for *traitors,* as I had come to think of the fallen leaves.

I particularly dreaded a morning following a windy night, but each day I was rewarded with the sight of leaves clinging tenaciously to the branch. True, their numbers grew ever less, but I had selected several that I thought of as *favorites,* and I became convinced that these would not fail me!

It was a silly game – and I often wonder now if perhaps at the time I wasn't a little mad – but it was something to concentrate on other than the approaching date of execution. And it worked!

On the last day of November five leaves remained on the

branch. And late that afternoon the kindly guard handed me a newspaper.

"There's great news," he told me, and he pointed to a small item at the bottom of the front page. It was a brief announcement that the date of my execution had been postponed until February 16 to allow an appeal to the Ontario Court of Appeal.

This was the first news I received that a stay of execution had been ordered. I often wonder when I would have been told, had it not been for that guard.

I was dazed and it was some time before the full significance of what had occurred got through to me.

I wasn't going to die! Hastily, I qualified my jubilance. I wasn't going to die as soon as I'd expected. But Pop used to say, "Where there's life there's hope," and I was alive! Perhaps there would be yet another miracle – an appeal, a new trial, even an acquittal.

Suddenly, for the first time, it seemed, I was aware of life beyond my 8' x 4' world. I could hear cars passing in the street outside, and now and then the honking of a horn or the screech of brakes. How good it was to be alive, even in captivity!

On her next visit, my mother appeared more rested and composed than I had seen her since my ordeal began. She had spoken to Frank Donnelly and he had assured her that a boy of fourteen would not hang.

Her optimism cheered me but I recalled that Donnelly had also predicted that the charges would be dismissed and that I would never come to trial – and later, having to stand trial, that I would never be convicted. Frankly, I found his assurances less than heartening. But I said nothing, determined not to undermine my mother's sudden good spirits.

* * *

December 25, 1959. The first of ten Christmases that I was to spend behind bars.

For dinner there were gray mashed potatoes and congealing gravy heaped on a slice of turkey, which I ate seated on the edge of my cot, balancing the heavy steel tray on my knees. Even on Christ's birthday I was not allowed the luxury of eating at the table in the corridor.

In the afternoon, members of the Salvation Army visited the jail and I could hear them singing carols with inmates in another cell block. A guard said that they wished to see me and asked how I felt about it. I told him flatly that I wanted no part of them.

Every Sunday morning they had come to the jail to hold services for the inmates, and not once had any one of them expressed a desire to see me. I saw no reason then why I should contribute to the saintly glow of satisfaction they no doubt felt at having sacrificed a Christmas afternoon to bring cheer to the unfortunates.

One person wished me a Merry Christmas that day. It was, of course, the guard who had been my friend throughout and when he arrived for the holiday shift he came directly to my cell, wished me all the best and gave me a bag of candy.

My friend had the good sense, a week later, not to extend the traditional greetings, and New Year's Day, 1960 passed without my noticing.

On January 12, my appeal to the Ontario Court of Appeal opened, conducted by John O'Driscoll. Mr. O'Driscoll had been recruited on my behalf by Frank Donnelly who, thirty-six hours after my conviction, had been appointed trial judge in the Ontario Supreme Court.

The hearing continued for three days but I was not informed of the outcome for some time.

My fifteenth birthday, January 18, was marked by a visit from my mother, who wished me many happy returns through the mesh screen in the visitors' room. I resented that screen, yet it had its advantages. The face of the person on the opposite side was little more than a white blur, thus aiding us in our little game of "everything is just fine," that we each played out faithfully.

Ken had sent me a wrist watch, which I attempted to examine through the screen, but I was not allowed to have it, nor was I allowed the chocolate that Mom had brought. I was permitted, however, to keep the birthday cards from the family and Pop and Granny.

There was little to talk about, the county jail hardly being conducive to birthday celebrations, but we managed to fill the allotted half-hour with cheerful, inane chatter.

Mom asked me if I remembered my thirteenth birthday. I did, and it was a pleasant memory.

Karen Hamill, who lived next door to us on Quebec Road, was born on the same date as I, and two years previous we had had a joint party. Mom had made a giant birthday cake, which she'd decorated and inscribed, "Happy Birthday Karen and Steve."

"She wore a white dress and after the party we went to a dance at the school," I reminisced. That had been my first real date, I guess.

It was the kind of conversation we might have had around the dinner table at home. Mom mentioned Karen's brother, Craig, and I remembered all the times that the two of us had gone fishing at the river for pike and bass. We'd gone hunting too, but with poor results. Neither of us ever seemed too enthusiastic about shooting anything. I can't recall ever having brought home so much as a rabbit.

"We were pretty unhappy when the Hamills left, weren't we?" Mom asked.

I had been unhappy all right. I had stood outside the house and watched the truckers load their furniture. And before Craig and Karen had left, we all went for a ride on our bicycles.

"Do you remember Carol?" Mom went on.

Of course. Carol Carter and I had been good friends. I guess my second date had been with her. At Saturday night get-togethers we danced to records, and once we went to a movie together.

Then the Carters moved away. That was the sad part of life on an air base. Families were always moving in and out. The moment you made friends with someone, the family was transferred. I often envied children of civilians who lived in the same community for years and made life-long friendships.

Mom had been an air force wife long enough to become accustomed to the moving. Getting used to living in a trailer in Goderich while Dad lived in Ottawa, however, was something else. But she never complained and any time I mentioned her separation from Dad, she would shake her head and smile and tell me not to worry about things like that.

* * *

On January 20, I was informed that my appeal before the Ontario Court of Appeal had been dismissed. Then, a few days later, I was told my sentence had been commuted to life imprisonment.

The courts were convinced of my guilt but the Cabinet, in its infinite goodness, had decided to spare my life – so that I could spend it behind bars.

So much for justice and innocence.

I felt a strange indifference to it all now. Those months in the death cell had left me with a kind of numbness and I was unable to rejoice. One takes so much, I guess, and then the body builds up an immunity to emotion.

My favorite guard was relieved to hear the news though and that day he threw open my cell door, and with a wide sweep of his arm, gestured for me to join him in the corridor. It was the first time since my conviction that I had been out of my cell, except to bathe or visit, and I walked for so long I was exhausted.

My gratitude to the Cabinet for sparing me from the gallows was exceeded only by my happiness at being allowed into the corridor.

My commutation meant, too, that I could once more go out into the yard for exercise.

My first day out was mild and the snow was sticky. I made a pile of snowballs and hurled them against the wall until my arm was sore. It felt wonderful. There were so many muscles I'd almost forgotten about.

Unfortunately, my trips to the yard were interrupted briefly by an incident involving two girls and a boy who had escaped from a training school in Michigan. They had been captured and housed for a time in the county jail.

One afternoon in the yard they erected a huge igloo, which they invited the chief turnkey, a strict and rather disagreeable individual, to inspect. Once they had lured him inside, they collapsed the structure on top of him.

Actually, the sight of the guard struggling up through the snow was most enjoyable, but as a result, no one was allowed into the yard for several days thereafter.

* * *

Governor Bell seemed genuinely happy when he announced on the last day of January that I would be transferred to the Training School for Boys in Guelph.

"You'll be taken first to Kingston Penitentiary but you'll be there only overnight," he said. "The next day you'll go to the school. It'll be fine there because you'll be with boys your own age."

I wasn't that enthusiastic about Guelph, but then the only place I wanted to go to was home.

On February 2, 1960, my eight months of confinement in the Goderich dungeon came to an end. I discarded my prison clothes, wondering briefly who would wear them after me, and put on the blue suit that my mother had bought me for the trial.

The last time I had worn that suit I had heard a judge sentence me to death.

CHAPTER IX

The sheriff and his deputy were waiting in the reception area to take me into custody. While one of them handcuffed my wrists the other produced leg irons.

"I don't think you'll need those," Governor Bell remarked casually, saving me momentarily from the irons.

I wanted to thank him for that gesture. I wanted to thank him too, for letting me watch baseball in his home but already I was being led to the iron door, flanked by the two officers, both of whom towered above me. They were huge men, well over six feet tall and weighing at least 250 pounds.

We walked down a somewhat frightening stone corridor and the officers, talking loudly to each other, listened for the echoes. Everyone who passed there must have played that game.

We went through the huge, creaking wooden gate and I felt the sharp, cold air of Gloucester Terrace. I breathed deeply, filling my lungs. I had done this so often in the yard, as if I could store it up until my next outing.

When we reached the car, the deputy produced the leg irons again. I had seen pictures of them in detective magazines but they looked even more ominous in real life.

"I think we're going to put these things on you," the sheriff announced. He now felt safe, out of sight of the governor. "You can probably run faster than we can and we don't want to take any chances."

I had no intention of trying to make a break for it but the sheriff was certainly telling the truth about the running. With all that weight, neither of them would have made it to the corner.

These officers were like most of the others in that they avoided talking to me whenever it was possible, preferring rather to motion in the right direction with a wave of a hand, the flick of a thumb.

They had a two-door Buick and getting into the back seat wearing handcuffs and leg irons was no simple feat. Fortunately there was no one else around as I shuffled to the door of the car, crouched with my wrists together in front of me and dropped onto the seat. Once inside, I couldn't seem to manoeuvre myself into a comfortable upright position, so I remained slouched.

We drove out of the Glouchester Terrace area and began picking our way across town. It had been a drab place when my parents took me there on the occasional Saturday and now, with piles of dirty brown snow everywhere, it was even dingier.

We pulled up in traffic near the courthouse and I took a quick look around at the Bedford Hotel, the Woolworth store and the various clothing shops. Nearby was the movie house and a couple of eating places. This was downtown Goderich where people went on Saturday nights.

We circled around in front of the courthouse and a couple of old men turned to look at our car. They had the same nondescript appearance of some of the good men who wanted to send me to the gallows. The deputy sheriff nodded and gave them a wave of the hand as we went by and they returned the greeting.

Somebody had named Goderich *The Prettiest Town in Canada.* He was either an over-zealous member of the local Chamber of Commerce – or he was crazy.

* * *

Lunch at a restaurant on the highway near Orangeville was something I was to dream of many times in prison. And it was years before I shook the memory of that ordeal from my conscious mind.

Standing in handcuffs and shackles before a dozen gaping faces does something to you inside. They can examine your anus and spray you with disinfectant – they can even look on when you're having a bowel movement in your cell. But when they denude you in public, they destroy you.

I've been told, and I believe, that some cops take a sadistic pleasure in publicly humiliating a captive but I'll give my guardians the benefit of the doubt. I think they were just too stupid to realize what they were doing when they pulled in to the restaurant for a meal.

"C'mon," the sheriff ordered, getting out of the car. "We're going to eat."

I placed my elbows on the top of the front seat and raised myself slowly. Getting out of the car proved more difficult than entering it but finally I made it.

The parking lot was full of cars, and I dreaded the prospect of entering the restaurant literally in chains. I asked the sheriff to remove the shackles but he refused.

"Let's go," he said.

I walked into the restaurant first and stopped beside a counter with a cash register and a display of candy and gum on it. They came up behind me and scanned the room. It was just a few minutes after noon and the place was crowded. Finally, a waitress waved from across the room to indicate she had a table for us. It was in a booth.

The sheriff walked toward her and I followed with the deputy behind me. I could only shuffle my feet and the shackles made an awful noise on the marble floor. Suddenly everybody in the room was looking at me and at one table, a man actually dropped his fork in surprise.

At the booth, the sheriff turned and motioned for me to sit down. He and the deputy sat opposite and they immediately picked up menus and began reading. When I looked around I could see people straining for a better look. I was a real freak, something they could talk about when they got home that night.

My first reaction was one of embarrassment. This was followed by a kind of boyish hurt, the sort a kid feels when he thinks he has been overpunished. Why, I wondered, would anybody do this in front of people?

The waitress came to our booth with pad and pencil and we all ordered steak. When it came, I realized I couldn't cut it so I asked the sheriff if he would remove the handcuffs, or else slice the meat for me. He had already started his lunch and couldn't be bothered. He grunted something and went on eating.

I noticed the waitress standing at the side of the room watching as I tried to use my knife and fork. The handcuffs kept hitting the plate and I couldn't manage the utensils at all. For some reason, I didn't object to her looking at me. She wasn't at all like the others who stared so rudely.

Finally, she came over and asked if everything was all right. She was in her late twenties, or early thirties, with deep red hair and a friendly smile. She watched me as she talked and I could tell she felt sorry for me.

"I can't seem to..."

I started to say that I couldn't manage the steak but she was way ahead of me. She took the knife and fork out of my hand and cut the meat into small chunks. She then put the utensils back in my hands.

"Can you make it now?" she asked.

"I'm sorry," I said, thinking of the trouble I had put her to.

"I'm sorry, too," she said. As she turned to leave, she sneered at the officers across the table from me but they were too busy eating to notice.

She returned a short time later to see if we needed anything else and again she addressed me. I said I had eaten enough and the sheriff cut in to say he wanted the bill.

The leg irons clattered on the floor again as I made my way to the door. I paused in front of the cash register while the sheriff paid the bill and I could see people staring from various tables. This time I felt defiant. I would never see those people again, so why should I worry what they thought?

The sheriff pointed to the door with his thumb and as I turned, I noticed our waitress standing there. She was smiling warmly.

"Come and see us again," she said.

"Yep," I replied. "Soon as I can."

* * *

In the dismal, gray light of that snowy February afternoon,

Kingston Penitentiary reminded me of the Tower of London, as pictured in one of my old English history books. Its massive stone walls and turrets and its grimly impressive entrance gate would have been the pride of any castle in the British Isles. Beside this impregnable mass of stonemasonry, the Huron County Jail in Goderich looked like the gatekeeper's house.

The sheriff pulled up at the gate and turned off the engine and again I stumbled out of the car dragging my shackles. He banged on the door and in a moment a guard opened it. It was a huge steel door, much bigger than the one at Goderich, and it had a terrible squeak. I don't think they bother oiling the hinges in those places. If the authorities think that a squeaking door has a psychological effect on inmates, they're right. The squeal of those hinges filled me with apprehension.

Just inside the door, I stepped into a very small, busy area where men were putting cards into a timeclock and putting on and taking off overcoats. The weather was a main topic of conversation. Was there snow coming? What was ahead for the weekend? They brushed past me as though I weren't there.

"It's all right to take them off," one of the guards told the sheriff, pointing to the handcuffs and shackles.

The sheriff took the key from his pocket and unchained me and I suddenly felt wonderfully relieved. The handcuffs had chafed the skin on my wrists but it wasn't the physical discomfort that bothered me. It was the psychological thing. I still hadn't recovered from the experience in the restaurant.

The sheriff gave my committal papers to the guard, saying he would return for me the next day. The guard then took me by the arm and led me through another door into a kind of yard.

I had become accustomed to being behind walls by now but this was such a huge place. In the semi-darkness I could see there were a number of buildings, all of them stone, and in one of the corner turrets there was a guard. He had a rifle and I imagined he had it trained on me. The wind whipped the snow around my neck and I felt cold – and terrified.

"In here," the guard said and we entered a big building across the yard. He spoke briefly to an officer at the entrance and I was taken to a small room and told to undress.

I went through the same procedure as at Goderich. My armpits and anus were inspected. I was told to take a shower, then I was sprayed with disinfectant. The experience was as degrading and humiliating as ever, and I felt physically ill. Finally I was given prison garb and taken to a cell in the hospital section of the prison.

Supper was brought on a tray by an inmate who nodded at me and stuck out his tongue at the food. He was a wiry little man, with hollow cheeks and a heavily-lined forehead. He didn't attempt conversation.

I couldn't quite decide what my tray held, but it appeared to be some sort of greasy stew, a few vegetables and one hunk of meat floating in a sea of gravy. The tray itself fascinated me, with its variety of hollows, and I decided that it must save a lot of dish-washing.

Among Canadian penal institutions, Kingston Penitentiary, or K.P. as it's often called, is one of the biggest and best-known, ranking with St. Vincent de Paul near Montreal. So enormous it seemed that that night I was too frightened to sleep. I sat on the edge of my cot until daylight, listening for signs of life in the deserted hospital.

In the morning, the inmate who had brought my supper returned with breakfast. He winked at me, looked at the porridge and held his nose.

Soon after breakfast, a guard escorted me out of the cell area. At the entrance to the hospital ward we paused while he spoke to an elderly inmate.

"How are you feeling now?" the guard asked.

"Well, just so-so," the man answered. "When a man grows old, he starts to fall apart."

"Who's old?" the guard asked.

The man laughed and the wrinkles almost obscured his eyes. He must have been close to sixty years old and seeing him like that in a prison hospital shocked me. There may have been people of that age in the County Jail but, being segregated as I was, I hadn't seen them.

Outside the building, three or four inmates were shovelling snow. There hadn't been much of a fall but the authorities obviously believed in keeping clean walks. At the administration building, another inmate was busy chopping ice from the steps. He was a young fellow of perhaps eighteen or so, I figured. I had no idea what he was in for, but I felt sorry for him. The fact that he was in a penitentiary rather than a jail, meant that he would have to be serving a minimum sentence of two years.

I was then taken to a small, sparsely furnished room, given my suit and told to change. I dressed quickly and followed the guard to the entrance gate of the penitentiary, where the sheriff and his deputy were waiting. There was no greeting. The sheriff snapped the handcuffs on my wrists while the deputy adjusted the leg irons.

Nobody spoke. My custodians didn't even look at me directly. It was as though they were preparing to move merchandise and were determining that it was properly crated for the journey.

The sheriff retrieved my committal papers and we walked through the penitentiary gates to the street. The sun was shining and the air was clear and sharp. I might have forgotten for a moment who and where I was. Then the deputy nudged me.

I stumbled into the back of the car. From my crouched position I could see the towering walls and turrets. Not many kids my age can say they've spent the night in Kingston Penitentiary, I thought.

To which I silently added, *thank God.*

CHAPTER X

If anyone had told me eight months earlier that I would some-day wind up in a reform school, I would have been pretty worried. But everything is relative and after all those months in the County Jail and my overnight stay in Kingston Penitentiary, the Ontario Training School for Boys in Guelph looked mighty good.

Its one spectacular feature, of course, was that it had no wall. Of all the unpleasant things of prison life, I found the wall the worst, not only because it shut out the view but because it was a constant reminder of captivity. It was the great demoralizer, the final humiliation.

The school had other good points, too, one of them being that it was situated on the rural outskirts of Guelph with lots of land around it and trees everywhere you looked. I was always a country boy at heart and my first thought as we drove up to the school was that this would be good farming land. At the time, of course, the landscape was piled high with snow.

The sheriff and his deputy escorted me through two electronically-operated doors into a big, bright visiting room. My shackles rattled loudly against the floor but this didn't bother me as much now. I was getting accustomed to the insult.

A few minutes later a big friendly man came into the room and introduced himself as Don Williams, the superintendent. He accepted the committal papers from the sheriff and told him to remove the handcuffs and leg irons.

After the officers had left, Williams told me to sit down. He himself sat down, crossed his legs and rubbed his hands. He was a relaxed individual with a knack for putting you at ease.

"I think you should get along well here," he said. "You will be with boys your own age and as long as you obey the rules you'll have no problems. I think you will find that we have an exceptionally competent and understanding staff."

Williams explained that I would be placed in a segregated section of the institution for a few days for classification. All new arrivals went through this. It was a matter of determining a boy's adaptability and deciding where to place him in the school program.

After our chat, Williams turned me over to the guards in segregation and I was assigned to a cell, which was considerably bigger and brighter than the one I had occupied in Goderich.

Then suddenly I became ill.

* * *

At first it felt like indigestion, then it became a stomach ache and two or three times that first night I vomited. There was nothing physically wrong – it was perhaps the aftermath of my harrowing months in Goderich.

I had been under such tension for so long in the County Jail, waiting and thinking all those months that I was going to be hanged, that likely I was now experiencing a type of delayed shock. I didn't sleep at all that first night, and only fitfully for several nights thereafter.

I tried to push the horrors from my mind but each night when I stretched out on my cot, I began to relive those terrible months.

In a kind of half-sleep, I saw a man, big and menacing, who shouted at me, demanding a confession. It was Inspector Graham, and with him were shadowy figures that materialized as the other detectives and Dr. Brooks. The place, of course, was the guardhouse at Clinton.

Often the scene changed and a female justice of the peace was reading a charge of murder. Then I'd see the guards in the jail, watching me as I cringed with fear in my rotten little cell. Finally, there was the judge, staring and solemn, ordering my death from the Bench.

The reaction set in then and I would feel cold all over and start to shiver. This lasted fifteen or twenty minutes but afterward, sleep was not possible.

It got so that I looked forward to morning when the guards came for the fellows to put them to work. Usually this meant washing floors and walls. I wasn't that fond of scrubbing but I welcomed the activity because it helped relieve the tension inside me.

I had been in segregation about a week when an English-born officer named Dave Mills came to see me. He was about twenty-six years old with jet black hair and he spoke with a pronounced English accent. He started out by calling me by my first name, something nobody else had done in jail, and I took an immediate liking to him.

Mills told me I was being assigned to the general school program and took me on a tour of the building. There were three shops in operation – the machinery, carpentry and sheet metal shops – and he asked where I would like to work. I chose the machine shop.

There were thirty-five to forty boys at the school, and living quarters were divided into four sections. Since there were never more than twelve boys to a section, I came to know those about me fairly well.

We were awakened at 7:30 a.m., did calisthenics, ate breakfast and went to the shops assigned us. Our work day ended at 4:00 p.m. and after supper we could read or play cards until 10:00 p.m.

There was an active sports program on weekends. In winter we played basketball, hockey and broom ball. The summer sports included softball, football and soccer.

Saturday was inspection day at the school, and after breakfast the boys washed the walls, scrubbed the floors and tidied up their cells. Later an officer inspected the quarters and awarded points for the cleanest and neatest. The section with the highest score was given a radio for two weeks and soft drinks and chocolate bars.

Being among boys of my age was good and having people like

Dave Mills around made life bearable. He was always kidding with us, cheering us up.

"You know, Steve," he said one day, "this isn't such a bad place when you think about it. You can learn a trade, you're well-fed, and sometimes you can even have a little fun."

The fun he was referring to occurred during a pre-inspection cleanup on a Saturday morning. A group of us were pretty wet, from scrubbing floors and we'd decided to have a water fight. One of the boys threw a pail of water at someone and caught Dave Mills who just happened to come in at the wrong time. He was completely soaked but instead of getting angry, he grabbed a full pail and went after the fellow who had drenched him. In a few minutes we were all wringing wet and laughing ourselves hoarse.

* * *

Visits were permitted every two weeks and these were much more relaxed than they had been at the County Jail. For one thing, we didn't have to talk through a metal screen. We could sit in big comfortable chairs in the visiting room and talk without supervision. The whole family was able to visit, too, which made it even more pleasant. The room was big enough for members of several families to visit their boys and on certain days there was so much talking going on it was difficult to follow a conversation.

My family had moved to Ottawa, where Dad was now stationed. Mom didn't say so, but I knew that she was happy living in a house again after that trailer. Dad had found a place in the country just outside Ottawa and Mom liked the location. She was glad to be away from the base.

The kids were doing well at school and Barb was very excited about Ottawa. Life must have been more interesting there than at Clinton because the schools were always organizing visits to the Parliament buildings and other places of interest.

Of course all the news I heard on visiting days was good. My family was always cheerful. I adopted the same policy and my family, too, heard only the good news. I told them about the fun I had with the other boys and how nice everyone on the staff was to me. And when it came time to say goodbye, we all pretended to be in such good spirits.

"I wish we had the trailer parked outside here," Barb would say every time she came. "Then we'd be real close to you."

"Haven't you had enough of that darn trailer?" my mother would ask.

We were such a close family. I guess perhaps this was the result of having moved around so much all over the country. The way the air force transferred people from base to base, it was not possible to cultivate long-term friendships. So we had come to depend on each other much more than do members of non-travelling families.

This relationship, of course, made parting all the more difficult and every time my family left I felt deeply depressed. The depression would last two or three hours and there was no antidote for it. I would go off by myself and wait it out. Eventually the terrible feeling would pass. I never learned to cope with these post-visit blues. They remained with me throughout my life in prison.

It might have been easier if I had been able to let go – to shout, smash a chair, set fire to a mattress, or even cry my eyes out. But back as far as the early weeks at Goderich, I had decided against emotional outbursts. Especially, I had made up my mind that I would never cry. I came close to crying several times.

Everyone had his down periods at one time or another and we made it a point never to intrude on an individual's privacy. But usually the boys tended to cling to one another, trying to find solace for their loneliness. This is the one thing we all had in common. We were utterly lonely.

The officers tried to ease things by organizing games for us in the evenings. It was a way of letting us blow off steam. Then on Saturday nights we were allowed out of our living quarters and into a basement room where we could watch hockey on television.

I took part in all the sports, but on Wednesday afternoons, the boys were allowed to go to the Guelph arena to play hockey. I was not. This upset me and I took the matter up with school officials. They explained that I was a federal prisoner and that they could not extend this privilege to me without authorization. Don Williams wrote to Ottawa asking permission two or three times but it was always denied. Federal authorities were obviously not going to take a chance on stirring up unfavorable public reaction.

Tired of spending every Wednesday afternoon alone in the school, I finally complained to Dave Mills. There was no logical reason, I said, why I should have to stay behind. No one was denied the outing, except for bad conduct. And I had a record of good conduct.

Mills was always willing to discuss problems but in this case he didn't know what to say. It wasn't his fault, nor even the school's. "You see," he tried to explain one day, "your situation is quite different to that of the other boys."

He was absolutely right there.

* * *

Spring came to Guelph and several of the boys I knew were released. How I envied them! April had always been one of my favorite months, a time for fishing, spotting geese, finding wildflowers in the woods and just plain dreaming. It was not a time for being locked up in an institution, that was for sure. I found myself thinking now about Ken and Bill and Barb and wondering what their first spring in the Ottawa area would be like. I hoped they'd find a good swimming hole.

In the warm sunshine of late April and early May, life became almost enjoyable. I spent as much time outside as possible, and while I longed often for my old solitary excursions to the Bayfield River, the days at Guelph were not without their small pleasures. The absence of a wall, of course, was the big thing. On clear days you could see for miles around.

School officials took pride in their property and almost as soon as the snow was gone, the flower beds in front of the building were bright with tulips. I enjoyed the flowers and I also liked having a potato farm on one side of the school and a woods across the road.

The nice weather meant outdoor sports and the boys began lining up their softball and baseball teams. They had to be good because they would be competing with teams from outside. Getting together a team wasn't always easy because most of the boys were serving terms of six to eight months and someone was bound to check out of the institution before the end of the ball season. I was always in demand, partly because I was good at sports, but mostly because everybody was pretty sure of my finishing out the season!

The tulips died and were replaced by petunias and phlox, and then by asters and marigolds. In the field beside the school, the plants bloomed and the potatoes were picked, and slowly but surely the summer was passing. I knew it was finally over when the trees in the woods across the road turned bright red and gold.

With ball games and family visits, and trees and flowers, it hadn't been too bad a summer. Only once in mid-June had I developed a case of the blues, recalling that it had been a year since my arrest. Now it was fall and I had a full schedule ahead of me.

Jim Corbett, an affable man in his fifties who was the machine shop instructor, had already shown me how to use various tools and how the machines worked. Now he was giving me a beginner's course in mechanical draughting. Later, he taught me how to apply my knowledge of draughting to the machines.

Regular education was compulsory at the school and I was enrolled in eighth grade night classes. Actually, it wasn't a full Grade 8. I attended two evenings a week and took only three subjects: history, mathematics and English. I guess we were taught what the authorities thought would be the most use to us.

My teacher was Cecil Reid, a big, husky man in his mid-thirties, who couldn't understand why I disliked Canadian history. Our course included both Canadian and American history.

I told him once that I preferred American history and particularly that dealing with the Civil War and he shook his head. It wasn't that he had anything against American history but he felt one should not read it in place of Canadian.

Actually, it wasn't the war I liked. It was the South. "If I lived in the States, I'd live in Tennessee," I told my teacher. When he asked why, I said I liked the idea of the rolling hills. The terrain simply appealed to me.

The truth of the matter was that I had always tended to side with the underdogs. And now, wrongfully convicted and imprisoned, I had become an underdog myself and sympathized with them all the more.

"In fact," I said, "if I had been an American during the Civil War, I would have been with the Confederates."

CHAPTER XI

The Guelph Training School had a number of good, helpful people on its staff. It also had a man named Wells. He was a baiter and it was not surprising to find him there since he has prototypes in every Canadian custodial center.

Every inmate knows that the moment he walks into an institution he loses most of his personal rights, one of them being the right to show disapproval. Even in a youth-oriented center like the Training School, he is not entitled to an opinion on anything. No matter how much he may dislike something, he will be wise to keep quiet because any disagreement with a guard invariably results in the inmate being put on charge.

Sometimes an inmate decides to assert himself, however, and this is what Glen did one Saturday morning. Glen wasn't a bad kid but he had a quick temper and he hated scrubbing floors.

Wells knew this boy and liked to get him riled. This time he came up alongside Glen and told him he was working too slowly. Glen wasn't over-exerting himself, but he was doing a good job. This was inspection day and he knew that the cleaner our section looked, the more likely we were to win radio and refreshment privileges.

"Hurry up," Wells ordered.

Glen went on scrubbing and didn't answer.

"You're pretty slow today," he said.

Glen dipped the brush in the cleaning mixture, squeezed it against the side of the pail and went on with his work as though no one had spoken.

"This floor will never be finished at the rate you're going," he went on.

Wells, obviously enjoying himself enormously, continued to annoy the boy. He kept it up for about fifteen minutes and finally succeeded in getting to Glen.

"I've done all the scrubbing I intend doing," Glen said, wiping his hands on a cloth and rising to face his tormentor. "Take that scrub brush and shove it."

"You're on charge," Wells snapped, in mock indignation. "Swearing and refusing to obey an order. Those are serious offenses."

Glen lost his privileges because of the incident and for several weeks he was prohibited from watching television on Saturday nights and from participating in sports. Loss of these privileges was serious since they were really the only pleasures we could anticipate.

We all knew that the officer had precipitated the situation, so we staged a slowdown to protest Glen's unfair treatment. It had no effect on Wells who didn't seem interested in tangling with us.

Then on Christmas Day, my first in Guelph, Glen was playing cards with some of us in the lounge when Wells walked in. The way he surveyed the room made it obvious that he was looking around for a reason to stir things up.

"Those bookshelves," Wells called over to Glen at the card table. "They need tidying."

"Yes," Glen replied casually.

"Straighten up those shelves," Wells ordered.

"As soon as I finish the game."

This time Wells exploded. "Straighten those shelves," he demanded.

Glen blew up, too. "I'm not going to do it until I finish my game," he snapped.

Wells, sneering now, took Glen by the arm and said, "All right, back to your cell. I'm putting you on charge."

At this point all the fellows in the lounge stood up and a boy named John said, "If you take Glen to his cell, you're going to have to put us all away."

John was no more than five feet tall but he was well-built and the school's best shortstop. The determination in his voice stopped the officer cold.

"All right," said Wells, releasing Glen's arm and stepping back, "I won't put you on charge this time but straighten the shelves after supper."

John had won the battle and we went on with our game, but that evening we were very quiet. Christmas is the saddest day of the year when you're locked up.

* * *

The Ontario Training School for Boys didn't officially celebrate New Year's Eve but we decided to mark the event.

We couldn't see the time from our cells, but when the night shift arrived, we heard the men punching the clock and knew that it was midnight. The moment the guards came on duty we grabbed our cups and shoes and banged on the bars, at the same time hollering at the top of our voice. We didn't actually say anything – we just screamed.

"Hey, you guys," one of the officers yelled, but we drowned out his voice.

"Hey, cut it out," he tried again. Other officers joined him, telling us to be quiet.

The more they cautioned us, the more racket we made. We experimented with the sheet metal lockers and discovered that they produced a satisfactory din when struck with a tin cup. Then someone had the brilliant notion of banging energetically on the sink or toilet. This was a one-piece unit and when it was struck, the noise carried throughout the building via the pipes, creating a sizeable din.

Someone hit on the idea of using rolls of toilet paper as New Year's Eve streamers, and every time a guard ventured into the cell block he was hit by a flying roll, forcing him to flee for an exit amid howls of laughter.

The guards didn't enforce their demand for quiet, knowing that we would eventually exhaust ourselves. This we did about 3:00 a.m., without bothering to wish one another Happy New Year. What was there to be happy about? From where I stood,

1961 looked like another very poor year.

* * *

I had just put away the Christmas cards when my birthday cards began to arrive, from Mom and Dad, of course, and from Ken and Bill and Barb, as well as from Pop and Granny, who never forgot a holiday or a birthday.

There were no more childish sentiments expressed. The boys pictured on the cards were young adults. Because I was sixteen and no longer a child.

I was unaware that anyone at the school had thought of my birthday, but about 8 o'clock that evening I was ordered to report to the dining room.

"Happy Birthday, Steve," someone shouted as I entered, and the group of boys and guards who had gathered in the room took up the cry.

I was terribly touched, particularly so when the wife of a guard brought in a cake she had baked and decorated, complete with sixteen candles. I extinguished the tiny flames with one breath, and a guard assured me that I'd get my wish. That I very much doubted.

The highlight of the evening was the presents. Because he knew how fond I was of jazz, a guard presented me with a trumpet, something I had wanted since I was twelve. And there was a photo album from Mom, who had sent it to the school, to be given to me at the party. This was a practical, as well as sentimental gift, because over the years I'd collected a lot of snapshots of the family and friends from the days of Edmonton and Clinton.

After the food and presents came the traditional birthday "bumps". They weren't too pleasant, because someone got hold of the rubber despatcher used to scrape the dishes. A few whacks from that could smart! Everyone made sure that I wouldn't forget my sixteenth birthday in a hurry!

Life at Guelph resolved itself into a series of uneventful days and weeks. Only the change of seasons marked the passage of time. Spring arrived and splashes of color brightened the grounds around the school. Then one day I noticed the haze that shimmered over the landscape and realized that it was already August.

Mom visited every second weekend, sometimes alone, sometimes with Dad. That year, Bill and Barb went to Vancouver and Mom brought their letters for me to read. There was a letter, too, from the Hamills, who were on summer vacation. Karen was fifteen, they said, and very tall.

Mom tried to make everything sound important and interesting. When she arrived Labor Day weekend, it was with tales of how the kids had outgrown all of last year's school clothes. On Thanksgiving the subject was pumpkin pies, and how she was teaching Barbara to bake. Early in December she spoke eagerly of Christmas.

Christmas Day at the school was the usual sad affair. Turkey and mince pie could not lessen the loneliness, and I became terribly depressed when I thought ahead to all the Christmas Days I would spend away from family and friends.

New Year's Eve found us once more going through the motions of celebration as we greeted another inauspicious year – 1962. And on January 18 the most exciting thing I found to pass the day was a copy of *Auto Mechanic*. A sixteenth birthday is important, the seventeenth just another day.

My mother remarked a change in my appearance soon after I turned seventeen. I'd had trouble with my eyes and was now wearing glasses. Perhaps that made the difference.

"It's not the glasses," Mom said. "But there *is* something..."

During the next couple of weeks I studied my face in the mirror, then I knew.

On Mom's next visit, I told her, "It's not that I look *different*. I'm simply *older*."

"Of course," she said, suddenly realizing what was happening. "You're growing up."

I was. I was growing up in prison.

* * *

That year I was granted a transfer from the machine shop to the carpentry department. Frank Horsefield was the instructor and I knew right away I was going to get along with him. He was tall and slim with strong, capable hands and he had endless patience with the boys.

He showed me first how to operate the machines and then launched me on architectural draughting. He was a quiet, methodical man who kept reassuring me when I found myself in difficulty. As was the case with most things, it took time to achieve perfection in carpentry and he kept reminding me of this. Horsefield didn't believe in rushing things anyway. He always maintained that it was better to see how well, rather than how quickly, a job could be done.

In the carpentry shop, I learned about home improvement. Horsefield showed me how to go about remodelling a kitchen, how to transform an ordinary basement into a recreation room.

I was always good with my hands and every now and then the instructor would point to something I had done and tell the other boys that that was the way to do it. I was pretty proud of myself and wrote my parents that once I got back home, I would be able to perform wonders around the house.

I made several china cabinets which members of the staff bought for their homes and a spiral staircase two storeys high. The latter project was a big one calling for a lot of planning and work, but I didn't like it because it reminded me of the spiral in the County Jail at Goderich.

It was in the art of cabinet-making that Horsefield seemed to derive his real pleasure and he kept bemoaning the fact that there were so few real craftsmen around. When I made a desk from some African mahogany he managed to acquire, he was over-joyed. I had shown good *craftsmanship* and this was important to him. Actually, the desk was good enough to be shown at the Canadian National Exhibition in Toronto that year.

At the close of the exhibition, they shipped the desk to my parents and a few days later I got a letter from my mother. "Steve, I had no idea you could do such good work," she wrote. It was a great letter and I read it several times. I needed bolstering like that every once in a while.

Time passed quickly at the school only if you were busy, so when one of the staff people asked if I would like to join a French class, I jumped. So did six of the other boys.

Our teacher was a well-dressed, good-looking girl in her mid-twenties who had just arrived in Canada from France and she really brightened up our Wednesday afternoons. We all thought she was pretty glamorous but there was more to it than that. She seemed to want to help us escape from our environment, at least in a spiritual sense.

She illustrated her language exercises with pleasant comments about the Seine and its bridges. She spoke of fanciful places like La Madeleine and Montparnasse and the palace of Versailles. And she had a rapt audience at all times. It was no surprise, of course, that our class was a happy one because she liked us and we sure liked her.

Early in January of 1963, Superintendent Williams called me to his office to make an announcement. He had been advised by Ottawa that I was to be transferred to Collins Bay Penitentiary in Kingston. I had known that that day must inevitably come, and I had dreaded the prospect.

My French teacher heard about my transfer and the following Wednesday she presented me with a gift, a pair of black leather, fleece-lined gloves. I tried them on right there in class and they fit perfectly.

"I'm sorry to hear you're leaving the class," she said. She spoke quietly and earnestly.

"I'm sorry, too," I said just as earnestly.

I didn't tell her that the thought of going to Collins Bay terrified me but she seemed to sense it. "I hope things will be all right for you where you're going," she said.

School officials regarded her as a good teacher and none of us had any argument with them on that point. But she was much more. Sitting there in that French suit, speaking softly of the Seine and smelling sweetly of perfume, she symbolized all the femininity of the unseen world beyond the electric doors.

CHAPTER XII

On January 13, 1963, just five days before my eighteenth birthday, I got my release from the Ontario Training School for Boys. I was now old enough to graduate from reform school to penitentiary and a federal penal officer was waiting to take custody.

They gave me a gray suit three sizes too big, a white shirt with the top button missing and a tie that didn't match the socks. It was the best they had in stock that day. I would have worn the blue suit and accessories my mother bought for the trial, but I had outgrown them in three years.

The officers joked with me as we walked to the visitors' room. "That's some suit," one of them laughed. "Don't forget to write," another said jokingly. "We want you to scrub the corridor floor before you leave," a third said.

They seemed to be sorry to see me go. And I guess maybe they were. During my three-year stay in the place I had never caused any trouble. Even Superintendent Williams appeared a little sad. He was in the visitors' room with the officer from the penitentiary when I came in.

"I hope you do as well at Collins Bay as you have done here," he said. "And I hope you won't be there too long."

He shook hands with me and then introduced the man beside him. He was Pat Patterson, a tall, slim officer with a warm, friendly smile who had happily come for me in civilian clothes.

He shook hands and then produced a pair of handcuffs. "Do we need these?" he asked. When I replied that he didn't, he put them away.

Pat Patterson was a far cry from the big, overweight sheriff and deputy who had insisted on making me travel in handcuffs and leg irons, and during the drive to the penitentiary he got me to talk about myself.

The prospect of Collins Bay frightened me, and he tried to make the place seem less forbidding than I imagined it. When I told him about working in the machine shop, he said I was in luck because the penitentiary had a well-equipped shop with a really top-notch officer in charge.

Whenever I was frightened, my stomach rebelled. Patterson seemed to sense this when we stopped to eat in a Trenton restaurant: "Take it easy," he said as I worked my way through a steak. "We have lots of time." He didn't seem the least worried about when we reached our destination.

It had started to snow while we were in the restaurant and there was a good half-inch covering the car when we went out. Patterson brushed the snow from the windshield while I scooped it off the rear window and then we took off.

"It's really not that bad a place," he said as we drove along a highway slowly clogging up with snow. "I mean a lot depends on the individual..."

* * *

Collins Bay Penitentiary was barely discernible through the swirling snow in the beam of the headlights.

We pulled up at the entrance, and not until I got out of the car could I see the outlines of the structure in the illumination of the building lights. It was a huge, dismal place of gray Kingston limestone with a stone wall twenty feet high.

Patterson rapped with the steel knocker and a guard opened the barrier. He closed it behind us and opened a second steel gate which he also shut as soon as we had passed through. The gates closed with a clanging sound which sent a shudder through me and I recalled how terrified I had felt the first time they had closed a door on me in Goderich.

In the reception area, Patterson talked to a couple of the guards and they looked over their shoulders at me and nodded. I imagined he was telling them who I was and that I was all right, or something to that effect, but I couldn't lose the feeling of fear that overwhelmed me. I felt perspiration forming over my upper lip.

"It's late, so you'll spend the night in the hospital," Patterson told me.

We climbed a dimly-lit staircase and three flights up we went through a steel barrier and then a heavy wooden door into the hospital area. An old guard was on duty and he asked Patterson my name, ignoring my existence.

"Quiet tonight?" Patterson asked.

"Any quieter, it'd be like the morgue."

The hospital guard flicked on a light over his desk, picked up a ballpoint pen and paused over a long sheet of white paper.

"Steven Murray Truscott," Patterson said.

The old man made some notes, put down the pen, went out of the room and returned with a pair of green pyjamas and a hanger. I took off my suit and hung it up and got into the pyjamas which proved much too big for me. I didn't bother trying to exchange them.

We passed through still another door into a room with ten beds, all of them unoccupied. "Use any one you like," the guard said. "You have unlimited choice of accommodation tonight."

I picked a bed at the end of the room and stretched out, holding my stomach which had begun to heave again. Only the night lights were on but it was sufficiently bright to see that the designers hadn't had the morale of the inmates in mind when they planned the hospital. It looked more like a storeroom than a ward, with walls painted a dirty yellow and bars on all ten windows.

At night, prison is an eerie, hollow fortress in which even the ordinary sounds of distant footsteps, clicking doors and running water are often distorted. That night, I lay awake trying to identify a whole assortment of noises. One of the persistent sounds was that of the wind, whipping the snow against the windows, and it made me think of the wind that November night in Goderich, when I had been waiting to go to the gallows. God! How long ago!

At one point, I heard several voices, laughing and talking and I heard barred doors opening and then clanging shut and I figured it must be the midnight staff change.

Courting sleep, I attempted to count all the doors I had passed through since that terrible night in Clinton. I remembered a book I had read at Goderich – *Death Has a Thousand Doors* – and the phrase stuck in my mind.

There had been so many doors, each leading me deeper into the maze of stone and steel. I had progressed from one cage to another, each larger than the last.

I fell asleep thinking of this latest labyrinth and woke to the sound of voices beyond the door. They were changing the guard (but this wasn't Buckingham Palace!) and an inmate assigned to the hospital brought me breakfast.

"You new?" he asked.

I nodded sleepily and he put the steel tray on the floor beside me.

There was soggy toast and jam, served on the tray without plates and a heavy steel mug weighing almost three pounds. The day before, at Guelph, I'd had bacon and eggs on a plate, with toast on the side, and milk in a glass. I was going to miss those meals.

After breakfast I was fingerprinted and photographed, told to undress, and examined for birthmarks and permanent scars. I had none. When I dressed, it was in penitentiary issue: gray pants, shirt, smock and socks, white T-shirt and black oxfords. Again the trousers were too big for me.

The clothing was drab, every article emphasizing the anonymity of my life. But it was the number stamped on each item of clothing that rankled. The digits 6730 were to become, in effect, my name.

I wondered if they had started with number 1. That would have been a long time ago and the inmate, if he were still alive, would be very, very old now. I wondered, too, about Number 6729, who must have preceded me. If he were young and new at this, he too must have been unhappy.

No one had to administer specific punishment to depress and demoralize me. The simple procedure of assigning a number represented yet another step in the process of de-humanizing, another effort to destroy me.

My new status was brought home to me the next day when a guard called, "6730 Truscott, report to classification." My first name had been replaced by a number and I didn't like it.

After dressing, I was taken to the *change room,* a depressing place painted the same sickly yellow as the hospital. It's strange how color cheers or depresses. That shade of yellow made me feel ill.

I was given another set of numbered clothes, and a pair of black leather boots. I also received a thin mattress, two gray wool blankets and a knife, fork, spoon and steel mug.

A guard walked me to an area he identified as Cell Block 3, a drab, colorless corridor lined with cells, each of which had a solid wooden door with a tiny peephole in the center. One of these was unlocked and I went in, dropping my gear on the floor. I had been in a sufficient number of cells to judge with authority, and after inspecting my new surroundings I decided that this cell was at least an improvement over that hole in Goderich County Jail.

"This is where you'll be bunking for now," the guard told me.

The cell was seven feet long, four wide and eight high. There was a bed that folded against the wall, a toilet and sink unit, and a small cupboard, the door of which could be lowered to provide a table for writing or eating.

At the back of the cell was a small barred window that looked out upon one of the prison yards. I glanced out and saw that the small square was almost dark, in the shadow of the ugly gray stone wall that all but blotted out the sky.

The guard told me to make my bed and he stood at the door to see that it was done properly. There were certain basic regulations, none of which I found difficult. I had to keep myself and my cell neat and clean at all times, fold back my bed each morning before leaving my cell, and make sure that the cupboard was tightly closed.

Later, I joined the prisoners from the other cells for the supper parade. These were older men, and after spending three years among boys my own age, I felt strange and alone.

I didn't speak to anyone, and no one spoke to me, although

several inmates stared at me because I was a newcomer.

A couple of days later the Kingston newscasters reported that Steven Murray Truscott had been transferred to Collins Bay Penitentiary. The men were then aware of the identity of the new character in their midst.

Supper was served through a series of wickets in the wall of a corridor and the men lined up in the tradition of the soup kitchen. The first wicket dispensed the main course, the second bread and the third coffee.

There was one word for that first supper – slop. There were no plates, just trays with hollows and the stew and dessert mixed freely in one big congealing mass. To make matters worse, it was necessary to carry the tray back to the cell, by which time the food, or what passed for it, was cold.

This was the penitentiary big-time and there was no coddling as there had been at Guelph.

I went to bed early that night with a headache and a feeling of nausea but my thoughts on the activities of the day prevented me from sleeping. *6730 Truscott.* It was stamped all over me like the Made in Canada stamps on merchandise.

And to think, if they enforced the letter of the law, I was there for the rest of my life.

CHAPTER XIII

In the lonely, barren world of the penitentiary with its great dividing line between inmate and staff, Joe Fowler was the proverbial beacon light, the good friend and wise counsellor who always had time to listen. To those of us who worked with him, he was the able machinist, the talented draughtsman and the painstaking instructor. But more than that, he was living proof that prisoner and officer could surmount that invisible barrier.

Joe Fowler ran the machine shop and thus became one of the first people with whom I had extensive contact. With my background in machinery at Guelph, it was natural that I should be placed in that shop and Joe was quick to approve my posting. We were destined to hit it off from our very first meeting.

Joe was in his early forties, a quiet, thoughtful man with strong features and crisp black hair that was going gray. He had an honest, friendly approach that I accepted at face value. One of the first things I noticed about him was that he had a good firm handshake and this to me was the mark of a dependable man. In my several years of association with him, I never had reason to find him otherwise.

"I think this work will prove very beneficial to you," he said to me the first day. "And if you like to work, there's a lot to be done."

The men of the machine shop carried a heavy workload, looking after all the machinery in the institution. This was no minor chore in a center of that size. They maintained the complicated prison kitchen equipment, and the machines at the Farm Annex and the Staff Training School, and sometimes they even got to do odd jobs at that sin bin on Palace Road they called the Women's Prison.

"A man gains enough experience in this shop to be able to fill any job on the outside," Joe said proudly.

He wasn't exaggerating, because, in addition to their regular work, the men were doing a lot of custom work. The fact was that the guards realized they had access to one of the most reasonable shops in the area and they brought their defective lawn mowers, outboard motors, washing machines and everything else to us for repairs. Judging by the number of custom items handled, it was obvious the guards were also doing favors for their friends and neighbors. Actually, it cost about five cents an hour in labor when they used us – and no arguments with the unions.

Joe didn't rush things, preferring rather to let me accustom myself to the equipment in my own good time, and it was not until my second week that he started me on maintenance.

He ran a tight shop and kept a close watch on how his men behaved. If he felt a man was unable to do the work, or didn't take a keen interest in it, or just didn't get along with the other fellows, he didn't want him around. He realized that such an inmate would simply make things difficult for everybody else. On the other hand, if a man did good work, he was commended.

Inmates have no sense of responsibility – and why would they when all their thinking is done for them? But Joe believed in encouraging initiative among his men and when someone was assigned a repair job, he was on his own until he ran into some specific difficulty.

He taught me how to handle a propane torch and showed me the intricacies of arc welding and draughting and it was not very long before he put me in charge of most of the custom repairs.

One day he came in with a bushel basket full of mechanical parts. "Here's something for you," he said. He laughed and added, "Let's see you put this one together."

It was a rotary tiller, but at this stage I had never seen a motor taken completely apart. It took me a couple of days to figure it out but eventually I put it together and Joe congratulated me. I think he was surprised that I was able to do it.

Joe was a good teacher and never worried about us doing a good job. The men in the shop had an excellent reputation throughout the prison and those who brought machines in for repairs knew every job would be satisfactory.

All the fellows liked working for Joe because they knew that if they got into any difficulty, he would go to bat for them. He believed that his men were responsible to him and no one else and he was willing to go to the warden on their behalf if necessary.

On one occasion, one of the men had a run-in with a guard, who promptly put him on charge. Joe went to the warden and said the man was a good worker, that he had never made trouble in the shop and that furthermore, he believed the officer was at least partly to blame for the incident. As a result of his intercession, the charge was dropped. It was this sort of thing that made him so popular and in return for his support, he knew he had our undivided loyalty.

I was never in trouble, probably because of his influence, but I always knew that if there *was* a problem, I could count on him. This relationship between an officer and his men was unique in the institution.

* * *

I spent my eighteenth birthday working in the shop with two new-found friends, a man in his forties named Hector and a fellow in his twenties called Satch. Joe introduced us to one another and we soon discovered we had a lot in common. We were all quiet types, all from Ontario and all serving long terms. Like most inmates, I had decided to make friends with people who planned to be around for some time.

Hector said he was from Windsor and I told him I had an aunt living there. Satch was from the Kingston area and joked about not having to travel far to get to the penitentiary. I told them about my living on air bases and how I had travelled over most of the country. But none of us ever discussed why we were in prison. That subject was entirely taboo.

Hector was the helpful, not to mention generous, type and he offered to help me financially if I found I couldn't manage. He knew I had been classified as Grade 1 and that I was thus earning only $1.25 a fortnight. I had taken up smoking by then and by the time I had bought tobacco and cigarette paper, there wasn't much left over for things like toothpaste, let alone soft drinks and chocolate bars.

Both Hector and Satch took turns showing me the ropes. Prison, they taught me, could be tolerable if you did your work and if you kept out of trouble. And keeping out of trouble was largely a matter of keeping away from certain people. Like every other institution, Collins Bay had its quota of troublemakers and my friends knew who they were.

If prison was tolerable in my case, however, it was just barely so. For one thing, I was always surrounded by older men and, for another, I could never see beyond the wall. After Guelph, that wall took some getting used to.

We were allowed to use the gymnasium in the evenings, but the fellows did nothing there but play cards and I wasn't interested in doing that every night. The library, too, was a disappointment with nothing better than a few outdated novels and useless technical books, the gifts probably of some righteous benefactors anxious to clean up their own bookshelves. There was not one volume dealing with the United States Civil War and, for that matter, no books on history at all.

I aired my beef about the lack of history books to Joe Fowler one morning in the machine shop and, as usual, he listened patiently, nodding and shrugging as the situation required.

"I've always felt sorry for the Southerners," I said. "They really had it rough."

"Yeah," Joe said. He didn't say any more but he knew that my own sad plight had something to do with my defense of the Confederates. He was a wise and perceptive man, whose years as a prison employee had taught him to recognize such things.

* * *

Inmates were allowed visitors for an hour once a month and each time my parents came we all put on our usual act. They told me of life in Ottawa, how well the kids were doing in school and how they liked their new home. I pretended that I was getting along well and doing interesting things.

"Take care of yourself," they would say, as they were leaving. I'd shake my father's hand and kiss my mother and say "See you next month." It was all very inane, but the fact was that none of us really knew what else to say.

As month succeeded month, I found myself drifting farther and farther away from my family and life outside. My mother and father asked the same old questions and I gave the same tired replies. None of us would admit it at the time, of course, but each time we got together we had less in common.

The summer visits were better because I could report on my sports activities. Collins Bay had several soft ball leagues made up of six teams each and we took our games seriously. My father was particularly interested and wanted me to relate all the details of each game.

Other times, conversation lagged and there were long periods of silence when we truly found nothing to talk about. And yet these visits were all that kept me going.

We had the same problem exchanging letters. I wrote home once a week and received a letter from my family every week. The contents never varied, but then what was there to write about? Well, occasionally there was news. That first fall, for instance, I applied to the Vocational Training Office for permission to take the machine shop course – the theory part of it – as a sort of refresher course. I wrote home about that, then wrote again later to say that permission for the course had been denied. The reason was that I was doing too much time and officials suggested that I apply again in a year or two.

* * *

In theory, there was much that an inmate could do to improve himself, such as continuing his education by means of a correspondence course. But in actual fact, things didn't always work out well, as I learned when I applied for a course in English.

I was very enthusiastic when I received my books and work

sheets. I studied hard and soon completed my first exercise, which I submitted for correction. Then I realized how much red tape was involved. My exercise went first to the library, then to the censor's office and on to administration, from where it was taken out and mailed. This took about a week, to which was added two weeks for correcting and another week coming back through prison channels.

The officer in the library was old and senile and he would hold the exercises for periods up to a week, thus delaying my next submissions. I tried to keep up with the course for some months and finally gave it up in exasperation.

Eventually, the Vocational Training department approached me about the machine shop course and I arranged to take the theory. This meant that I spent the mornings studying and the afternoons back in the shop doing practical work.

"By the time you graduate, you're going to know a lot about machinery," Hector said one day.

"He knows a lot right now," Satch put in.

Actually, I wasn't that anxious to increase my mechanical knowledge. What I really wanted more than anything was to keep busy because that way the time passed more quickly.

I complained a lot to Joe Fowler about how slowly the time went, but one day they started playing Christmas music on the radio and I realized that almost a year had gone by. Like a lot of other inmates, I grew quiet as the day approached and hardly spoke to anyone.

There was an air of depression throughout the institution and it accentuated my own feeling of loneliness. I received cards from my family and, for the first time, I got some from strangers who had read about my case and obviously felt sorry for me. I kept them all together in my cupboard because to have them up on the wall in full view would have been just too depressing.

New Year's Eve was our opportunity to express dissatisfaction and vent our hostility. The celebration was not unlike the ones at Guelph. We waited until guard change at midnight and then we picked up our cups and shoes and banged on the bars and yelled as loudly as we could. The guards, obviously accustomed to New

Year's Eve merrymaking in the penitentiary, made no attempt to silence us. The noise went on until nearly 3:00 a.m. but I flaked out on my cot long before that. I couldn't seem to work up the enthusiasm for this mock merrymaking that others could.

I had by now accepted the fact that this would be my life for a long time to come and every day the outside world became a little more remote. Yet I could never really become a part of prison life because I was not like the other men. I was not a criminal.

The result, I suppose, was predictable, I became a loner.

CHAPTER XIV

The important thing about January 18, 1964, was not that I celebrated my nineteenth birthday, but that I said goodbye to a chubby little guy in his forties named Gord, who was being paroled. I inherited his job as head of the Collins Bay Penitentiary radio room.

It was a small room across from one of the guard stations, but it was equipped with a television set from which the sound could be sent over speakers in the cells, three AM and FM receivers, a control panel, two record players and three amplifiers. It also had a record library of 1,000 45 RPMs and 200 LPs, not new but in good shape and donated to us by local radio stations.

Gord had turned the room into something of a nerve center. He had devised a system of public announcements and had even organized a kind of disc jockey show in the evenings. I had been impressed the first time I visited because of certain little professional touches. For instance, he had managed to find some red leather material which he had tacked around a table, making it look like a reception desk in a commercial radio station.

The radio room was an extracurricular job which I did in conjunction with, not instead of, my regular work. I wanted it this way because the busier the day, the quicker it passed.

I rose now at 6:00 a.m., opened up the room a half-hour later to warm up the amplifiers and went on the air at 7:00 with martial music and a few wake-up words for the inmate population.

At 7:30, I announced it was time to get up because the guards were coming for the count. After breakfast, I turned to stations that played music during the day. In the evening, I manned the receivers, switching from one station to another to provide the kind of broadcasting the men liked best.

Friday nights were best because then I became a disc jockey, playing requests from the inmates. "And now, for Paul from John, here's Elvis Presley singing *Wooden Heart...*"

Western music was most popular at the Bay, and since most radio stations featured it at one time or another, I could keep my audiences pretty well satisfied. Later, when a new inmate named Charlie joined me, the radio operation took on an extra load.

Often there were sports events in the evening – outside in the summer and inside in the winter – and we'd break in on programs at 5:00 p.m. to announce the events. At the same hour, we also broadcast any special bulletins the administration wanted to air. Since there were television sets in the gymnasium and dormitories, we also read program listings from *TV Guide* magazine.

Charlie and I received a lot of gripes from inmates who thought the programming could be improved, but we also got a number of compliments, most of them deserved, we thought. We were always searching for new ways of being useful to the population, such as bringing in a French-language radio station 200 miles away in Montreal so that our Quebec boys would feel at home.

"You know what we are?" Charlie asked one night as we sat at the controls trying to decipher the comments of a French announcer.

"Dunno," I said.

"We're public-spirited," he explained. "Just downright public-spirited."

* * *

About this time, I also undertook to look after the kitchen machinery at the farm annex, that big, sprawling agricultural department of the penitentiary which provided us with most of our vegetables and dairy products. This was part of my determination to keep occupied for as many hours as possible.

I looked forward to my Wednesday morning visits to the annex, mainly because it was located beyond the walls. It was strange but I could actually feel a decrease in tension as I went through the gate on my way to the farm, and then feel it mounting as I returned.

My country-boy mentality made it possible for me to feel at home at the annex right away. My work was inside, of course, but I always had a few minutes outside, and sometimes someone would ask me to do some mechanical repairs in one of the barns. I felt comfortable where there were cows and tractors and the smell of earth.

"You must be the busiest guy at the Bay," Joe Fowler said when I returned from the annex one day.

"It's your fault," I laughed. "You taught me so well I'm in demand all over the place." I made the remark jokingly, but it was absolutely true.

Joe understood my need to keep busy and when there was a slack period in the shop, he would encourage me to work on a private project.

On one occasion, I found a couple of old cars and dismantled them for parts. From an old cement mixer, I got a gasoline motor and from a dilapidated stone-crusher in the quarry, a clutch. With these I built a tractor that became the pride and joy of the shop. Nobody worried that it had a transmission from Ford, a rear end by Pontiac and a motor from a cement mixer.

It had a practical value, too. Every Wednesday when I went to the annex, I had to lug my 70-pound tool chest along and that was pretty exhausting. With the tractor, I could toss my tools on the back and the trip was a cinch. (The contraption must have been a good one because long after my release, it was still in running order and had never even required repairs.)

Everybody took a keen interest in the tractor and often the guards stopped to watch us tooting around outside the shop. It was definitely an attraction.

Putting a tractor together from spare parts reminded me of another occasion back in Clinton, a few years earlier, when the scoutmaster and I had built a go-kart that ran on a gasoline motor. It could do fifteen miles per hour and Ken and I chased around the base until the gas ran out. Gas was expensive but Dad or one of the farmers would often give us a couple of gallons.

* * *

In the fall, I was transferred from the cell block to a dormitory with thirty-five inmates. It was a major change. Instead of being by myself in a cell with a peephole to look through, I was now in an open dorm where I could talk to people.

"You'll be less lonely here," Satch, who had been in the dormitory for some time, said the day I moved in.

I nodded, but with my schedule, there would be very little time for fraternizing, wherever I was billeted.

Inmates never discussed their cases with the result that we really knew very little about one another. It was sufficient to know that we were all caught in the same rat trap.

But my case had attracted more than ordinary attention from the media and everybody at Collins Bay knew who I was. Consequently, when the papers started carrying reports on Isabel LeBourdais' investigations into my case, they were passed on to me. The inmates in my dormitory were from Kingston, Peterborough, Toronto, Hamilton, London, Ottawa and Montreal, and since they all received their hometown papers, I had quite a cross-section of reading matter.

Mrs. LeBourdais, a Toronto writer and wife of a prominent author, had come to see me when I was in Guelph. Believing in my innocence, she had made an extensive study of my trial and had gone on to investigate some of the doubtful procedures that preceded it.

No one in the dormitory commented on the news, but I knew the fellows were sympathetic. They had all been through the mill themselves, and naturally enough, many of them didn't think too highly of the courts.

Only once do I remember someone mentioning anything to me – and that was short and to the point. It came from a fellow named John, who was serving two years for armed robbery.

"I hope it works out for you," he said, and knowing him as I did, I knew he meant it.

John had already been at Guelph for some time when I arrived there and had given me the new inmate routine – that is, he took me over, showed me around the premises, tipped me off about certain officers and bought tobacco and cigarette paper for me when I had none. When some years later he was sent to Collins Bay, I was already there and *I* was the veteran who showed *him* around and looked after *his* needs. It was the general practice in all the institutions to try to set newcomers off on the right foot. A shortage of money was a usual complaint among new arrivals and, in the case of John, I supplied him with necessities like toothpaste.

Poor John! He had been such a happy-go-lucky fel'ow at Guelph, so good-natured and fun-loving, taking things as they came and never complaining. Following his release from the school he had been in a robbery. He had waited long weeks in the County Jail for his trial, and then when he was convicted, he had been pulled apart by the newspapers and described as the lowest of criminals. The news reports were so lurid, in fact, that I had trouble recognizing him from them.

I knew a number of people like John during my years at the Bay, poor unfortunate kids who might never have gone astray except for a faulty set of circumstances, and I always tried to remember the adage, *There but for the grace of God go I.....* Yet, while I wanted to see a fellow get a fair deal from the courts, I could never really approve of him breaking the law in the first place. I didn't possess any criminal tendencies myself and thus found the lawbreaker's way of thinking foreign.

Sometimes in the dorm I would get all choked up listening to somebody talking about his boyhood. Some of the stories were sad and I always felt sorry for boys from unhappy homes. I remember wishing at the time that everybody could have known a home as happy as mine had been.

But then, on other occasions, I would hear the fellows planning what they were going to do when they got out and this annoyed me. They were going to break into this place and knock off that place and always there was this boast about how clever they were.

I didn't say anything to them but I kept thinking to myself, "If you guys are so smart, how come you're in here?"

CHAPTER XV

The guard at Guelph who gave me my trumpet couldn't possibly have known what far-reaching therapy he was making available to me – but I said many a silent thank you to him over the years at Collins Bay.

That trumpet was my salvation many times. It allowed me to blast off when things went wrong and I was blue and the whole massive stone fortress threatened to close in around me and crush me.

Several of the inmates could play musical instruments and some of us formed a band made up of trumpet, saxophone, clarinet, trombone and bass fiddle. We had jam sessions in a little room off the gymnasium and every evening after supper we started off with some bars of *Bourbon Street Blues,* our favorite piece.

Most of our fellows liked jazz and we all got together around the radio whenever Queen's University broadcast a concert. This was the one kind of music we could really feel, perhaps I guess because we could identify with the musicians and composers. Like them, I think, we sought an escape from the unhappiness and frustration of life.

Anyway, whether I was listening to jazz, or blasting away on my trumpet, I'd feel the tension in me decreasing.

Jazz was one of the things that kept me sane during the early years at the Bay. That and the hope that some day I would walk through the gate a free man.

Freedom. No one appreciates its meaning until he no longer has it.

Perhaps because I was innocent, I found it more difficult to adjust. In any event, my desire for freedom became a sort of obsession. It was all I thought about by day and all I dreamed about at night.

And I shall never forget – nor forgive – the National Parole Board for dangling the prospect of freedom before me, and then when my hopes had soared, denying me the parole they had led me to believe I would get.

I hadn't gone begging. The board had come to me. In August, 1964, a little more than five years after my arrest, it had sent a notice in the mail, informing me that I was eligible for parole and saying that I could apply for one on a form available through the classification department of the penitentiary.

I secured a form, filled it out, and in desperation to gain my freedom, did something very stupid. In the space reserved for my personal comments, I wrote that if I were released I would not be in trouble again. By this I meant that I would not be in trouble *period.* But I had been thinking in terms of all those people who believed me guilty and, since I knew they took my guilt for granted, I wrote the word *again.*

Then I began to worry, would the Parole Board consider my statement as an admission of guilt? As it turned out, the Board did *not* accept this as an admission of guilt. Years later, I would wonder about something else. Why would I be eligible for a Parole anyway? Under the regulations, a person who is sentenced to hang and whose sentence is commuted to life may *not* be paroled in less than ten years. In any event, in January, 1965, I learned that my application had been deferred.

I was shocked by the news but I was curious, too. Why would they allow me to apply for parole and then deny it? I put the question to the classification officer and he shrugged. The board, he said, was not obliged to give me, or anyone else, a reason.

The next time my mother visited, she said she had written to the board, inquiring about my status and asking whether any further action was being considered. The board, in its reply, made it clear it was not required to furnish explanations. It was accountable to no one.

My mother was extremely upset. "They didn't say so in so

many words but they were, in effect, telling me to mind my own business," she said.

I tried to explain that I had made inquiries with the same results but she just stood there shaking her head. "I don't understand," she said. "I just don't understand."

"Mom, something will work one of these days," I said, knowing I was lying. "For now we can only wait and hope."

I didn't really know what to say to her. The truth of the matter was that in prison you had to sit there and take what they gave you, no matter how unjust it might seem.

The denial of my parole had been a blow in every sense and for some weeks after, I hardly spoke to anyone. I guess the other inmates recognized my symptoms because they didn't talk to me either. In prison you get to know when a fellow wants to be alone and you respect his privacy.

* * *

The hostility grew in me now as it had never done before and after my twentieth birthday, I decided I had suffered enough injustice and declared my own private war against the administration.

My fight was really with The System – that big, cold, impersonal machine called Justice which had put me behind bars and which insisted on keeping me there even though I was innocent.

But it wasn't possible to fight the police, the courts, the Parole Board, the whole of the Justice Department. So I had to lower my sights and content myself with a kind of guerilla warfare, carried on stealthily inside the penitentiary, in little, clandestine ways that delayed and frustrated but could not be detected.

It was shadow-boxing really, hitting out at intangibles, striking at people who, because of the tremendously complex nature of The System, were never directly responsible for anything that happened. There was no one person anywhere you could go to and say, *I am innocent and I want you to correct the injustices that have been done me;* no one powerful figure to whom you could say, *I need help. Please do something...*

I was trying to even things up when I knew it was not possible to even them up. But it gave me the feeling of getting back at them and this had its momentary satisfactions.

When a guard brought a vehicle to the machine shop for repairs, I took as long as possible to fix it, thus putting him off schedule. If a machine broke down in the kitchen, I was slow to repair it and the whole business of preparing menus was complicated. When a guard called the shop to inquire about delays, I dodged the call. Later, I would explain that he would have to wait because there was other work ahead of his.

One day an officer from the boiler room brought in a part for repair and I told him I was busy and that he would have to wait. I stalled over the job I was doing and the officer kept after me to hurry.

"If he doesn't stop bugging me, I'll walk out of the shop and somebody else can do the job," I told Joe Fowler.

I immediately regretted speaking this way to Fowler but he just nodded and winked. He then told the guard to lay off and get out, that he would have his repairs done when I was through with the job I was currently doing.

There was always a certain amount of friction among the guards and this aided my rebellion. Any time I could add to the dissension with a word or two, I did, and sometimes this resulted in a fight. The guards especially disliked hearing that other officers considered them incompetent, so I tried to think up all kinds of incidents in which they might be accused of falling down on the job.

I suppose it was poetic justice that I was never caught doing any of these things, but was charged with an act I had not committed.

It happened one night when some of the boys were working late. A member of the kitchen staff made them coffee but could find no milk, so I provided a can which we always kept in the radio room. The next day the kitchen steward replaced my milk but, instead of putting the can away in the radio room, I stuck it in my coat pocket. That night the guards conducted one of their periodic frisking operations and found the milk.

No one asked me for an explanation as to how the milk got into my pocket. I was simply charged with stealing it from the kitchen.

I refused to argue, and ignored the whole thing.

The next day Deputy Warden Allen called the shop and told me he was taking thirty days good time away from me for theft. A person doing life doesn't have any good time, so I promptly told him that if he could find any, he was welcome to the whole lot. He called back later and Joe Fowler confirmed what I had told him, that I had no good time.

"You're a good fellow, *sir,*" I told Joe.

He didn't answer. When he didn't want to comment on something, he pretended not to hear.

CHAPTER XVI

Even today they come back to haunt me, a sizeable corps of psychiatrists and psychologists, probing my subconscious with drugs and drawings, trying desperately to establish my guilt so as to justify my detention.

I don't like these people crowding in on me during the quiet of the night but then how can I stop them? They are, after all, still a part of my life, and why wouldn't they be? They harassed me for nearly five years.

They couldn't resort to physical punishment, so they relied on the more subtle subterfuges of their trade. They gave me sodium pentothol to find out the truth, and when they found it, they refused to believe it. They put me through the nightmare of LSD, thinking they might bare me as a killer, and had to give this up, too.

Except for one man, all the psychiatrists started their questioning in the same way. Had I killed Lynne Harper, they all wanted to know? When I said I hadn't, they were disappointed, even annoyed.

On behalf of The System, they wanted me to repent and cleanse my soul. A confession was what they needed to relieve their consciences.

The psychologists wanted me to reveal my innermost secrets by telling them what I saw in a series of ink blots and one, a Spanish woman, was vitally interested in how inmates went about satisfying their sexual needs. I am no expert in this field but it occurred to me she was trying to satisfy herself through some kind of voyeurism. I guess she didn't expect me to be so blunt with my answers, because she went beet-red when I told her that some of the men turned to homosexual acts or masturbation.

* * *

Of all the psychiatrists I saw, George D. Scott is the one I remember best. He was chief psychiatrist for the whole Kingston penal complex, which meant that he saw several thousand inmates. Every inmate sees the psychiatrist at least twice, once soon after admittance and again before release.

Scott was a short, compact and wiry man who wore his white hair in a brushcut and he had the kind of agile mind that kept him continuously two paces ahead of the person he was interviewing. He was the man who saw me first and most often.

Dr. Scott seemed friendly when I first met him but I soon began to think the friendliness was a surface thing. In his white, or green, smock, he was always the psychiatrist, the representative of the penal establishment. In front of him on the desk, there was always an open file, and while I automatically assumed it was mine, I wondered where he had collected so much information about me.

He was casual when beginning an interview, sometimes cupping his hands, other times resting his head in an open hand, playing with a pencil or an elastic band, giving me quick, close looks as I sat there across from him, tense, cautious, unrelaxed.

Then, matter-of-factly, as though he were inquiring about a field day or a baseball game, he would ask, "Did you kill Lynne Harper?"

I wouldn't answer immediately, waiting until the first surge of anger had gone through me and I was able to speak calmly. I never let my emotions show because then I would be vulnerable.

"No, I did not," I would answer with what seemed like complete composure.

The question made me antagonistic right from the start. He, naturally enough, took the administration's attitude that if I wasn't guilty, I wouldn't be in the penitentiary, and I took the view that Justice in Canada was anything but infallible.

Dr. Scott was often impatient and sometimes, when I was

156

answering a question, he would repeat the word, "Yeah," every few seconds as though he was trying to hurry my sentence along.

I didn't mind what he said – until he brought up the subject of my family. Then he was treading on dangerous ground. I had long ago decided that my parents and my brothers and sister were no one's business.

Dr. Scott first interviewed me late in 1964 and neither of us thought much of the other. I was never rude but neither was I very communicative. Then after a few meetings, he asked if I would be willing to take some tests on the understanding that if they revealed nothing to indicate my guilt, he would come around to my way of thinking. It smacked of one of those childish deals that prison officials sometimes make, but since I was innocent, I had nothing to fear, so I gave my consent.

One day we went into a small room in the hospital area and Scott handed me a glass of clear liquid that looked and tasted like water.

"All right," he said, "go ahead."

I sat on the edge of the bed and drank the contents. At first I felt no effects at all but then my tongue became swollen and heavy and I felt groggy, as though I had had too much to drink.

Dr. Scott sat on a chair beside the bed, going through the file, and every so often he would look up and ask me how I felt.

What he had administered was sodium pentothol, the famous truth serum, but after about half an hour, he had to admit that there had been no conclusive results.

It was not until much later that I learned from him that, while I was under the drug, he had discussed the offense with me and had also questioned me about my father and mother. I had apparently shown no emotion, but I had expressed an interest in what had been going on in the back of my mind. Because of this interest, he said, he had been prompted to suggest that I try the LSD adventure.

My most vivid memories of the sodium pentothol test were the bright lights that flashed before my eyes and then later, as the drug wore off, the sensation of pain in my leg.

My LSD trip, however, was something else.

157

I felt no effects from my first dose of LSD, injected into my arm with a hypodermic needle. A few minutes later Dr. Scott injected me again, this time with a double dose, and this one did the trick.

I could feel myself getting sleepy and my head began to roll a little. Dr. Scott, aware the drug was working, put a strap around my waist and fastened me to the bed, explaining that this was standard procedure. Some people became violent under the influence of LSD.

I had no desire to argue with him, or even to ask what he was doing. I was conscious, but just too sleepy to be anything but apathetic.

Suddenly I was out in space somewhere and there were tens of thousands of colored lights, some of them big, others mere pinpricks, dancing around me. They kept flashing on and off and from my position, seemingly suspended somewhere in mid-air, the effect was strikingly beautiful. I remember thinking at the time that every inmate should be allowed to make a trip like this at least once.

Still lying on my back on the bed, I could now see an image in front of me. It had the physical features of a human, yet there was an ethereal quality about it that surprised and frightened me. As the image became clearer, I saw it was that of a boy of perhaps three or four years of age.

I stared at him but he didn't go away and finally I recognized him. He was me – years and years before.

I felt a bad pain in my back at this point and found that it eased a little when I held myself in a rigid position. I don't know if the pain was real or imagined.

When I turned my head to the side, I could see a staircase. I looked at the floor and every tile was a step on that staircase.

As the effect of the drug wore off, Dr. Scott undid the strap and I sat up. I swung my feet over the side of the bed but the distance to the floor seemed greater than I had anticipated and I clung to the bed for security.

I finally stood up and everything began to spin, the walls, the pictures, the furniture. I staggered across the room. There were now three doors where before there had been one. I tried to go

158

out through an imaginary one and hit the wall.

Years later, Dr. Scott explained that while I was under the influence of the drug, he and a psychiatrist named Mark Hewson questioned me about the dreams or daydreams I was having. They wanted to know what bubbled to the surface when my mind was free. Had I thought about my parents, my life in the institution, my hostilities, sex?

According to Dr. Scott, LSD produces one of two results. The person involved either goes outside himself and talks about his experience, or he considers it so terribly personal that he keeps it entirely to himself.

In my case, he concluded the experience was a psychological, emotional reaction of a pleasant nature, rather than a revelation of things past. He was surprised to find that I gave no indication whatever of what was going on in my mind. In his own words, "Watching you was similar to watching someone completely absorbed in a TV show."

My LSD trip must have been pretty colorful compared with the rest of my cold, gray life because, according to Dr. Scott, I emerged from the drug-induced world saying, "Whew, that was some ride!"

During my years of confinement in Goderich, Guelph and Collins Bay, I was interviewed by a dozen or more psychiatrists and psychologists and not many inmates could boast of having that kind of attention. Actually, publication of Isabel LeBourdais' book, *The Trial of Steven Truscott* (McClelland and Stewart Limited), brought on the first real barrage. Somebody had apparently decided suddenly that some positive answers were needed in my case.

Scott was the doctor in charge at the time, and, as he explained later, he felt that no matter what he did, he was bound to be considered *persona non grata* by one faction or another. With the authorization of the then-Commissioner of Penitentiaries, Allen J. MacLeod, he called in a group of psychiatrists, including Drs. Briggs, Hunter, McCauldron and Pratten, and gave them a set of questions to ask me. My answers, he felt, would enable him to make certain decisions.

Dr. Scott wanted to know if I had a disability treatable through psychotherapy, what the group thought of the use of sodium pentothol and LSD, how I felt psychologically about the LeBourdais book, my parole prognosis, and whether it should be recommended that I have psychiatric treatment after release to help me adapt to the outside.

He wanted to know, too, if I should be interviewed every few months after release, if a private psychiatrist should be called in without having to make a report, if the woman psychologist (who questioned me about sexual habits in prison) should continue seeing me and if the results of the drug experiments should be recorded.

The report of the group was, in part, to the effect that I displayed no clear-cut psychiatric problem, that psychiatric contact would be advisable to assist me in future adjustment and that there should be no further probing into the past.

One of the procedures that occurred to Dr. Scott was that perhaps I should be sent to a mental institution, the Ontario Hospital in Penetang for further tests. He mentioned this to me and, although the prospect frightened me, I said nothing. Later I learned that he was making arrangements to have me sent there and I told my parents. A Toronto lawyer, E.B. Jolliffe, who had been interviewing me at the request of my parents, took strong objection to the proposal and I heard no more about Penetang.

I was civil with all the doctors who questioned, me but I managed never to say more than necessary. This seemed to satisfy them, so I guess they just figured that I had no imagination.

Two of the psychiatrists I rather liked. Dr. Hunter, a six-footer in his mid-forties, was one. Unlike some of the others, he had no stuffy, pseudo scientific air about him. He wore an open-necked sport shirt, which I liked, and pleased me no end by not asking the inevitable question. In fact, he made it clear at the start that he wasn't interested in my guilt or innocence but rather in my plans for the future.

Another man I liked was Dr. Szatmari from Toronto who, I believe, had been sent by the Parole Board. He was Czechoslovakian and he struck me as a bit of a rebel.

160

One of my defenses against the psychiatrists and their endless repetition of the same question, was to concentrate so hard on something else that eventually I managed to put them completely out of my mind, and although physically we were in the same room, I wasn't giving them a thought. I managed to control most of my frustrations through sheer concentration.

I knew it was important that I conceal how I really felt because they were certain to construe any hostility on my part as guilt. I don't think any of them ever suspected that I was annoyed by their questions.

* * *

For a time I came close to hating George D. Scott.

I disliked him for asking that initial question but I also resented his whole approach to my case. He kept telling me that there were four possibilities as he saw it: (1) I had committed the crime and remembered committing it; (2) I had committed the crime but had buried the fact in my subconscious; (3) I had *not* committed the crime but knew who did and remained silent out of loyalty; and (4) I did not commit the crime and had no idea who had.

Then one day he asked a question that so shocked me I couldn't answer for some minutes. He asked, without so much as a blink of the eye, if it were possible that my father had committed the crime, and I was covering for him!

As calmly as I could, I replied, "No, this is *not* possible."

Strangely enough, since I had never shown the least fondness for him, it was without hesitation that Dr. Scott later approved a request from me that I be transferred out of the main, walled penitentiary to the farm annex beyond the wall. That transfer was the greatest therapy imaginable.

After my release from Collins Bay, I met Dr. Scott and thanked him for arranging my transfer. Two things still bothered me, however, and I took them up with him.

The first was his remark about my father having perhaps committed the crime. From what he remembered of the incident, he said, he had been trying to goad me into showing some emotion.

The second was my belief that he had devoted his time to obtaining a confession. He thought that was true enough. "Most of us were busy playing detective when we should have been concentrating on basic psychiatry," he said.

It was a surprising comment from him – and yet not so strange. It may have been that as time went on he felt less and less convinced of my guilt.

He said, too, "When I finally got around to being constructive, you and I got along fine." This was true.

Anyway, I know now that I don't hate George Scott. By sending me to the annex, he may have saved my life and sanity.

CHAPTER XVII

The long years in prison had been filled with an overwhelming sadness and despair, and 1966 promised to be worse. That was the year I became twenty-one, and realized that I had virtually grown up behind bars.

It was hard to believe that I had had seven birthdays in custody, and frightening to conjecture how many more there might be. It was difficult to console myself with the knowledge that persons serving life sentences commuted from death penalties were eligible for parole after ten years.

If there was anything good about the early months of 1966, it was that on Easter Sunday morning I met a man who was destined to become my very good friend. Had anyone suggested, prior to that meeting, that I should someday make friends with a minister, I'd have said he was out of his mind. I hadn't forgotten the R.C.A.F. chaplain at Goderich.

But Mac Stienburg was something else. He was young, not only in years but in ideas, a United Church minister who smoked and drank Whiskey Sours and was often in hot water because he invariably supported the inmates against the penal Establishment. If he'd been a Hollywood hero, they would have billed him as the *fighting padre*.

Physically, Mac was a very ordinary man. His hair and eyes were a deep shade of brown, his features pleasant but not striking. He was not tall, yet there was an illusion of height.

He never displayed a superior attitude to the inmates. He was always casual, and he had a talent for prison jargon that the men appreciated. His speech, often delivered out of the side of his mouth, invariably contained references to the *joint* (penitentiary) or the *screws* (guards).

Partly because of his age, but no doubt mostly on account of his avowed interest in the welfare of the inmate population, Mac soon discovered that he was an extremely popular man, and his services were attended by overflow congregations.

One day he called me into the chapel and told me that while he didn't believe in bothering people with questions, he was always available if someone wanted to discuss a problem. He was always available for a game of crib, too, he remarked.

I didn't want to talk but I rather fancied myself a superior crib player, and took him on. To my surprise, he skunked me first try.

"You're sure lucky at cards," I joked. "Is Somebody Up There giving you some help?"

He looked over his shoulder then turned back and winked at me.

"Now you know what you're up against," he grinned.

I attended services every Sunday and visited his office in the chapel every week or two. There were plaques on the walls of the chapel that interested me and he explained their significance.

I was especially intrigued by one on the wall beside the pew in which I sat each Sunday, and Mac told me that the glowing lamp on it represented the lamp of life. Then he quoted from St. John:

"Then spake Jesus again unto them saying, I am the light of the world; he that followeth me shall not walk in darkness but shall have the light of life."

Again, referring to a wooden sculpture of a ship, Mac quoted:

"Paul said to the centurion and to the soldiers, Except these abide in the ship, ye cannot be saved."

"Is that true?" I wanted to know.

"Is what true?" Mac asked.

I suddenly felt foolish for asking the question and changed the subject. "Want to play some crib?" I asked.

"Sure do," he replied, dropping the original subject immediately. He was always fast on the up-take.

We saw each other frequently over those first few months, often at the chapel but occasionally in the radio room where he liked to look over the long-plays. He would sometimes visit as I turned on the supper hour music, or he might drop in during the evening. He was always interested in what I was doing.

I was going through a good many psychiatric sessions about this time and one evening, feeling disgruntled, I snapped at him.

"Aren't you going to ask me the question?" I wanted to know. I was thinking of that first question asked by all the psychiatrists, "Did you kill Lynne Harper?"

"What question?" he asked casually.

"Oh, never mind," I said, realizing that, in his own way, he was telling me he didn't want to know anything I didn't care to tell him.

In 1966, Isabel LeBourdais' book about my trial came out and immediately went on the prohibited list at Collins Bay. My mother tried to get a copy to me but the warden refused to let it through. I finally got one through a guard who felt indebted because I had repaired his lawn mower. It was a fair deal: he got the mower repaired free and I got the book at less than twice its retail value.

The book wasn't that big a surprise. It simply brought home to me once more what a tragic farce the trial had been, and how prejudiced the people of Huron County had been at the time.

There is always friction between the personnel of an air base and the population of a small town in the vicinity. But it would be hard to match the bigotry, hate and vindictiveness of the citizens of Huron County.

I had considered the people of Clinton and Goderich little better than a lynch mob but Isabel LeBourdais' book drove the point home again. It made me realize that there would never be any place on earth I would despise with the same intensity that I loathed the communities of Clinton and Goderich.

There the nightmare started – and there, I felt, it would sometime end.

The longer I remained in penitentiary, the more embittered I became. I lived only for the day I would be free. But when would that be? All I could do was wait.

Mac did what he could to make things pleasant. Inmates who

attended chapel regularly were allowed to invite a friend, or family member, to Sunday service every so often, and he arranged for my parents to join me soon after he took over the padre's job.

After the service, we had lunch in the gymnasium and I introduced him to Mom and Dad. He had other guests to talk to, but it was with my people that he spent the most time. He later told me that because of all the stories in the press over the years, he felt he knew me. I often wondered if Joe Fowler hadn't also felt he knew me in this way.

Mac liked my parents and kept in touch with them after that, relaying messages from them to me, and vice versa. It was a nice arrangement because he was doing it on his own, as a minister of course but as a friend as well.

"I appreciate what you're doing," I said one day.

"I'd rather work with the family as a unit than with just you in a kind of vacuum," he replied.

As a minister, Mac had a lot of unpleasant duties to perform, among them informing inmates every now and then that a wife, or a parent, had died. These experiences had made him a pretty perceptive person and when he said something to me I usually listened.

One day, for instance, he said, "I always keep it in mind that your parents are going through a bad time, too." The comment, said casually like that, made me feel warm all over. He was genuinely interested in my people and I shall never forget this act of simple human sympathy for others.

Mac was always so casual that you never were sure whether what he did was accidental or planned therapy. There was the chapel visit one Sunday, for example, when his wife Mary showed up with their two youngsters, Trevor and Andy. My brother Ken had come up with my parents that day and after service the Stienburgs and the Truscotts sat down to lunch together.

We chatted until the kids began to act up and Mary decided she'd better take them home.

I really hadn't given the children much thought then, but Mac brought them in one Saturday morning for another visit and they were so full of life and good spirits that I suddenly took a great liking to them.

When I was sent to prison, Barb and Bill had been small, and now I recalled how nice it was to have children around. The sight and sound of those two youngsters playing and laughing in a prison was a wondrous thing. It restored my hope in the future.

A few days later I ran into Mac, and I told him how much I'd enjoyed being with Trevor and Andy. "It's difficult to explain," I said, "but it was as if they were pointing out to me that there's something beyond those walls, a life that's waiting for me."

Mac was pleased.

"Well," he said, "those boys sure took to you. You've become their big brother, in their minds."

"I feel old enough to be their grandfather," I quipped.

Mac never preached except on Sunday mornings. But he was tuned in to the lonely and unhappy and was never at a loss when it came to finding some appropriate inspiration.

As we walked out of the chapel, he stopped in front of one of the plaques and said, "I suppose you know about the old Roman torch?"

"Torch?" I asked stupidly.

"Look it up sometime," he said, suddenly going into his corner-of-the-mouth-tough-guy routine. "Matthew 5-16."

I didn't look it up and that was the first thing he asked me next time we met. This time he quoted it:

"Let your light so shine before men, that they may see your good works, and glorify Your Father which is in heaven."

CHAPTER XVIII

My mother made no effort to hide the joy she felt as we sat in the visitors' room. "The whole of Canada is behind you," she said, not caring how much she exaggerated.

Poor Mom. I had never seen her so happy, so full of hope. First there had been the LeBourdais book, urging a re-examination of my trial. And now a group of people, angered by the injustices in my case, were demanding no less than a formal review by the highest court in the land, the Supreme Court of Canada.

"They've sent petitions across Canada, to the United States and even to Europe," my mother said. "Thousands of people have signed in support of you. Do you know what that means, Steve? It means the government won't be able to ignore you any more. They'll have to look into your case."

She spoke with such sincerity and conviction that I took her hand and said, "I wish I had had you to defend me in Goderich instead of Frank Donnelly. I might not have been here now."

At the same time the petitions were being circulated, people started writing me direct, addressing their letters of support simply to *Steven Truscott, Collins Bay Penitentiary, Kingston.*

Because of penitentiary regulations entitling me to mail only from persons on an approved list, these letters were never given to me. Instead, they were turned over to my mother who divulged their contents when she visited. Invariably the messages sympathized with me and expressed the hope that I would soon be released.

"I don't know when I have been so encouraged," my mother said one day. "The letters have been marvellous. And don't forget that for every one addressed to you, three others were sent to the government."

My mother had built up a protective wall of hope about her and nobody was going to break it down. She was so certain that my case would go to the Supreme Court that when the announcement was finally made she accepted it without surprise.

Her great confidence had inspired me and I, too, experienced little surprise at the news report. It said simply that by virtue of an Order-in-Council dated April 26, 1966, the Government had referred to the Supreme Court for hearing and consideration the following question:

"Had an appeal by Steven Murray Truscott been made to the Supreme Court of Canada, as is now permitted by Section 597A of the Criminal Code of Canada, what disposition would the court have made of such an appeal on a consideration of the existing record and such further evidence as the court, in its discretion, may receive and consider?"

* * *

The public clamor for an official review of my case and the Order-in-Council itself had made me something of a celebrity, with all the papers and magazines carrying pieces about me. But inside the institution, the fellows held to the tradition that every man was an island and you didn't go ashore exploring. Everyone had his own set of problems and didn't want to get involved with yours.

As for me, I had my ups and downs. I wasn't surprised that the case was going to the Supreme Court nor was I blasé about my situation. One day I worried a lot, another I shrugged and forgot about my plight. Generally speaking, I didn't have too much time to mope about because my radio room and machine shop work occupied me from 6:30 a.m. until midnight.

Mac was always there when I wanted to talk something out and he was a good listener. He never explored the case itself but often discussed my attitude toward it.

"I suggest you be cautiously optimistic about things," he said during a chat.

"Are you optimistic?" I asked.

"I don't know enough about the case to say I'm optimistic," he replied. "Let's say I'm hopeful."

I had to admit (when my spirits were up) that I was rather looking forward to having my case heard by the country's highest court. It was a unique thing to appear before such an august body.

"You have to be realistic," Mac said when he thought I was getting overly-optimistic.

And when he thought I was in the dumps, he said, "Come on. I think things look pretty good."

Sometimes we were joined in the chapel by other inmates and we discussed the implications of my case. "Imagine the impact on our whole legal system if the Supreme Court reversed the decision of the lower court," somebody said. Of course, we really didn't know what we were talking about but we talked anyway. Discussion was always good therapy.

Mac was careful about his comments, pointing out that he didn't know enough about the legal machinery to offer concrete suggestions. Like most other people, though, he had a sort of blind faith in the workings of Justice.

I had learned over the years to expect, and to accept, adverse decisions, and sometimes I would say, "You know very well, Mac, that even with enough supporting evidence, the Supreme Court would never reverse the finding of a lower court."

To this Mac would reply, "I don't think the court would take that attitude. After all, it *is* the highest court in the country – and it is very much respected."

We would sit over a game of crib after this and then say goodnight. Then, in the quiet of the dormitory, I would go over all the arguments in my mind and often keep myself awake half the night in the process.

Some nights I would have given anything to know whether or not I would be set free.

* * *

One evening I was called into the warden's office and introduced to John R. Matheson, Liberal M.P. for Leeds, Ontario.

Matheson, who was Parliamentary Secretary to Prime Minister Pearson, came right to the point. He asked me if I'd accept a parole in lieu of the Supreme Court Hearing.

I was frankly amazed. "I applied once for a parole – and this was denied," I said. "I'll do nothing that might in any way be construed as an admission of guilt. I want that hearing – I deserve it."

I don't think that Matheson was really surprised. He didn't push the offer. He simply handed me his card and told me to get in touch with him should I change my mind.

"I won't," I snapped. Then I called the guard and asked to be returned to my quarters.

The Steven Truscott affair was rapidly becoming a *cause célèbre* in the political arena. A few weeks later, I received another visitor, James Byrne, Liberal Member of Parliament for a Vancouver riding. Again we met in the warden's office but this time there was no *deal* in the offing. This man talked to me about the trial in Goderich and asked me how I really felt about it.

Well, that was my cue. If the treatment I received was an example of Canadian justice, I pointed out, I wasn't too impressed. He agreed, strangely enough. He then said he was convinced of my innocence and added that when he got back to Ottawa, he would tell the newspapers he was willing to stake his seat in the House of Commons on my innocence.

A few days later, the report was in the papers. Mr. Byrne had kept his promise. He had discussed my case in the House and declared his belief that I was innocent. He had even staked his seat on it – just as he had said he would.

People such as Mr. Byrne kept my hopes alive.

* * *

Every time my mother came, she brought new letters. The messages of hope and support came now from as far away as France, Germany, Sweden and Australia.

The reaction was gratifying because I had been hearing in recent years that people were wanting less and less to be involved in other people's problems. So many people, I had learned, had

171

adopted the attitude that, well, if it didn't concern them, it was none of their business.

The fact that so many people had signed the petitions and had taken the time to write letters to me and to the government restored my faltering faith. I began to think that perhaps a lot of people did care after all.

Some of the letters I received were from young women proposing marriage. I was sure they were serious and I was touched by them, but even if I had been in a position to consider marriage, it would have been the thought farthest from my mind.

I had been confined for so long that my one thought, when I considered the prospect of my release, was that I would never stay too long in one place. I would travel and when it came time to settle down, it would not be in a city, or even a town but somewhere out in the country.

One letter, I recall, came from a young widow with two small children who told me she lived in a nice Canadian urban neighborhood and owned her own car. She said if I was thinking of marriage, or if I just needed a place to stay, she would like to meet me.

Another letter came from a twenty-three-year-old secretary in Europe who said that she had travelled all over Canada and had followed my case from the beginning. It occurred to her that when I was released, I might be happy for an opportunity to leave Canada. If so, she said, I was welcome to stay with her in her country.

Some of the letters absolutely amazed my mother. She couldn't understand why complete strangers would want to marry me.

CHAPTER XIX

It seemed so strange, early on a crisp October morning in 1966 to put on a civilian suit that had no numbers and a white shirt and tie, to get into a car, to drive through the gate, leave the walls behind and drive slowly along a roadway flanked by trees whose leaves had turned to brilliant reds and golds.

Almost three years and nine months before, I had arrived at Collins Bay in a raging snowstorm. Now, bound for Ottawa and the Supreme Court hearing, I was being driven through country lush with the vegetation of early fall, past fields of ripening pumpkins and yellow-brown cornstalks, past orchards bright with the redness of autumn apples.

I should have been thinking of what lay ahead in Ottawa but all that mattered just then was that hundred-mile drive from Kingston, along the fringes of the Rideau Lakes country. Ray Singaard, the penitentiary officer who was my escort, and Bill Sands, the Farm Annex officer who was our driver, had agreed that my first excursion into the outside world should be as pleasant as possible. To make it so, they had decided to take it easy on the way up, making short detours off the highway now and then to let me have a look at some of the small towns.

The morning was filled with the wonderfully-exciting *little* things of free, everyday life, things I had almost forgotten existed.

I found myself fascinated with the people on the street. They all seemed so busy, carrying parcels out of food stores, sweeping the sidewalks in front of their homes, hanging out the wash, shaking rugs, getting in and out of their cars.

I was intrigued, too, with the sounds that came from all directions – the hum of car engines, the squeal of tires, the shrill cry of a woman calling a child, the unmistakable clunk of a screen door being slammed shut somewhere in the distance. Noise – it was wonderful. I would never have supported an abatement program.

The restaurant in Smiths Falls combined a lot of strange sensations. We sat at the counter with strangers all around and there was music blaring away and the smell of food cooking in the back and I suddenly felt uncomfortable.

"What will you have?" the waitress asked, giving me a quick, casual glance as she ran a cloth over the counter.

"Just coffee," I replied shakily.

Hungry though I was, I was much too nervous to eat. As it was, I gulped the coffee. Ray and Bill knew I felt strange because they kept exchanging glances. But they made no comment.

Outside in the car, I slumped way down. It had been a good morning but an exhausting one. As Dr. Scott explained to me later, I was reacting to a new environment in a very normal way. It was a question of sensory deprivation.

I had lived so long in the terrible grayness of prison, isolated from the sight, sound and tactile stimulations of ordinary living, that it was difficult for me to face up to that first barrage beyond the walls. Some inmates, barely vegetating over a period of years, are actually terrified by the outside world, so perhaps I hadn't done so badly.

"I didn't know what to say to that girl," I told Ray and Bill as we drove along. "It's been a long time since anybody bothered to ask me what I'd like to have."

My address in Ottawa was the Carleton County Jail, an old dungeon of a place that reminded me a little of the jail in Goderich, and my cell was a place four feet wide and seven feet long, containing a narrow bed and lavatory pot.

It was a rotten place where the lights went out at 7:00 p.m. and where, in the morning, they gave me a razor with a blade that had been used all over the cell block and no hot water. They even refused to let me use a fresh blade which I had remembered to bring along from Collins Bay.

Ray Singaard came for me early that first morning and drove me to the Supreme Court Building where I spent the day in an anteroom playing cards with him. There was one bonus: my parents and my brother Ken visited me during the lunch hour recess.

My mother was surfacely optimistic as usual. "The lawyers have high hopes," she said. "They feel sure things are going to turn out right." I wondered if, in their legal wisdom, Arthur Martin and E.B. Jolliffe and R.J. Carter did indeed feel that hopeful.

Ken wanted to know if things were reasonably comfortable at the jail and I said they were passable. We spoke of jail the way other people talked about hotels. It was weird.

I returned to the jail and the next morning, after an icy cold shave with the usual blunt razor, I joined Ray on a wild car drive to the courthouse. A news photographer had waited for us to leave the garage under the jail and had followed us. On Rideau Street, we tried to lose him but he accelerated and in a few minutes he was travelling alongside us with his camera on the window ledge. I don't know how he managed it but he was close enough to reach out his window and tap on ours to attract my attention.

The officers did their best to protect me from photographers but they didn't always succeed. Actually there were so many of them in Ottawa for the hearing, it was impossible to dodge them all.

* * *

The Supreme Court of Canada is an old and august body which has traditionally considered the appeals made to it on the basis of transcripts of trials and arguments of counsel. But in my case, it decided to shatter precedent and hear witnesses. More than thirty were called – and I was one of them.

The newspapers said my testimony would be the high point of the hearing and I suppose that might have been so since I had not been called to testify in my defense during the trial in 1959.

But sitting there in the anteroom playing cribbage with Ray, I had made up my mind that if I were questioned on details that were hazy to me seven years later, I would simply say that I didn't remember. That way no one could twist my testimony, nor say that I hadn't said this, that or the other thing years before.

I am sure the Supreme Court would take a dim view of my recollections of the day I was called to give evidence. But two things stand out: (1) I was deeply involved in a game of crib with Ray when I was called; and (2), I was returned to the County Jail for lunch and had some awful fried bologna served with stale bread.

Walking into the courtroom took me right back to 1959. True this room was more elaborate and now there were nine Justices when before there had been but one judge. But the lawyers were there, and the clerks and the police and the spectators – all of them staring at the freak who had come before them professing his innocence.

It was this constant staring that had so disturbed me back in Goderich. It became a sort of phobia and I imagined everyone was staring at me, a situation which persisted to a certain degree for some time after my release from prison.

The papers said I stood erect with shoulders back before the nine robed Justices, that I looked trim, though pale, that I hesitated before answering questions and that sometimes I spoke so quietly the judges asked me to repeat what I had said. In a sense, everything they had said was true.

But perhaps in the whole of that packed courtroom, only a few people, such as my mother and father, really believed me when I swore I had not killed Lynne Harper.

I am innocent! How often I had said that.

Arthur Martin was the man who asked me to tell my story – and it was the first time it had been told in my own words.

I kept my composure as I told of the events of that June night. This was something I had learned in prison: never let them know they're getting to you.

I told about meeting Lynne near the school, about taking her to the highway on the crossbar of my bicycle, about stopping at the bridge on my way back and watching as she got into a gray 1959 Chevrolet.

I said she had wanted to visit a house on the highway where

there were ponies.

"Did you have Lynne Harper in the bush?" Martin asked at one point.

"No, sir," I answered.

Once or twice, I looked across at my parents and felt badly for them. They looked so sad sitting there, wishing good things for me.

The questions went on and I continued piecing the old story together again. Yes, Lynne had been in my class. I had once gone to a birthday party at her place but I had never gone out with her on dates.

Yes, we had exchanged words during our bicycle ride to the highway. She had asked me if there was a fishing hole nearby and later she had mentioned being angry with her father for not letting her go swimming.

Every now and then there was a lull in the questioning while the judges and lawyers discussed a point. I gazed out the window. It was only mid-afternoon but the October sky was already showing signs of darkening. Then the questioning resumed.

Yes, it was still light when I took Lynne to the highway...

Yes, it was a Chevrolet. I was interested in cars at the time and knew all the models. I couldn't be mistaken about that...

Oh, the interminable story!

I had gone home to baby-sit...

The first knowledge I had that something unusual had happened to Lynne was the morning after our bicycle ride. Her father came to our house inquiring about her because she hadn't been home all night...

The hearing gave me a chance to take a swipe at the psychiatrists. They had wanted me to admit guilt but I wouldn't, I said.

It gave me an opportunity, too, to disagree with the doctors who examined me after my arrest and testified I had sores the size of 25-cent pieces on either side of my penis. The Crown argued they had resulted from an attack on Lynne.

I testified the sores were considerably smaller than described by the doctors and added that they had developed six weeks before my arrest.

They kept going back to the same tired old questions. The Crown, for example, produced two maps of the Clinton area and asked me to point out the route I had taken with Lynne and the one I followed back alone.

One of the judges asked how long it had taken me to make the trip to the highway and back and I said it had taken about fifteen or twenty minutes.

Later the lawyers argued over the testimony of Jocelyn Godette at the trial. She said I had asked her to go looking for calves with me. Was this true, I was asked? The story was a lie, I said.

At one point, Crown Counsel Donald Scott reviewed certain testimony given at the trial and I said I couldn't remember it. How, he wanted to know, could I forget testimony that incriminated me? I hesitated. How do you answer a question like that?

"Because I've forgotten," I said finally.

* * *

The hearings lasted the better part of two weeks, and since my presence was seldom required at the proceedings, I spent most of the time either in the County Jail or in the anteroom of the court building. I liked the latter because there I could play crib with Ray. I got running accounts of what was going on from my parents and lawyers and from the newspapers which gave the hearings extensive coverage.

My mother continued to be optimistic. Experts had been called in for my defense and they were demolishing a lot of the damning evidence of my trial. The defense had even gone to the United States for one of its experts, she said. He was a man named Charles Petty, assistant medical examiner for the state of Maryland, and he established positively that Lynne's death could not have occured earlier than midnight.

Every time Mom visited, she told me about a new witness who had rallied to my support. But something inside was telling me that things were not going well. It was nothing I could put my finger on, but it was there. Call it intuition, but I had a feeling the proceedings were not doing me much good.

The hearings were finally adjourned with instructions to legal counsel to prepare their arguments for presentation at a later date. I was relieved because I was beginning to think I couldn't stand much more of the County Jail. I didn't think I would ever want to return to Collins Bay Penitentiary once I had left the place but a few nights in the Ottawa jail made the Kingston institution look pretty good.

The morning Ray came for me at the jail was bright and crisp and I was looking forward to the drive back to Kingston. Again Bill Sands was the driver and I asked if he thought we could go via Richmond because I had never seen my parents' new house.

Bill agreed and, I gave him the address. We coasted slowly past the house. It was painted white and sat back in the autumn grass about a hundred yards from the road. There were good-sized yards both front and back.

I was glad I had seen the house because now, when my parents spoke of it, I could visualize it. But seeing it made me feel sad. I thought of all the years I had lost.

CHAPTER XX

November had always been a long, lonely month but this one seemed longer and lonelier than all the others, perhaps because of misgivings about the Supreme Court hearing. I had disciplined myself not to show my feelings but my nerves were raw and my temper flared easily now.

I lost interest in work, both in the machine shop and the radio room, and I found it difficult to concentrate on reading and playing cards. Something was going to have to happen to break the monotony. Somehow I was going to have to get out from behind that wall.

The wall had driven a lot of guys crazy over the years – and it was beginning to drive *me* crazy now.

I applied to the warden for a transfer to the Farm Annex. This was just behind the institution but it was on the other side of the wall, surrounded by open fields. My request was rejected because the Supreme Court decision was pending. They didn't want to be bothered with a transfer when a new trial might be ordered and I might eventually be acquitted.

Mac Stienburg kept dropping in on me, thus helping me retain some vestiges of sanity. His friendship was important because I had no real friends in the penitentiary population.

"I have some more literature designed to save your soul," he joked one night.

He was referring to spiritual tracts from every imaginable religious order and sect in the country, which were addressed to me. Officials channelled them through him.

"It's curious how many people are interested in saving my soul now," I said without joking. "I don't think there was one truly concerned individual in the country during the trial in Goderich. Where were all those good people then?"

"Public opinion was against you at the time, primarily because of the nature of the offense," he answered. "Also there was no question of any prejudice or irregularities in the trial."

"Surely someone of importance must have wondered," I suggested. It had bothered me that no one among the so-called just and intelligent people of the country was interested enough to look further into my case immediately after the trial.

Mac wasn't surprised. "Once a man is found guilty," he said, "the public accepts him as such. After all, a jury *said* you were guilty and, under our system, innocent men don't go to prison."

* * *

It was strange, opening a newspaper and reading about myself. So strange, in fact, that I sometimes had the feeling I was reading about somebody else. The news report about English actor Michael Rennie, for instance. How could things like that be happening to me?

Rennie had been in Ottawa in December and had announced plans for a movie about my case, which he would direct. He told reporters he had been following the Truscott story since the trial in Goderich.

I was in the news again early in January of 1967, with an announcement from Ottawa, that Crown and defense counsel had submitted their written factums to the Supreme Court.

I was encouraged by the defense contention that my conviction should be quashed or that a new trial should be ordered for a number of reasons, one of them being that there was conflicting medical testimony about the time of Lynne Harper's death.

On the other hand, I was pretty downcast about the Crown summation. The prosecution maintained that the only new evidence at the October hearings was my own testimony and it added, "With respect to Truscott's evidence, it is submitted it is not worthy of belief."

Late in January, the lawyers argued the pros and cons of the case in person before the justices, and the court subsequently reserved judgment.

During the next three months, my name was hardly ever mentioned in the papers. The big news everywhere was Canada's Centennial. The country was one hundred years old and I was twenty-two.

* * *

On May 4, 1967, the Supreme Court, with one judge dissenting, upheld my conviction. It made its decision public at 10:30 that morning without any advance notice to me. I learned my fate at the same time the rest of the country did.

Again Mac Stienburg played a part by asking me to meet him in the chapel that morning. I didn't know it at the time but Mr. Jolliffe had suggested this because he wanted me to hear the news in an official way and not by chance on a radio broadcast.

From the chapel, we walked to the warden's office. Deputy Warden Duff was on duty that morning and we went into his private office. About 10:30 the telephone rang in the general offices outside and Mac went out to answer it.

He returned a few minutes later and I could tell right away the news was bad. He addressed himself to the deputy warden.

"It was Mr. Jolliffe," Mac said, "The verdict is unfavorable."

Mac then directed me to the telephone. Mr. Jolliffe capsuled the decision for me. The court had decided eight to one against me. Then my mother came on the line.

"Hello, son," she said. There was a long pause and oh God, I felt sorry for her.

She wanted to know if I had heard the news and I said I had. Then she said she would be seeing me soon. I wanted to talk to Dad but he was too upset to come to the telephone. Isabel LeBourdais was with my parents and I spoke to her, too.

Mac and I then went back to the chapel for coffee. I didn't talk much except to say that I was glad Mom was coming that afternoon. Later, Mac went out to answer telephone questions from reporters and I got my lunch tray and went to work in the radio room. A guard we called Glue Snoot Johnson kept coming in and

I guess he thought I might try to hang myself.

Later, an assistant deputy warden looked in. He was quite upset. Another officer then asked if I wanted to wait for my mother in the hospital, thus avoiding possible questions about the verdict from other inmates. I said I would.

It was a strange situation. Some of the staff were taking it harder than I.

Mom arrived late and Mac walked me to the visitors' room. He had got permission to supervise the visit, replacing the normally-assigned officer, thinking we would feel easier with him than with a stranger.

Mom was upset, as I knew she would be. She hadn't counted on a rejection by the court. Dad was so upset he couldn't even make the trip.

"We're not giving up," she said, unconvincingly.

Then we sat in silence. Neither of us knew what to say.

* * *

That night in the radio room, I kept hearing the reports. "The Supreme Court of Canada today rejected..."

It was later that I sat down with the papers and sorted out the details. It was an unhappy mess.

"There were many incredibilities inherent in the evidence given by Truscott before us and we do not believe his testimony."

The eight learned judges – Chief Justice Taschereau and Mr. Justices Cartwright, Fauteux, Abbott, Martland, Judson, Ritchie and Spence – took up nearly one hundred pages of legal paper to back up this statement.

"We find it impossible to accept Truscott's evidence given before us that he and the girl (Lynne Harper) left at 7:30 p.m....

"Our conclusion is that Truscott's evidence...does not and cannot disturb the finding implicit in the jury's verdict that after passing Gellatly, Truscott and Lynne went into Lawson's Bush...

"It is also implicit in the jury's verdict that the girl died where she was found...and that she was not picked up at the intersection and subsequently brought back dead or alive by someone other than Truscott...

"On a review of all the evidence given at the trial, we are of the opinion that on the record as it then stood, the verdict could not be set aside on the ground that it was unreasonable or could not be supported by the evidence...

"Indeed, it being implicit in their verdict that the jury completely rejected the evidence of those witnesses who said that they had seen Truscott pass over the bridge with Lynne Harper, and Truscott's statements as to having seen Lynne Harper enter a motor car, we are of opinion that the verdict was in accordance with the evidence...

"We are also of opinion that the judgment at trial could not have been set aside on the ground of any wrong decision on a question of law or on the ground that there was a miscarriage of justice."

Eight judges had drawn a circle around me and there was no getting out of it. The ninth, Mr. Justice Hall, would have given me a chance to clear myself. In his dissenting opinion, he wrote:

"Having considered the case fully, I believe that the conviction should be quashed and a new trial directed...

"I take the view that the trial was not conducted according to law. Even the guiltiest criminal must be tried according to law...

"That does not mean that I consider Truscott guilty or innocent...

"The determination of guilt or innocence was a matter for the jury and for the jury alone as its dominant function following a trial conducted according to law."

* * *

My faith in Canada's judicial system had been badly shaken in Goderich but after hearing the decision of the Supreme Court, I had nothing but contempt for what passes as justice in Canada.

That May night in Collins Bay Penitentiary, I was filled with anger. Anger at the government and at everyone who believed in the integrity and impartiality of our courts.

Perhaps what bothered me the most was the knowledge that the last legal opportunity to prove my innocence was gone.

<hr>

CHAPTER XXI

<hr>

The Steven Truscott case had been disposed of by the Supreme Court and, from a legal point of view, the government considered it closed. The Prime Minister of that time, Lester Pearson, made it clear in the Commons that he had discussed the matter with Justice Minister Pierre Elliott Trudeau and Solicitor-General Larry Pennell and that it had been decided no action would be taken.

The clamor continued, however. Conservative Leader John Diefenbaker wanted to know in the House if the Parole Board was considering my case and, if so, when a decision might be expected. He also suggested that the *Queen's Mercy,* extended in years of celebration, might be given me as a centennial gift.

New Democratic Party member Stanley Knowles introduced a bill which would have granted me immediate parole without a Parliamentary view of my guilt or innocence. He believed the court had made a "shocking decision."

Liberal Member of Parliament James Byrne had once suggested a Royal Commission to investigate my case and now he said he still favored it. It was Byrne who had staked his seat in the House on my innocence when he tried to get me a hearing.

Hardly a day went by without a mention of my name in one connection or another in the papers and over the air, and two or three times a week, Mac and I would review developments.

About this time, he had begun to suspect that attempts were made to listen in on our chats. His suspicions seemed to have been well-founded because, on two occasions, the chapel cleaner spotted an officer coming out of the duct work that ran under the chapel office. In any case, we decided after this to sit in a pew in the middle of the chapel where eavesdropping was difficult.

We were never able to prove anyone had been trying to over-hear our conversations and we agreed to treat the matter as a joke. The chapel cleaner saw the humor right away and every time he passed a register he would bang on it and shout, "Are you listening, Charlie?"

Early in June, Mac went off on a course in Windsor and there he met my aunt and uncle. There was nothing unusual about him wanting to meet them. He was one of those dedicated penal people who had to know everything about his subject and who eventually wound up being a part of his life.

When he returned to Collins Bay, he had an announcement to make. He was giving up his work as prison padre to become a parole officer, a change he undoubtedly figured would give him more scope within the penal framework. He conducted a couple more services, however, and after one of them he asked me to stay.

"When do you join the parole service?" I asked.

"July 1," he answered.

"My Dad's birthday," I said absent-mindedly.

It was the cue he had been hoping for. "Steve," he said, "I want to talk to you about something..."

* * *

I suppose one of the great shocks of my life was hearing that my beloved mother and father had decided to separate.

Mac had *had* to tell me. There was no other way. And yet he hesitated and this had made me feel sad. Poor Mac! He had his quota of dirty jobs.

"Mrs. LeBourdais called me at home last night," he said. "She was worried you might find out accidentally and thought that perhaps I should break the news to you."

I think he realized my shock but there wasn't much he could do to soften the blow. He said, "Your parents have agreed upon a separation."

The rest of the day I spent wandering around the dormitory,

desolate over the news from home. That night I wrote Mom:

"I had a talk with the padre today and he said...that things aren't going very good. I know that things have been pretty rough lately and hard on the nerves.

"Those people in Ottawa can't hurt me anymore. You and Dad are the only people in the world who mean anything to me and who keep me going. I don't know what I'll do if anything goes wrong at home as I feel that most of this is my fault. All this heartache and strain because of me. Things are so mixed up and I just don't know what to do."

The terrible thing about it all was that I was locked up unable to help in any way.

On July 1, I wrote Dad, wishing him a happy birthday. We used to joke about how lucky he was to have a birthday the whole country celebrated. Then I told him I had heard the news from the padre. And I wrote:

"You and Mom are the only people who mean anything to me..."

"The people in Ottawa can't hurt me anymore but what *can* hurt me is something wrong at home."

The words varied a little – but not the thoughts. They were always about my family.

Something wrong at home. What an understatement. The years of tension and disappointment had finally destroyed my family.

* * *

I kept as busy as possible during the long unhappy months of 1967 and somehow time passed.

"I received a very nice letter from Karen," I wrote my mother one day. "I haven't heard from her since they moved but she said everybody was fine and she wanted me to say hello."

Karen – what wonderful, pleasant old memories. Let's see now, when had we had that joint birthday party in Clinton? Oh yes, I was thirteen and she was twelve.

There is a tendency in prison to remember things as they were, rather than as they are, especially if you are in for a long stretch. But I tried to keep up with things.

Ken was married now and had a son named David. It was hard to believe because such a short time ago we used to bicycle down to the Bayfield River.

Bill was living with Dad now that our home was broken up and I couldn't convince myself that the kid brother I sat with at night was old enough to make decisions like that.

Barb made me most conscious of time. I remembered Mom and Dad bringing her home from the hospital in Edmonton – and here she was, all grown up.

"Barb really surprised me when she was up," I wrote my mother. "She talked all the time."

It was August and she had just returned from British Columbia with a batch of pictures for my photo album. She was a real shutter-bug, that one. Many of the places I knew around Vancouver had changed but my grandparents looked the same. There was my grandfather working on the roof of a new house he was building – and my grandmother looking on approvingly. There was Granny driving a small bulldozer. There was Pop repairing a bridge.

It's not easy writing interesting letters in prison but I tried to keep Mom informed:

"I watched the Ottawa game. They sure didn't put up much of a fight. I guess Barb was glad. The West will come through and take the Grey Cup..."

"I had a visit from Isabel and she said to say hello. We had a nice long visit. It's good to have friends like her..."

"Dad came up and we had a good visit. His nerves are still quite bad. It makes me feel awful sitting here and not being able to do anything but I guess this is something he'll have to work out for himself. My nerves weren't too good for a while but nothing anyone said helped..."

"I've been getting cards from all over. They let cards come in to me. My cupboard is full, so we are putting them on the walls..."

December came and I told my mother not to take chances making the trip to Collins Bay if the weather was bad. As it turned out, the snow and cold didn't interfere with any visit.

And I continued writing:

"I hope you and Barb have a nice Christmas. I hope things will be better next year. I guess they *have* to get better..."

"We had a pretty fair Christmas. Lots of shows and I gained five pounds. I never got to bed before 3:00 a.m. over the holidays and I sure feel it now. This morning I fell asleep leaning against a door and almost landed on my head..."

Barb and I exchanged cards in January and once again I was reminded of the passing of time.

"I hope Barb enjoyed her birthday," I wrote Mom. "Imagine her being fifteen."

* * *

In April, 1968, the warden advised I would be eligible for parole on June 11, 1969 – just ten years to the day of my arrest.

I immediately re-applied for transfer to the Farm Annex and on the morning of May 7, Dr. Scott called me to his office. He approved my transfer immediately and that same day I was on my way.

I had one regret about moving so quickly. If I had known the night before, I would have taken my trumpet into the radio room and announced my departure with a blast loud enough to rock the wall.

CHAPTER XXII

The May fields were greener and thicker than I had ever remembered them from childhood, and for a long time I stood there, watching the grass bend softly in the wind, inhaling the scents of spring and listening to the now half-forgotten sounds of farm animals.

Then that night at the dormitory window, I stood fascinated by the multi-colored lights of the newly-opened Frontenac Shopping Mall, just across the highway from the institution. It was strange, knowing that any night of the week, I could look across a civilian parking lot full of cars to a Woolco department store, a Dominion supermarket, a Pontiac car dealer, a steak house and, beyond them, a high-rise apartment building with lights in most of the windows.

My transfer meant a lot of good things, like being able to eat from plates in a cafeteria (instead of from a sloptray in a cell or dormitory), and being free to walk about the property after supper, and being able to wear the watch Ken bought me for my fifteenth birthday in the County Jail at Goderich.

Goderich! What a long time ago that was!

It meant more and longer visits with my family and summer picnics on the lawns with Mom bringing a lunch that always included either lemon pie or chocolate cake, my favorite boyhood desserts. I had separate visits from my parents now that they no longer lived together. One day, Mom would come with Barb, and sometimes Ken; and another day, it would be the turn of Dad and Bill.

It meant being with my friend John, who had also got a transfer from the main institution. It was a unique situation in that John and I were the first inmates under life sentence to be housed in a minimum security camp. We figured it was one of those experiments they sometimes try, but we didn't question it.

But most of all it meant that the wall, that ugly, gray mass of stone that had been my great psychological enemy, was no longer there to remind me of my captivity.

The Farm Annex wasn't everybody's cup of tea, but for farm boys such as John and I, it was made to order. Except for the fact that it was still part of a penitentiary.

* * *

The annex was a huge operation with eighty milch cows, five bulls, some twenty or thirty calves (the number varied) and more than 5,000 chickens. The whole of the regional penal complex, including Kingston Penitentiary, the Prison for Women, Joyceville Institution and Collins Bay Penitentiary, depended on it for milk, cream, eggs and vegetables.

They didn't go easy on us but then we didn't expect farming to be easy. There was choring to be done every day of the week because cows were no respectors of weekends. Then there were the back-breaking jobs: the silo to clean, the fence posts (all 4,000 of them) to be painted.

We rode the tractors and worked the land, cultivating, disking, harrowing and seeding and then haying. It was real farm life – up with the sun, and during seeding and harvesting, working well into the hours of darkness.

The first season, we brought in 50,000 bales of hay and 30,000 of straw, which meant a lot of handling since the hay was cut green, brought back to be spread on dryers, then baled and stored in the barns. But John and I developed muscles we didn't know we had and soon we were tossing 100-pound bales at each other for the fun of it.

We made the most of our new-found freedom and one night we decided to take advantage of the fact that there was a drive-in movie just beyond the fence that closed in one of our fields. It was so situated that when we sat on our tractors at the fence, we were behind the last line of cars and directly facing the screen.

A Jerry Lewis comedy was showing and it looked as though it was pretty funny. But it was like sitting through a silent movie, since we had no speakers. After a few minutes of this we called to the occupants of one of the cars to turn up the speaker. They ignored us, so we turned on our tractor lights and that started a furor with people jumping out of their cars and shouting to us to turn them off. We decided then to slip quietly away in case someone called the police.

A couple of nights later we left the hayfield nearest the drive-in to the last so that we could work it after dark. That night John Wayne's *Rio Bravo* was showing and for this we didn't need the speakers. The action spoke for itself.

We saw several soundless movies in this way and considered them as just rewards for many hours of really back-breaking work.

I had blisters on my hands and feet and my back ached and at the end of the haying season, I had dropped from 189 pounds to 154.

But that first summer at the annex was the best I had known in years. In a way, it reminded me of those now-remote summer days on Bob Lawson's farm.

* * *

The annex covered 1,000 acres and this was a sizeable enough area in which to play hookey. John and I had two favorite spots we managed to visit with astonishing regularity.

One was the quarry which was always full of water. Our swimming hole even had a natural diving board, made by a jutting rock. The only drawback was that the pool was adjacent to the highway and we were visible to the occupants of passing cars. We figured, however, that if anybody wanted to watch two fellows swimming in the nude, well it was their business. After all, *we* couldn't make use of the pool at the Holiday Inn.

Our other hideaway was the little river at the edge of the property. Here, with improvised lines and using worms (and occasionally flies made by the inmates), we caught catfish and sunfish and

Steven Truscott approximately one year before his trial. (Canada Wide)

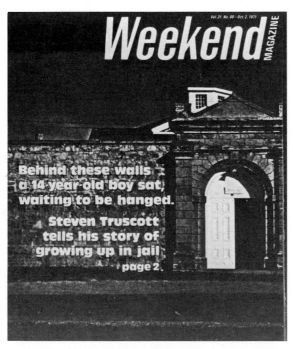

Collins Bay Penitentiary (Frank Prazak – Weekend Magazine)

Betty Galbraith-Cornell's sketch of Seaforth — the town where people claim Lynne Harper was seen on the night of her murder.

The body of Lynne Harper

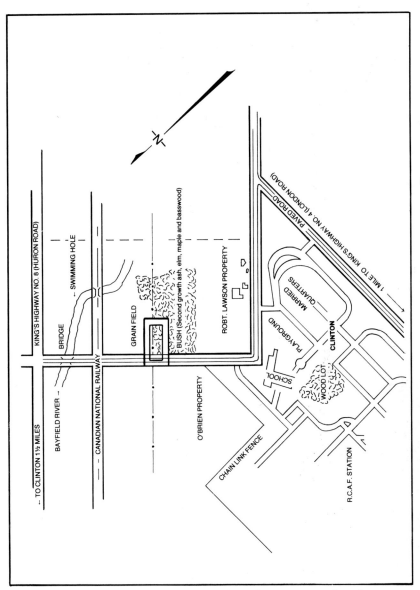

The area surrounding Lawson's bush where the victim was found.

An aerial view of Kingston Penitentiary.

Mac Stienburg – The United Church minister who befriended Steven Truscott in prison and later became his parole officer.

Justice Emmett Hall, who wrote the dissenting opinion in the Truscott case before the Supreme Court of Canada. (Canadian Press)

Steven's family, in April 1966, following the government's announcement to refer the Truscott case to the Supreme Court of Canada. Surrounding a chair, empty since 1959 when Steven was convicted of capital murder are (from left) sister Barbara, Mr. Truscott, brother Bill, and Mrs. Truscott. Steven's elder brother Ken lived in Montreal at the time. (Wide World – Canada Wide)

The author Bill Trent (left) talks with Dr. Scott, chief psychiatrist at Kingston Penitentiary.

From a bridge near Clinton, the town where Steven grew up, Steven visualizes his lost youth. (Frank Prazak – Weekend Magazine)

some unidentified specimens we took to be pike.

Then one night as we wandered around the farm, John and I saw water oozing from the ground. We figured it was a spring, got shovels and started digging. Two guards came over, and when we said we were making a fish pond, they shrugged and went off.

We worked until we had a pond ten feet in diameter and three or four feet deep, and from then on, all the fish we caught in the river went into the pond. We fed and looked after them all that first summer and they were still there the next year.

Sometimes during our evening walks, John and I would become serious and talk about our futures. He had his Class A mechanics' papers and a car company had a job waiting for him when he got out. I had no plans. I just wanted to catch up on all the living I had missed.

But usually we talked about how we could devise new ways of eluding observation when we wanted to swim or fish in the river. We had a number of escape routes across the fields, but access to them depended on our timing.

The guards came around every hour for the count, except during lunch-break. On weekends, we ate at 11:00 a.m., gulping our food in fifteen minutes. Our officers and the guards in the high towers of the main institution had lunch between 11:15 and 1:00 p.m., so that gave us nearly two hours to fish or swim. We watched our timing but occasionally something went wrong.

One morning, we were swimming nude about a quarter of a mile down river when a guard began the count. We couldn't go back across the fields because we would have been spotted. We noticed a big log by the river bank, put our clothes on it, crouched behind it and dog-paddled our way back up the river until we were opposite the annex. As we approached, an inmate who had been watching out for us was up on a fire escape, waving like mad to tell us the coast was clear and we could make it back across the fields.

There was a wide marshland along the river bank and we waded through this in mud up to our waists. Finally, caked in mud, we crawled up the bank and dashed to the annex.

In the shower we discussed our near-disaster. We weren't sure it had been worth the effort. Yet there was the wonderful excitement of it.

* * *

I suppose you might have called us naturalists but John and I loved the outdoors and we were always getting involved with the wildlife. Often, of course, it was by accident, as was the case with the rabbits. One of the fellows in the haying gang had accidentally run over and killed a mother rabbit and we decided to look after her three young.

We took them to a remote spot on the property and built a shelter and three or four times a day we fed them milk through an eye-dropper provided by one of the inmates. When they were old enough to eat by themselves, we brought them milk, sweet clover, carrots, lettuce and cabbage leaves. We took such care of those animals that we even exercised them during our lunch-hours.

Then one day we were on our tractors and we came across a young groundhog. We chased him to his hole and I got there ahead of him and rammed a stick down so that he couldn't get too far in. John, wearing work gloves, put his hand into the hole and pulled him out by his stubby tail. He was pretty vicious at first but after petting him for a time and talking gently to him, he calmed down and we took him back to the annex.

We decided to lodge him with the rabbits overnight but when we put him in, one of them hopped over to sniff him and he snapped at it. The rabbit didn't appreciate that – after all, it was his cage – and, since he was more than a foot long himself, he reared up on his hind legs and began to kick the groundhog. In a few moments, he was joined by the other rabbits and that poor little groundhog took quite a beating.

We realized we couldn't leave him there overnight, so we rescued him and put him into a makeshift cage we fashioned from a garbage can and some wire netting. The next morning we took wire from a chicken coop and built our friend a permanent home. We had this fellow for a long time and during the summer we caught several full-grown groundhogs. Catching them was a risky business because they could give a nasty bite, so we devised a trap that made it easier for us *and* the animal. It was simply a small wire cage with a spring-loaded door and we set it up at night.

The trap, set in the long grass, worked the very first night we tried it, but it was not until we were right on top of it the next morning that we realized we had captured a full-grown skunk.

John and I must have stood in one position without moving a muscle for half an hour, trying to decide what to do next. Finally we picked up a big piece of sheet metal that was nearby and, using it as a shield, advanced on the trap. We got the thing open all right but the skunk refused to leave.

John was a spunky kid who wasn't going to let it go at that. First he peered cautiously around the edge of the shield and, when the skunk ignored him, he stepped out from behind it altogether. Still nothing happened. I was pulling for John – but that was all. I had no intention of getting close to the cage, preferring to stay well behind the shield. Finally John got tired of staring at the animal and he turned around to leave. And that must have been what the skunk was waiting for because the moment John turned his back, that skunk got him square on the leg.

By this time, a small crowd had gathered at a safe distance, and when John was hit, we all cleared out in a hurry.

"Hey, wait for me," John bellowed but nobody wanted to be within thirty feet of him.

"You're on your own, pal," somebody called to him from a safe, odorless distance.

One of the fellows ran back to the annex and returned with fresh clothes and a can of tomato juice. John stripped off all his clothes, and while everyone from the annex who had come out to watch the fun laughed and applauded, he poured the juice all over his legs to kill the odor.

* * *

By late summer we had more animals and fish than we knew what to do with but nobody ever bothered them. This didn't surprise us because the inmate code, a sort of unwritten law, called for a show of respect for those who had spent a long time behind bars.

Our rabbits were our favorite friends and eventually we wound up looking after fifteen of them, all of them jacks and all of them in the husky fifteen to twenty-pound class. But by early September, there was a hint of frost in the air and we knew we would soon have to lose our friends. There was no way we could care for them in the winter.

"I think we're going to have to let them go," John said one day. "We could, you know, actually kill them with our kindness." He was right, of course. We would have to set them free so they could learn to forage for themselves before the winter.

Well, one day we said goodbye to our jacks and watched them scurry off to wherever it is that jack rabbits go in the last warm days of fall – and suddenly we were sadly alone.

John and I had both gone to prison at an early age and, perhaps because of that, we had a lot in common. Of course we would go off looking for rabbits and groundhogs. We were kids in search of our childhood.

CHAPTER XXIII

The word *parole* annoyed me. It implied that a generous group of people had agreed to release me before expiration of my sentence, on a promise that I would behave myself and report to a parole officer for the rest of my life. It was ironic that I would have to promise good behavior when, in fact, I had never been guilty of any *mis*behavior.

Only an innocent person who has gone to prison can know the incredible frustration of trying to convince people that he is innocent.

It was with the certain knowledge that I had no other choice that on September 9, 1968, I filed my second application for parole. It was worded simply – and this time, nothing was ambiguous.

"I still maintain my innocence," I wrote, "but realize that, under the law, the only way that I can obtain my release is through parole."

It was a small price to pay for freedom. Humbly, I added the following to my application:

"I feel that further incarceration would make my adjustment to society more difficult. I feel that I have a good future ahead of me."

In October, Dr. Scott asked if I had thought of furthering my education. He was quiet, interested and anxious to help, emphasizing that an inmate's academic standing was important when his case was before the National Parole Board.

My old antagonism for Dr. Scott was gone now. I no longer dwelt on the psychiatric sessions, thinking of him rather as the man who made possible my transfer to the farm. I was grateful for that.

I said I was interested in improving myself and a short time after he arranged for Professor Barry Thorne, of Queen's University, to visit me at the annex. We talked about extension courses and I settled for one on political science. My classes were an hour a week, to be held in the visitors' room at the annex. Thorne and another Queen's professor, David Cox, would be my teachers.

I wrote essays and we discussed them and the meetings often got spirited, especially with Cox. I defended the New Democratic Party against all comers. Why wouldn't I? It was NDP people who had come to my aid first, when I needed it. But then Cox would begin an analysis of my arguments and we would get hopelessly embroiled in semantics. The course was designed to determine how government *should* conduct its affairs, he emphasized, not necessarily how it *does*.

After dealing mostly with penal people, it was stimulating talking to a lively man like Cox.

"What have you read?" he asked one day.

"Enough to know we haven't got much to be proud of among our politicians."

"Negative."

"Well, look at Sir John A. MacDonald."

If my books were correct, he had accepted a sizeable gift from the Canadian Pacific Railway to convince the government to look kindly on a CPR plan for a transcontinental route.

"Hmmm," said Cox.

"Sir John resigned, which was sensible," I said.

"Well?"

"What I can't fathom is why the people of Canada voted him back in the next election."

We didn't always come up with answers but we probed things. And for me, half-way to a vegetable, this was good. It made me think.

We reviewed the Canadian Constitution, the British North America Act, the Canadian Bill of Rights. Cox talked about the freedom and dignity of man. *Safeguards.* He used that word and I cut him off. I remembered Clinton and Goderich.

"The Bill of Rights is a farce," I said.

In November, Dr. Scott arranged for me to visit Queen's and the classification officer, a kindly man named Mr. Paine, drove me there. It had always seemed strange going out of the institution but this time, walking among hundreds of students, it was downright unnerving.

Professor Thorne gave me a tour of the campus and afterward, for an hour, I sat in a classroom among a lot of young people, listening to a discussion of Indian affairs. No one knew who I was and no one spoke to me. They whispered messages among themselves and passed things to each other across me as though I weren't there. I suppose there was nothing unusual in their behavior since they didn't know me. I was an anonymous and wholly unremarkable figure who had simply turned up in class one day.

This, I reasoned, would be the way I would start life over again after my release. Some day, I would simply turn up somewhere – and start over. Quietly. Anonymously.

It was no surprise that the Parole Board assigned Mac Stienburg to my case. He did, after all, know me and my family better than anyone.

My parole situation was more complicated than some and consequently would require more investigation.

For one thing, they were dealing with a person who had been incarcerated since the age of fourteen. How does an individual such as this cope with a world he doesn't know? And with me, there was an added complication. My parents had separated, so where would I go?

"When you start life again on the outside," Mac said, "it must be under the best possible circumstances."

He was speaking for the Parole Board, which didn't want me set adrift in a hostile environment. But he was also speaking for himself. *He* wanted the best for me.

Mac saw me often and when he arrived smiling, I knew there was good news. One day he looked particularly pleased.

"The reports are favorable," he said. "I've seen them all."

"What about Dr. Scott's report?" I asked.

"Also favorable," he said.

"Son of a gun," I said. "How's that?"

I brushed the question aside. I had been thinking of George Scott and talking to myself. Dr. Scott – he had certainly come through for me in different ways during the last couple of years.

Mac was there on January 18, 1969, to wish me a happy twenty-fourth birthday and to tell me not to worry about the parole because his investigations were going well.

"I'd prefer you studied and did well in your examinations," he said.

In the spring my exam papers came and Mr. Paine let me write them in the quiet of the visitors' room – and I passed. Mac, of course, was pleased.

In April and May, I had several psychiatric interviews, the results of which I knew were going into my parole assessment file. But there was no word from the Parole Board and I could feel the tension mounting.

John was in the same situation. He had applied for parole a month earlier and hadn't received word. We were both pretty edgy, losing our tempers easily, often becoming unreasonably irritable. We recognized the symptoms, however, and never prodded one another.

On June 12, I got word that the board had reserved judgment in my case. That night, I took a long after-supper walk around the farm. Back in the dormitory, John sensed there was something wrong with me. He didn't have to ask about the parole.

We sat down in front of the television set and watched a commercial for the A & W Drive-in restaurants. Somebody was eating a hamburger and gulping down a Hires.

"I'd love one of those burgers right now and I'd tell them to pile on the onions," John said.

"We'll send over," I joked, remembering there was an A & W just across the road.

John and I were very quiet during the next few days. We worked the land until way past dark and the only time we spoke was when one of us came across a rabbit. We had a passion for those animals.

Then one day at lunch, Mac came to me with a plan. How, he wanted to know, would I like to spend my first few weeks of freedom in the Stienburg household? It was a unique plan. He had never heard of a parolee going into his parole officer's home.

I didn't answer right away. I was thinking of my own home. Well, my own home as I had once known it. I was thinking back ten years and that was a long time. Nothing was the same anymore.

"If you think you could stand the noise, I know the kids would like it," he said.

Trevor was three and Andy was five now and those were great ages for kids. I remembered when Barb and Bill had been that young and I had been their baby-sitter.

"I think," I said, "that I could stand the noise."

When the Solicitor-General announced in the House of Commons that the Cabinet would soon consider my parole, I knew the Parole Board had approved my application. I still didn't want to get my hopes up but Mac was as excited as an expectant father.

"I've had disappointments before," I said.

"Ninety-nine times out of 100, the Cabinet goes along with the board," he assured me.

Mac was so optimistic about my release that now he was discussing the procedure for leaving the institution. It would be without fanfare. Only certain key people in the institution would know my actual departure time. That way, we might avoid running into news reporters and photographers.

The keyword of my future was anonymity. If I was to make a successful start on my new life, I would have to pass through the gates of the institution – and vanish.

At the picnic table one Sunday, Mac and I went over a list of names and finally settled on one. When I left the penitentiary, it would be under an assumed name. Mac repeated it several times and it began to sound quite normal.

No one knew when the decision would be handed down, but Mac explained that if I happened to be in the fields at the time, an official car would be sent for me. I would then be returned to the main institution to sign the necessary papers and I would be released immediately. I liked the word *immediately.*

For several days after that, I watched the road from my tractor – but no official car showed up.

Then at noon on October 21, 1969, I got down from my tractor and went into the farm cafeteria for lunch and an officer advised me to report to the warden's office in the main institution at 1:00 p.m. A decision had obviously been reached by the Cabinet. But the question was – had they approved a parole? I doubted it.

At exactly 1:00 p.m., I reported to the office. Mac was standing there with Acting Deputy Warden C.H. Allen and a couple of other officers. They were smiling, but still I was pessimistic. Then Mac stepped out of the group and held some papers out to me. They were the parole documents. Nobody had to explain that to me.

"If you'd like to sign these, we'll be on our way," Mac said. He was wearing that tough-guy smile.

I signed two documents and a kind of numbness set in and I couldn't talk. I was taken to the discharge center and photographed in my prison garb with the number 6730 stamped all over.

To avoid contact with guards returning from lunch, or anyone else who might spread the word that my parole had come through, I was allowed to leave in my prison clothes. Mac had already stashed my civilian clothing in his garage so that I could change the moment we arrived at his house.

By the time I had been photographed, Mac had scouted the area outside. There was no one around. It was safe to go. He was a real mother-hen when he wanted to be.

Murray Peacock, a custody clerk, walked me to Mac's 1964 Volkswagen and wished me good luck as I got in. Mac accelerated immediately, running the gate as though he were a fleeing inmate.

As we drove alongside the farm, I looked across the fields. If John was out there on his tractor, he'd have to quit soon. It was beginning to snow.

BOOK III

In the Matter of
Steven Murray Truscott

CANADA

LAW REPORTS

Supreme Court of Canada

SUPREME COURT .... Cited as [1967] S.C.R.

PART V — 1967

IN THE MATTER OF A REFERENCE RE:

STEVEN MURRAY TRUSCOTT

Criminal law – Murder – Youth of 14½ years convicted of murder – Circumstantial evidence – Whether proper trial – Reference to Supreme Court of Canada – Supreme Court Act, R.S.C. 1952, c. 259, s. 55.

In 1959, the accused, a boy of 14½ years, was found guilty by a jury of the murder of a girl of 12 years and 9 months. Most of the evidence was circumstantial and the accused did not give evidence at his trial. The conviction was unanimously affirmed by the Court of Appeal. An application for leave to appeal to this Court was refused in February 1960.

Pursuant to s. 55 of the *Supreme Court Act,* R.S.C. 1952, c. 259, the governor general in council, in April 1966, referred to this Court for hearing and consideration the following question: "Had an appeal by Steven Murray Truscott been made to the Supreme Court of Canada, as is now permitted by Section 597A of the *Criminal Code* of Canada, what disposition would the Court have made of such an appeal on a consideration of the existing Record and such further evidence as the Court, in its discretion, may receive and consider?"

At this hearing, the Court received a large body of evidence, much of it relating to the medical aspects of the case and also heard the oral evidence of the accused who had not given evidence at the trial.

Held: Taschereau C.J. and Cartwright, Fauteux, Abbott, Martland, Judson, Ritchie and Spence JJ. would have dismissed such an appeal; Hall J. would have allowed the appeal, quashed the conviction and directed a new trial.

Joint opinion of the Chief Justice, Cartwright, Fauteux, Abbott, Martland, Judson, Ritchie and Spence JJ.: The verdict of the jury, read in the light of the charge of the trial judge, makes it clear that they were satisfied beyond a reasonable doubt that the facts, which they found to be established by the evidence which they accepted, were not only consistent with the guilt of the accused but were inconsistent with any rational conclusion other than that he was the guilty person. On a review of all the evidence given at the trial, the verdict could not be set aside on the ground that it was unreasonable or could not be supported by the evidence. The verdict was in accordance with the evidence. Furthermore, the judgment at trial could not have been set aside on the ground of any wrong decision on a question of law or on the ground that there was a miscarriage of justice. It follows that the judgment of the Court of Appeal dismissing the appeal made to it was right. The effect of the additional evidence which was heard by this Court, considered in its entirety, strengthens the view that the verdict of the jury ought not to be disturbed.

Per Hall J., *dissenting:* The trial was not conducted according to law. There were grave errors in the trial. Nothing that transpired on the hearing in this Court or any evidence tendered before this Court can be used to give validity to what was an invalid trial.

---

*PRESENT: Taschereau C.J. and Cartwright, Fauteux, Abbott, Martland, Judson, Ritchie, Hall and Spence JJ.

Reference by His Excellency the governor general in Council (P.C. 760, dated April 26, 1966) to the Supreme Court of Canada in exercise of the powers conferred by section 55 of the *Supreme Court Act,* R.S.C. 1952, c. 259, of the question stated above.

G.A.Martin, Q.C., E.B. Jolliffe, Q.C., and *R.J. Carter,* for Steven Murray Truscott.

W.C. Bowman, Q.C., and *D.H. Scott Q.C.,* for the Attorney General for Ontario.

D.H. Christie, Q.C., for the Attorney General for Canada.

Joint opinion of THE CHIEF JUSTICE, CARTWRIGHT, FAUTEUX, ABBOTT, MARTLAND, JUDSON, RITCHIE and SPENCE JJ.: – On September 16, 1959, Steven Murray Truscott, a boy of 14½ years, went on trial for the murder of Lynne Harper, a girl of 12 years and 9 months. The trial lasted until September 30, 1959, when the jury returned a verdict of guilty with a recommendation for mercy. An appeal to the Court of Appeal for Ontario against the conviction was dismissed on January 21, 1960. On the same date the sentence of death was commuted to a term of life imprisonment. An application for leave to appeal to this Court from the judgment of the Court of Appeal was refused on February 24, 1960. At that time this Court had jurisdiction to entertain an appeal only in two cases: (a) where there was dissent by a judge of the Court of Appeal on any question of law (there was no such dissent in this case), or (b) on any question of law with leave of this Court.

By Order-in-Council P.C. 1966/760, dated April 26, 1966, pursuant to s. 55 of the *Supreme Court Act,* His Excellency the Governor General referred to this Court for hearing and consideration the following question:

Had an Appeal by Steven Murray Truscott been made to the Supreme Court of Canada, as is now permitted by section 597A of the Criminal Code of Canada, what disposition would the Court have made of such an Appeal on a consideration of the existing Record and such further evidence as the Court, in its discretion, may receive and consider?

Section 597A of the *Criminal Code* of Canada was enacted by 1960–61, c. 44, s. 11, in the following terms:

597A Notwithstanding any other provision of this Act, a person

(*a*) who has been sentenced to death and whose conviction is affirmed by the court of appeal, or

(*b*) who is acquitted of an offence punishable by death and whose acquittal is set aside by the court of appeal,

may appeal to the Supreme Court of Canada on any ground of law or fact or mixed law and fact.

It came into force on July 13, 1961. On this Reference, therefore, we have power to review law or fact or mixed law and fact.

The Court also received a large body of evidence, much of it relating to the medical aspects of the case. It also heard the oral evidence of the accused. He had not given evidence at the trial.

The case against Steven Truscott was that he met Lynne Harper in the school grounds on the Clinton R.C.A.F. Station at about 7.10 on the evening of June 9, 1959; that he travelled north with her on the cross-bar of his bicycle on the county road; that he turned into Lawson's bush, which is about half way between the school grounds and Highway No. 8; and that he murdered the girl there. His defence was that the girl had asked him to take her to the intersection of Highway No. 8 and the county road; that he took her to this intersection and left her there, and when he was part way on his return journey, he saw a car stop at the intersection and pick her up, and that he never saw her again.

For an understanding of the evidence, it is necessary to describe the neighbourhood, a sketch plan of which is attached to these reasons. The R.C.A.F. Station is at the southerly end of a county road which goes north to King's Highway No. 8. This highway runs east and west. On leaving the Station, immediately on the right is the Robert Lawson farm property. Close to the road there are the usual buildings, including a barn. On the left is the O'Brien farm property. At the northerly limit of the Lawson property there are 20 odd acres of bush, mostly second growth ash, elm, maple and basswood. The wire fencing between the bush and the road is not in very good condition. There is an entrance to the bush along the northerly limit. It is referred to throughout the evidence as the "tractor trail". From the southerly end of the county road to the tractor trail is 3,366 feet. 1,568 feet farther north the Canadian National Railway crosses the road at right angles. Then, 491 feet farther north there is a bridge over the Bayfield River. This bridge is referred to frequently in the evidence. Then 1,300 feet farther north is the intersection of the county road with King's Highway No. 8. East from the bridge over the Bayfield River and visible from the bridge there is a swimming hole about 640 feet away.

We will first describe the movements of Lynne Harper in the late afternoon and early evening of June 9. She arrived home from school between 5.15 and 5.30 p.m. and she had finished her supper by 5.45 p.m. After supper she left the house for a short time to apply for a permit for the swimming pool for that evening. She could not get the permit because it was necessary for an infant to be accompanied by a grown-up person. Her parents were unable to go with her that evening. About 6.35 she went to the schoolhouse to assist a Mrs. Nickerson, who was conducting a meeting of Junior Girl Guides. Mrs. Nickerson confirms the time of her arrival. Mrs. Nickerson said that Truscott came along shortly before 7 p.m. and that Lynne Harper went over to speak to him and that after a few minutes they left together on foot in a northerly direction, Truscott pushing his bicycle. She puts the time 7.00 and 7.10 p.m.

An estimate of the time was also made by a Mrs. Bohonus, an officer of the Brownie Pack, who came to assist Mrs. Nickerson. Mrs. Bohonus said that shortly after she arrived, she looked at her watch and it was ten minutes to seven. According to her, not more than five or ten or, at most, fifteen minutes later, Steven Truscott appeared and talked to Lynne Harper. Mrs. Bohonus does not say how long they talked or at what time they left.

Three boys, Hatherall, Westey and McKay, were at the football field adjoining the school and the county road. They saw Truscott and Lynne Harper come from the school area to the county road. Lynne Harper got on the cross-bar of Truscott's bicycle and the two went north on the county road.

We will now deal with Steven Truscott's movements during the early evening of June 9th before he met Lynne Harper. We

216

begin with the evidence of Jocelyne Goddette. She, Lynne Harper and Steven Truscott were all in the same class, Grade VIII, at school. Jocelyne Goddette's story was that Steven Truscott had made an arrangement to meet her at Lawson's wood to show her a new calf. He told her to keep the arrangement quiet because Mr. Lawson did not like people trespassing on his property. She says that he called at her house about 5.50 p.m. and that she told him that she could not come out at the moment because of domestic duties and that she would meet him later if possible. Truscott denies that he made such an arrangement and the call at the house. Jocelyne Goddette's father said that there was a call such as his daughter described but that he did not know who the caller was.

Truscott arrived home for supper between 5.15 and 5.30 p.m. His mother sent him to the store at the end of the street to get some coffee. She fixes the time as close to six o'clock because there was need to hurry in order to get there before closing time. He obtained the coffee and returned home. After supper he went out. His mother had told him that he had to be back by 8.30 p.m. because she and her husband were going out and he was needed for baby sitting.

Paul Desjardine, a fourteen year old boy, rode north on his bicycle to go fishing at the bridge over the Bayfield River at about 6.10 p.m. He met Steven Truscott a short distance south of Lawson's bush. Steven was alone and was riding his bicycle around in a circle on the road. There was no conversation. Truscott denies that there was such a meeting.

Mrs. Beatrice Geiger left her house in the married quarters on the Base riding one of her sons' bicycles to go to the bridge. This was about ten minutes past six. On the way to the bridge Steven Truscott passed her in the bush area riding his bicycle. They were both going north. Steven went as far as the bridge, stopped a second or two, took a look around and headed south again. She met him the second time at about the railroad tracks. This would be around twenty-five minutes past six or half past six. Truscott said that he did not remember seeing Mrs. Geiger.

Kenneth Geiger, the twelve year old son of Mrs. Geiger, left

217

his home about a quarter or twenty minutes after six to go swimming. He walked to the school and met Robb Harrington and the two boys rode double on one bicycle down to the river. On the way down from the school area to the bridge he saw Steven Truscott. He was sitting on his bicycle in the middle of the road almost opposite the "tractor trail", which is on the northerly limit of Lawson's bush. He was facing towards the station. They passed Steven at about 6.25 or 6.27 p.m. Steven said to Kenneth Geiger that Mrs. Geiger was at the bridge and Kenneth Geiger said that he knew that. Robb Harrington estimates the time as being a quarter to seven. Truscott denies that he ever saw or spoke to Kenneth Geiger.

Ronald Demaray saw Steven on the bridge just before he went home. He believes that he got home between 6.30 and 7 p.m. and that it would take him ten minutes to get home from the bridge. As far as he could see, Steven was alone and just seemed to be looking around.

Richard Gellatly, a boy of twelve years, was at the river on the evening of June 9. He had to return home to get his swimming trunks. He met Steven riding Lynne Harper towards the bridge on the county road about one-quarter of the way from O'Brien's farm. Gellatly was riding south on his bicycle and Steven Truscott and Lynne Harper were riding north. He met them on the station side of Lawson's bush, that is, on the south side. He gives the time as 7:25 p.m. He says that he could be a few minutes out. He put on his trunks at home and returned to the river. It was about ten minutes after he passed Steven and Lynne that he went back to the river. He did not see Steven again. He was familiar with Steven's bicycle. He did not see the bicycle. He said that if it had been lying alongside the road by Lawson's bush or anywhere alongside the road, he would have seen it.

Mrs. Donna Dunkin drove to the river on the county road from the married quarters on the evening of June 9. She travelled from the married quarters at the station and pulled off the road just north of the railroad tracks. She saw Richard Gellatly riding his bicycle towards the station just as she pulled off the road to park. She also saw Philip Burns, who was walking behind Richard

Gellatly. At the time she saw them, they were between the railway tracks and the bridge over the river. Philip Burns would be no more than ten feet behind Richard Gellatly. She placed the time between 7:05 and 7:15 p.m.

Philip Burns, a boy of eleven years, who was unsworn, started to go south to the Air Force Station from the bridge on foot. He was behind Richard Gellatly. Gellatly started from the bridge on a bicycle. Burns left at approximately 7 o'clock. He fixes the time because he asked Mrs. Geiger what time it was. She did not have a watch. Sergeant McCafferty was close and he said it was around five to seven. Sergeant McCafferty gave evidence on the point and said that when Mrs. Geiger asked him for the time he looked at his watch and said either ten to seven or ten past seven, he could not remember which. Philip Burns says that he swam over to the south side of the river, put on his clothes and went up on the bridge where he waited around for five or ten minutes after being told the time, then he started for home.

Gellatly had left the swimming hole at about the same time. He went along the north bank of the river and Burns along the south bank of the river. Both were on their way home. They left the bridge at about the same time, Burns on foot and Gellatly on his bicycle. This was between 7 and 7:15 p.m.

Gellatly gave evidence that he met Truscott and Lynne Harper south of Lawson's bush at a point between the bush and O'Brien's farm. Burns says that he never did meet Truscott and Lynne Harper or either of them. While walking on his way home, he did meet Jocelyne Goddette and had some brief conversation with her. She was on her bicycle and she was near the south side of the bush closest to the station. She was going north towards the river. Further south along the road near O'Brien's farm and about two minutes later, he also met Arnold George, who was also going north and was behind Jocelyne Goddette.

When Burns met Jocelyne Goddette he had been walking for about ten minutes after leaving the bridge with Gellatly. Michael Burns, a brother of Philip Burns, says that Philip got home about 7:30 p.m.

Jocelyne Goddette, who was thirteen years of age at the time, says, in more detail than we have already outlined, that on Monday, June 8, she had a conversation at school with Steven Truscott. She said to him that on Sunday, the day before, she had gone to Lawson's barn and had seen a calf there. Steven asked her if she wanted to see two more new-born calves. She said "Yes" and he asked her if she could make it on Monday, and she said "No". He asked her if she could make it on Tuesday and she said she would try. Then on Tuesday, he repeated his invitation and she told him she did not know whether she could go and he invited her to meet him if she could go on the right-hand side of the county road just outside the fence by the woods. He repeated his warning not to tell anybody. The time for the appointment was six o'clock. She says that he called at the house at ten to six when she told him that she could not go but that she would try later. She had her supper and left the house about 20 minutes after 6 or 6:30, and went towards Lawson's barn to see if Steven was there. It would take but a few minutes to get to Lawson's barn. She stayed there for about five minutes. Steven was not at Lawson's and she went to see if he was at the meeting place. The meeting place was on the right-hand side of the county road just outside the fence by the woods. She met Philip Burns at the southerly limit of Lawson's bush and had a brief conversation with him. She bicycled north and got off her bicycle and walked slowly looking into the woods. She turned in the tractor trail and went three-quarters of the way in and then looked towards the railway bridge. She shouted Steven's name twice and then looked towards the woods and shouted it three or four times. She turned her bicycle around on the hard part of the ground and at that point she saw Arnold George going past. Arnold George also saw her on the tractor trail forty feet back. She did not see any sign of Steven on the tractor trail. When she saw Arnold George he was just going past the entrance to the tractor trail. She and George were both looking for Steven Truscott and they had a brief conversation. While they were talking Bryan Glover passed on his way to the bridge. He noticed them but did not stop. She came out of the tractor trail and went towards the river to the bridge. She did not see Steven at the river. She stayed there five or ten minutes and went back to Lawson's farm. She estimated that she got back to Lawson's a little before seven. She remained in the barn with Mr. Lawson for an hour and a half while he was doing his chores. The next morning at school she asked Steven why he had not been there and he just shrugged his shoulders.

Bryan Glover says that he arrived at the bridge a minute or two before George. He then looked for some friends on the west side of the river and about five minutes later returned to the bridge, saw his friends on the railway bridge over the river and went to join them. When George arrived at the bridge he says that he went over to the swimming hole, still looking for Truscott.

There is obviously something very wrong with Jocelyne Goddette's times. The jury would have to test her estimate of time along with the evidence of the time when Philip Burns and Arnold George were on the road and spoke to her and Bryan Glover who passed and noticed her, and also the evidence of Mr. Lawson. Lawson says that she first arrived at his barn at approximately 7:15. She left at 7:25. He fixes this time because she asked him the time before she left. She returned in twenty minutes to half an hour later.

Teunis Vandenpool, a boy of 15 years of age, lived on a farm on Highway No. 8 about a mile and a quarter east of the county road. On June 9 after supper he went swimming. He left his home at five or ten minutes after seven. He went west on Highway No. 8 and then down the county road. He was travelling by bicycle and was at the junction of Highway No. 8 and the county road about 7:15 or 7:20 o'clock. He didn't see any persons at or near the corner. He didn't see a car stopped. After he reached the corner he went down towards the bridge.

Between the bridge and the railroad is a field and he went down the path leading towards the river. This would be west of the bridge. He had his bathing suit on and he took off his clothes and went in the water. He remained in the water for ten or fifteen minutes and went home. He estimates that he made the return trip to the intersection of the county road between 7:30 and 7:35 o'clock. He arrived home at a quarter to eight. He noticed that when he started to do his homework, which was immediately after he got home. He didn't know Lynne Harper or Steven Truscott. He did not see a girl on a bicycle on the county road or a boy in red jeans. Truscott was wearing red jeans that evening. There were bicycles parked on the bridge but no persons on the bridge.

Steven Truscott was back at the schoolyard at 8 p.m. or shortly after that hour. He was back at home by between 8:25 and 8:30 p.m. according to the evidence of Mrs. Truscott, and he was seen at his home by his friend Arnold George about 8:45 p.m. We deal later with the conversation between these two at that time.

Truscott admitted that he had met Gellatly. He made this admission to F/Sgt. Johnson and Sgt. Anderson of the Ontario Provincial Police on Wednesday, June 10, and to Sgt. Wheelhouse of the R.C.A.F. and Constable Hobbs of the O.P.P. on Thursday morning. June 11. F/Sgt. Johnson said that Truscott's definition of the place of meeting was "just about the brow of the hill," which is a short distance south of the tractor trail; Sergeant Anderson that it was "halfway between the intersection at the school, the public school and the bush", which is about where Gellatly said it was; Sergeant Wheelhouse that is was "about halfway between where I had picked up Lynne and the crest of the hill", which is much the same as the admission to Sergeant Anderson.

The case went to the jury with five witnesses saying that they did not see Truscott and Lynne on the road. Two of these were actively looking for him.

The Crown's submission was that after he passed Gellatly he turned into the bush with Lynne and that this accounted for the failure of the other witnesses to see him on the road with Lynne. On the other hand, three witnesses who were called by the defence, Douglas Oats, Gordon Logan and Allan Oats, say that they did see Truscott on the road. The first two, Douglas Oats and Gordon Logan, say that they saw him cross the bridge with Lynne on his way to the highway. Allan Oats says that he saw Steven on the bridge alone some time between 7:30 and 8 p.m.

Douglas Oats, aged 11 years, said that he was on the bridge over the Bayfield River on the evening of June 9 looking for turtles. Steven Truscott and Lynne Harper came by him on the bridge. He turned around and put up his hand and said "Hi". Lynne was seated on the cross-bar of the bicycle. They were going north towards No. 8 highway. He did not see Lynne again and did not see Steven again that night. He stayed on the bridge until about 7:30 and got home about a quarter to eight. The only time that he saw Steven that night, Lynne was with him.

Gordon Logan, aged 13, first heard that Lynne Harper was missing on the morning of June 10 just before school started. The previous evening he had been down at the Bayfield River fishing and swimming. He saw Steven and Lynne go by on the bridge on Steven's bicycle. Lynne was sitting on the cross-bar on the bicycle. He made this observation when he was down at the swimming hole. He was out of the water. The two were near the north side of the bridge when he last saw them travelling towards Highway No. 8. He was standing just by the bend in the river on a big rock. This rock is 642 feet from the bridge at water level. He saw Steven about five minutes later when Steven rode back to the bridge, stopped and got off his bicycle. He does not know what Steven did from then on.

The presence of Gordon Logan at the swimming hole at 7:30 p.m. was confirmed by Beatrice Geiger, who was at the swimming hole at that time. She also said that there were people on the bridge. She could not tell whether they were men or women or children, or boys or girls. She did not pay too much attention. She thought that from where she was, had she been looking for someone she knew, she could have recognized him.

Allan Oats, 16 years of age, says that he went for a ride on his bicycle towards the river. He turned back when he was about 800 feet from the bridge. He saw Steven standing on the bridge wearing red pants and a light coloured shirt. He places the time between 7:30 and 8 o'clock.

The prosecution suggested that Douglas Oats was mistaken; that on his own admission he only saw Truscott once that evening and that the time must have been 6:30 p.m., when Douglas Oats was looking for turtles at the bridge and Truscott was alone at the bridge. This was based on the evidence of Mrs. Geiger and

Demaray.

Gordon Logan's evidence was questioned on the ground of credibility and ability to make the observation that he claimed to have made.

The credibility of Allan Oats was also attacked. He had evidence highly favourable to Truscott on Tuesday, June 9. He said that he mentioned it to nobody except his mother and no one else knew about it until Tuesday, June 16, when he was approached by Mrs. Durnin at the request of Truscott's father.

This conflict between evidence pointing to a disappearance into Lawson's bush and evidence asserting that Steven Truscott had crossed the bridge with Lynne Harper on his way to the highway and had returned alone, was the critical issue in this case and it was entirely a jury problem. The Judge's instruction to the jury on the issue was emphatic and clear:

> Now then, it is the theory of the Defence, and they brought evidence to show that, as I say this little Douglas Oats saw them going across the bridge and then, in a few minutes, according to the boy by the name of Gordon Logan – Gordan Logan also says he saw them going north on the bridge and in about five minutes he says he saw Steven return alone. Well, as regards Gordon Logan, it will be for you Gentlemen to say whether you believe his evidence, and it is very important, Gentlemen, because if you believe the Defence theory of this matter and believe Steven's statement to the police and to other people, that the girl was driven to Number Eight Highway and entered an automobile which went east; it is my view that you must acquit the boy if you believe that story.
>
> In other words, I will put it this way. In order to convict this boy, you have to completely reject that story as having no truth in it, as not being true. You have to completely reject that story.

Arnold George says that on the evening of Lynne Harper's disappearance he went to Truscott's house about 8:45 p.m. He gives the following account of their conversation:

> Q. What was said?
> A. Well, I asked him where he had been that night and he said: "Down at the river". I said: "I heard that you had given Lynne a ride down to the river," and he said: "Yes, she wanted a lift down to Number Eight Highway." and I said: "I heard you were in the bush with her." And he said: "No, we were on the side of the bush looking for a cow and calf." And he said: "Why do you want to know for?" and I said: "Skip it and let's play ball."

At the preliminary hearing he had not said anything about Steven saying that he was on the side of the bush looking for a cow and calf.

Truscott in his oral evidence denied that there was ever any such visit from Arnold George or any such conversation.

Next, on the evening of Wednesday, June 10, Arnold George says that he had another conversation with Steven:

> Q. And what was said on that occasion?
> A. Well he said that he – like the Police had questioned him and that he had told them he had seen me down there, and it wasn't me, it was Gordie Logan; and he thought that Gordie was me and he said that I had seen him, so he told the Police that. And down there at his house he told that to me and he said that Police were going to go down to my place to check up, so I agreed that I would tell them what was just said.

George did support Truscott's story in his statements to the police but after the discovery of the body the following day, Thursday, July 11, he retracted them. His evidence at the trial we have already outlined. It was that he had been looking for Steven and had not seen him.

Truscott, on the reference, denied that this conversation ever took place either on the evening of Wednesday, June 10, or at any time.

On Wednesday evening, June 10, there was talk about the disappearance among five boys who were together at the bridge. These were Paul Desjardine, Arnold George, Thomas Gillette, Bryan Glover and Steven Truscott. Paul Desjardine was telling Truscott that he had heard that he had taken Lynne into the bush. The account of the conversation varies from boy to boy but there is no doubt, according to these witnesses, that a suspicion was being voiced and that Truscott was appealing to Arnold George in support of his denial and that George was supporting him to the extent of saying that Steven was at the side of the bush looking for the cow and the calf.

Truscott did not give oral evidence at the trial. His defence that he had taken Lynne Harper to the intersection where she had been picked up by a strange car was before the jury in the form of exculpatory statements given to the police. On the reference he did give oral evidence in more detail. He described his movements from the time he left school until he went home to supper. Before supper and just before the store closed, he went to get the coffee for his mother. He left home about 6:30 p.m. and went first to the school grounds. He found no one there and rode

225

down to the railroad tracks on his bicycle. He could see no one at the river so he turned around a couple of times and went back to the station. He said that he met no one on the way down or back. He stopped at the end of the school and was watching the Brown-ies. Lynne Harper came over and asked him for a lift down to No. 8 Highway. After a few minutes they walked to the county road and then got on the bicycle. He says that they left at 7:30 p.m. He fixed the time by the school clock. On the way down to No. 8 Highway he passed Douglas Oats on the bridge. He let Lynne Harper off at the highway and rode back to the bridge. When he arrived at the bridge, he looked back and saw "there was a car pulled in off the highway and she got in the front seat." He said the car was facing northeast. He described the car as a 1959 grey Chevrolet with what appeared to be a yellow coloured licence plate. He next said that he stayed at the bridge for five or ten minutes and from there saw Arnold George and Gordon Logan at the swimming hole. He then went back to the school, arriving there about 8 p.m.

On Truscott's return to the school grounds there is evidence that there was some curiosity among a group of children about what had happened to Lynne Harper. Several children had seen him leave with her. He came back alone. When asked whether they made any comment to him or whether there was any conver-sation with them, he replied in the following words:

> I believe one of them asked me – they said "What did you do with Harper, feed her to the fish?" and I replied that I had taken her and let her off at High-way No. 8.

When Truscott returned to the schoolyard at approximately 8 p.m., no one noticed anything unusual about his demeanour, con-duct or the condition of his clothing. Most of his conversation appears to have been with his older brother Kenneth. This con-versation was testified to by three witnesses who were standing fairly close. These witnesses were John Carew, Lorraine Wood and Lyn Johnston. It had to do with an exchange of bicycles and an exchange of shoes. Kenneth Truscott had with him a smaller bicycle belonging to a younger brother. Steven Truscott was going home and he left his own bicycle and took the smaller one with him. There was also some conversation between the two about shoes. Steven Truscott was wearing crepe-soled canvas shoes belonging to Kenneth. Kenneth was wearing a pair of Steven's high boots. No exchange was actually made.

The crepe-soled canvas shoes did not enter into the trial because of a ruling of the trial judge that the prosecution had no right to call more expert evidence. But on the reference a photograph was introduced of the impression of a shoe near the girl's body. The marks of the rubber in a foot impression near the body of Lynne Harper corresponded with the marks of the shoe worn by Truscott to this extent: The shoes were of similar manufacture, the marks resembled each other, but the most that the evidence proves is that someone wearing shoes similar to those worn by Truscott on the night of the disappearance made a foot impression close to the body of Lynne Harper. There was no further identification. The evidence does not prove that the impression was made by the very shoes worn by Steven Truscott.

Truscott was unable to state the exact time of his arrival at home but his father and mother were still there. He says that he spent the rest of the evening at home and that the first occasion on which he knew that anything unusual had happened to Lynne Harper was when her father came to the house the following morning, which would be June 10, before he had left for school. The following is his account on the brief conversation at the house:

Q. What happened when he came?
A. He asked me if I had seen Lynne.
Q. Did he ask you or did he ask your mother?
A. I believe he asked my mother and my mother called me over and I informed him that I had given her a ride to the highway.
Q. Anything else?
A. I don't remember anything else.
Q. Do you remember when the first time you mentioned, if you did mention it, a grey 1959 Chevrolet car to anybody?
A. I don't remember who the first one was that I mentioned it to.
Q. Do you remember when you mentioned it, even if you do not remember who you mentioned it to?
A. I believe it was the police.

Mr. Harper's account of the conversation is that Truscott did say on this occasion that Lynne "had hitched a ride on No. 8 Highway." There is nothing in the record to indicate that Truscott had mentioned the car to anyone on his return to the school-yard.

We have already said in dealing with the evidence of Arnold George that George said that he visited Truscott soon after Truscott's return to the house to enquire about Lynne Harper. He also gave evidence of another conversation the following evening when he said that he was asked to say that he had seen Truscott at the bridge. We have also mentioned Truscott's denial of both these conversations.

Truscott gave his own version of the conversation among the five boys at the bridge on Wednesday evening, June 10. It differs from the account given by the boys at the trial. Their evidence is summarized above. This is Truscott's account:

Q. Was there any conversation about Miss Harper?
A. One of the fellows mentioned something about it, yes.

Q. Do you remember what it was he said?
A. He said, "I heard you had Lynne in the bush".

Q. What did you say?
A. I asked him who had told him this and he said Arnold George did. I went over and asked Arnold George and he said he had never told anybody that.

Q. Were you in the bush with her?
A. No, sir.

Q. How was this said when it was said, that he heard you had her in the bush?
A. More or less kidding with each other.

Q. Did you make any statement that you were not in the bush, you had just been at the edge of the bush looking for calves, or anything of that nature?
A. No, sir.

Q. Had you been anywhere near the bush looking for calves with Miss Harper?
A. No, I wasn't.

Q. Do you remember any discussion about that time about calves in the bush?

A. No, sir.

Truscott denied any conversation with Jocelyne Goddette concerning the making of an appointment to go looking for newborn calves. He denied that he called at Jocelyne Goddette's house about 5:50 p.m. to confirm the appointment. He denied that on the trip down to the river between 6 and 7 p.m. he met Ken Geiger and Robb Harrington. He denied any conversation with Geiger about his mother being at the river. He denied that he had seen Mrs. Geiger or Paul Desjardine during the course of that trip and said that he did not remember any of them giving evidence at his trial. He denied having seen either Robb Harrington, who was with Geiger, or Ronald Demaray, who says that he was at the bridge while Truscott was there. These were all people who gave evidence that they met him and described his movements on the road between 6:30 and 7:00 p.m.

He denied that he had met Gellatly on the highway and said that he did not remember telling the police that he had met Gellatly. At the trial Gellatly's evidence had not been challenged on cross-examination.

He denied that Arnold George came to his house at 8:30 p.m. on June 9 and that he had any conversation with George at any time during that evening. This was the occasion when George said that he had heard that Truscott was in the bush with Lynne and when Truscott had replied that he was on the side of the bush looking for a cow and a calf.

He denied that he had any conversation with George the following evening, Wednesday, June 10. This is the occasion when George said that he had agreed with Truscott to tell the police that he, George, had seen Truscott at the bridge on Tuesday evening.

Truscott told the police that when Lynne entered the car at the highway intersection, it was facing northeast and that he could see the colour of the licence plate when he was standing on the bridge looking towards Highway No. 8. The police questioned this. Constable Tremblay, Ontario Provincial Police, stood on the bridge on Wednesday, June 10, with Truscott and his mother. From the bridge Tremblay noted that he could not see any licence plates on cars proceeding along Highway No. 8 and also, that when a car with black and white plates travelled north on the county road and reached the highway, he could no longer see the licence plates. The bridge is 1,300 feet from the highway intersection. A photograph was introduced which seemed to support the police evidence.

On the reference this photograph was described as being highly distorted and not representing what could be seen by the human eye standing where Truscott said he was standing. Also on the reference, evidence was given by a team of private investigators who had various colours of licence plates that identification of colour could be made from the bridge. The Crown did not introduce evidence to contradict this.

In the final argument, Crown counsel said he accepted the evidence such as it was. His criticism of the evidence was that on the admission of the witness who drove the car, it could only be placed in the position where it was photographed by driving east across the intersection, stopping and backing up to place the car in a northeasterly position where it would catch the late afternoon sun, and that no car travelling from west to east would get into that position in the way Truscott described to pick up a hitch-hiker standing on the southeast corner of the intersection. The evidence given on the reference proves no more than this, that if a car is placed in this position at a certain time with the sun shining on the licence plate, an investigator standing at the bridge and knowing what he was looking for could identify colours, but not entirely without error.

The evidence at the reference upon this topic would seem to weaken the Crown's submission to the jury as based on the evidence adduced at the trial that Truscott could not have seen from the bridge what he alleged he had seen, i.e., that Lynne Harper entered a 1959 grey Bel-Air Chevrolet with a yellow licence plate, as it would seem that if that car had been in the one position in which the vehicle used by the witness LaBrash to carry out his test had been placed, Truscott could have made such observation. The purpose of that evidence at trial, however, was to attack the credibility of Truscott on this important part of his defence. Since the evidence was given at trial, Truscott has testified on the reference. We refer herein to the parts of his testimony which simply cannot be believed. In such circumstances, the evidence given at the reference in relation to the possibility of making the observation of an automobile so placed becomes of much less importance.

The body of Lynne Harper was found on Thursday, June 11, 1959, at 1:45 p.m. in Lawson's bush some distance in from the tractor trail. The evidence strongly pointed to this as the place where she was raped and murdered. We have already quoted from the instruction of the trial judge to the effect that the jury could not convict unless the jury entirely rejected the evidence of Douglas Oats and Gordon Logan that they saw Truscott on the bridge with Lynne Harper on their way to the highway intersection. All the evidence, including the medical evidence, has to be related to this critical issue.

An outline of the problem facing the jury at the trial seems to be this. First of all, they had the time of departure from the school grounds fixed with reasonable certainty by the evidence of Mrs. Nickerson and Mrs. Bohonus at not later than 7:15 p.m. Then, on his own admission, Truscott met Richard Gellatly between the school yard and Lawson's bush. He did not meet Philip Burns as he should have done if he had continued on his way to the highway. He was not seen by Jocelyne Goddette and Arnold George as he would have been if he had continued on to the highway and had returned alone from the intersection to the bridge. The jury's conclusion must have been that after passing Richard Gellatly and before Philip Burns, Jocelyne Goddette and Arnold George had an opportunity to see him, he had disappeared with the girl into Lawson's bush.

Before they could come to this conclusion the jury had to reject the evidence of Douglas Oats and Gordon Logan and they must have done so with the emphatic warning of the trial judge in their minds. On Truscott's story, the girl was proposing to go to a place where there were a few ponies. This was about 500 yards east of the intersection. Yet according to him she was still at the intersection when Truscott had returned to the bridge 1,300 feet to the south, from which point he says that he saw her getting into a car, although she was only proposing to go 500 yards. If this were true, then whoever picked her up or some other person would have had to bring her back to Lawson's bush, either dead or alive, unnoticed by anyone. If dead, he would have had to place her body in the bush and create the appearance that she had been murdered at that spot.

We do not think that there is any doubt about the place of death. The position of the body, the scuff marks and a footprint at the foot, and the flattening of the vegetation between the legs, indicated that the act of rape took place there. There were a number of puncture wounds on her back and shoulders, some of which were caused before and some after death. Under the wound in her left shoulder, which she suffered before death, was a pool of fluid blood lying on the vegetation. The wounds were consistent with their having been made by twigs scattered around the ground. A small quantity of blood was found on the dandelion leaves at the fork of the body. Under her left shoulder was a button from her blouse. According to the evidence of Elgin Brown, this button would be ripped from her blouse when it was torn to form the ligature with which she was strangled. Her clothing was in the area where the body lay.

There was evidence on the reference but not at the trial given in support of a theory that the girl had been killed elsewhere and her body subsequently brought back to the woods where it was found. This evidence was based on an observation from photographs of the body of what appeared to the witness to be a condition of blanching. This will be dealt with later.

We will do no more at this point with the medical evidence than attempt to summarize what was before the jury and what the issues were. The first witness was Dr. J. Ll. Penistan, who held an appointment as pathologist in the Attorney General's Department and was pathologist in charge of the laboratories at the Stratford General Hospital. He arrived at Lawson's bush at 4:45 p.m. on June 11. He described the position of the body on the ground and the state of the body and the clothing. The girl's blouse had been torn up one side and was tied tightly around the neck and secured by a knot under the jaw on the left side. There was a pool of blood under the left shoulder, enough to enable him to take a sample amounting to a dessert or tablespoonful. He described the condition of the ground below the fork of the body and took samples of dandelion leaves.

The body was removed to Clinton where he conducted an autopsy the same evening. He certified the cause of death as strangulation by a ligature. He removed from the stomach about one pint of a meal of mixed meat and vegetables. Very little of the meal had passed from the duodenum into the small intestine. His conclusion on the time of death is contained in the following extract from his report:

> *Note on time of death:* This opinion, which would place the time of death between 7.15 and 7.45 p.m. on 9th June, 1959, is based on the following observations and assumptions: –
>
> 1. The extent of decomposition, which is entirely compatible with death approximately 45 hours prior to identification, having regard to the environmental and climatic conditions.
> 2. The extent of rigor mortis. This had almost passed off, a finding again compatible with death at the suggested time.
> 3. The limited degree of digestion, and the large quantity of food in the stomach. I find it difficult to believe that this food could have been in the stomach for as long as two hours unless some complicating factor was present, of which I have no information. If the last meal was finished at 5.45 p.m., I would therefore conclude that death occurred prior to 7.45 p.m. The finding would be comparable (sic) with death as early as 7.15 p.m.

The other medical evidence given by the prosecution related to the condition of Truscott's penis. On the evening of Friday, June 12, 1959, in the presence of his father, Truscott was examined by Dr. Addison, the family physician, and Dr. Brooks, Senior Air Force Medical Officer. They found what they described as two lesions, one on each of the lateral sides of the shaft of the penis, about the size of a twenty-five cent piece, oozing serum. These lesions were immediately behind the glans. The penis appeared swollen and slightly reddened at the distal end.

Dr. Addison said it looked like a brush burn of two or three days' duration. He was of the opinion that there was nothing inconsistent with the injuries having been caused by entry into a young small virgin. The injuries could have been caused by a boy of Truscott's size and age trying to make entry into an underdeveloped 12 year old girl.

From his examination of the penial injuries, Dr. Brooks was of the opinion that they had been incurred between 60 and 80 hours previously. In fixing the time he allowed for the fact that the injuries would not be exposed to the air.

The medical evidence for the defence was given by Dr. Berkely Brown. He is a specialist in internal medicine and a member of the staff of the Department of Medicine, University of Western Ontario Medical School. His opinion was that normal emptying time of the stomach after a mixed meal would be three and one-half to four hours.

As to the condition of the penis, he thought that it was highly unlikely that penetration would produce the lesions described. His opinion was that it is rare that the penis is injured during rape and that if it is, the injury is usually to the frenum.

We do not wish to give any impression from this brief summary that the medical evidence at trial was in any way perfunctory. It was, in our opinion, careful and detailed, and it was tested by careful and detailed cross-examination. Our purpose at the present time is to show that the medical issues before the jury were well defined. These issues were the time of death and the condition of Truscott's penis as implicating him in the commission of the crime. On the reference many more witnesses were called. Some supported Dr. Penistan's opinion on the time of death, some Dr. Brown's. Some said that the condition of Truscott's penis was consistent with rape. Others supported an innocent explanation, including Truscott himself. This evidence will have to be analysed in detail. The prosecution submits that the whole of the evidence, including the medical evidence given at trial, after being weighed by the jury leads inevitably to the conclusion of guilt and that there was no room for any other rational conclusion. The Crown's further submission is that there were no new issues raised on the reference in connection with the time of death and that there was simply more evidence relating to it and that the weight of this evidence supports Dr. Penistan's opinion that death occurred within two hours of the last known meal, that is, before 7:45 p.m.

We next set out the following more detailed summaries of the medical evidence:

(a) Medical evidence at the trial as to the time of death.

(b) Medical evidence at the trial and on the reference relating to the condition of Truscott's penis.

(c) Medical evidence on the reference taken witness by witness.

(a) *Medical evidence at the trial as to the time of death*

From the opening of the trial the attention of the jury was sharply focussed on the importance of the medical evidence as to the time of death.

In opening the case to the jury Crown Counsel referred twice to the medical evidence as to the time of death as follows:

On this day, Tuesday, June 9th, you will hear witnesses tell of Lynne's movements after she left school, playing football as some member of the school team. Some playing field on or near the locale of this, being driven home by her teacher, having her supper with her mother and father, and being seen walking away from her home after the completion of supper. I am avoiding, quite deliberately, giving you times in there of when she arrived home. When she had her supper. When she finished her last meal. When she left the house. I will simply say it was about the supper hour. These times are important, Gentlemen, and I want you to note them as you hear from her parents. They won't follow one another probably. The mother first and perhaps a little later the father, but I would ask you to note, when they are in the box, what she had to eat. Also when she finished her meal, and I will tell you why. You will later hear from a Provincial Pathologist who did a post-mortem on her body, and he will give you an opinion on the time of her death, based on his observation of her stomach and its contents. His opinion will be based, probably the time of death, to the time of finishing the last meal, so I will prefer you to hear that, because it is of such importance, from the lips of the witnesses, themselves.

* * *

The body was later removed – when I say later, that same afternoon, that later afternoon, to Clinton, where Doctor Penistan, who arrived on the scene at the bush did a post-mortem. He will testify as to the cause of death and also the probable time of death.

As witnesses were called for the defence, Counsel for the Defence was required to address the jury first. His address commenced at 10.00 a.m. on Tuesday, September 29th, 1959, and concluded at 4.40 p.m. the same day. There was an adjournment for lunch from 12.45 p.m. to 2.15 p.m. and during the afternoon there was a short recess.

All that Counsel for the Defence said as to the time of death as shown by the medical evidence was as follows:

Now then, there is the question of the time of death. The opinion of an expert is only as good as the facts on which it is based, the opinion is based. If the opinion of an expert is based on facts that are incorrect, then that opinion should carry no weight. When Doctor Penistan said to you Gentlemen: "I place the time of death between seven and seven-forty-five, and I place it at that time because a stomach with a normal meal should empty in from one to two hours, but this meal was poorly masticated and that would increase the time which would be taken to digest this food and I allowed an extra hour because of the poorly masticated meal, and allowing that hour I have placed the time of death at seven to seven-forty-five, because I concluded this food had not been in that stomach more than two hours". And you heard about his examination. The stomach was emptied into this quart sealer, and then he and Doctor Brooks took the sealer and turned it around like this, and looked at it. And they say they saw this and they saw that. Now, what in the world kind of examination is that on the contents of the stomach to base a time of death? To give evidence on a serious charge such as this?

Here was a Government Pathologist making his examination by looking at the contents in a bottle with the light against him and the light behind him. There was no chemical examination of the contents of that stomach. There is no evidence of any chemical examination of the contents of that stomach. Doctor Penistan was asked if there was any examination to determine the hydrochloric acid content of the stomach, which is a good gauge as to the time to which digestion had progressed. No such test was made.

Now, you heard the evidence of Doctor Brown. He graduated in 1940. He spent a year in pathology and five years in the Army, doing post-graduate work for two years at London, Ontario. He took two more years in London England. He received a degree of Member of the Royal College of Physicians. He is on the staff of the Medical school of Western University. He specializes in diseases of the stomach. He is a consultant to the Ontario Cancer Association. Consultant to the Department of Veterans' Affairs and consultant to the Ontario Hospital, but not on mental problems, but the internal physical problems. Now, there is a man of very considerable standing and must be a man who knows his specialty or he wouldn't have attained such prominence, and his specialty is the stomach. And what did he tell you? He said that the stomach normally empties in between three and a half and four and a half hours, not one to two hours, as Doctor Penistan said.

Now I suggest to you that a man who specializes in the problems of the stomach is in a very much superior position to help you as to the emptying time of the stomach, rather than a pathologist who does not specialize in the stomach or its problems, and I ask you to accept the evidence of Doctor Brown when he said that the normal emptying time of the stomach was three and a half to four hours. And he said further, because of this poorly masticated food, it would require a further hour and it would take four and a half to five and a half hours for the stomach of this girl to empty.

Now, Doctor Penistan based his estimate that this food had not been in this stomach more than two hours, on the assumption that the stomach normally empties between one and two hours. I suggest to you that if the stomach emptied in one to two hours, that people would be extremely hungry before the next meal, four or five hours later. I suggest to you that it is only proper that you accept the expert opinion of Doctor Brown. If his opinion is accepted, then you must reject the estimate of the time of death by Doctor Penistan, because it is not based on proper facts. The time of death may be very important. You heard Doctor Brown also say that it was the effort to determine the time of death by the progress which had been made in the digestion of the meal of the stomach was quite unreliable and an unsatisfactory way of determining the time of death. You heard him say that a complete examination of the small bowel would be helpful in determining how much food had passed from the stomach. You heard Doctor Penistan state that the stomach was distended with one pint of food. Now, we have no information as to how much food was consumed. I asked Mrs. Harper how much meat was served to the girl and she didn't know. Her husband had served it. So none of the witnesses gave you any information as to how much food had been consumed. Surely it would take considerably longer to digest a big meal than a small meal. You heard Doctor Brown say that if a pint of food is consumed, that the stomach will produce a pint of digestive juices and you then have two pints in the stomach, and according to him the stomach wouldn't be fully distended – the stomach of this girl wouldn't be fully distended unless it contained three or four pints.

And then, again, Doctor Penistan may be in error in his estimate of the contents of the stomach. You saw the jar. About a half a pint. A quart sealer, about a quarter of the sealer is filled with the contents. Now, it may be said that some part of that was used up in tests, but we know of no tests. The doctor certainly didn't use any up. I suggest to you it would be dangerous to assume that the doctor removed more that that quantity of food from the stomach. And I do, with all sincerity, suggest to you twelve men, on whose shoulders rests the question of the guilt or non-guilt of this accused, that it would be highly dangerous, in view of the evidence of Doctor Brown, to accept the evidence of Doctor Penistan on that point.

Counsel for the Crown dealt with this question of the time of death as follows:

On Tuesday, June 9th, Lynne Harper, age twelve, played ball after school, was driven home by her teacher, Miss Blair, and then had her supper of turkey, peas, etc., finishing at a quarter to six. You have the evidence of both her parents on that. When her body was found in the bush, Thursday, June 11th, Doctor John Penistan, a Provincial Pathologist with a highly specialized education and training, and years of experience in determining causes of death and time of death, and all the particulars can only be arrived at by a doctor trained in a specialist field.

He arrived soon after the body was found and attended at the scene where it was found in Lawson's bush. He made a study of the position of the body, the surroundings, calculated the climatic conditions that applied. The marks, the terrain, made some observations on what he noticed about the flattening of vegetation between the legs. Marks, I said. This blouse about the neck. He was at a great advantage to find it there and see the body at the scene. And then he had the body removed to a Funeral Home in Clinton and performed a full post-mortem examination there. From careful study he gave the opinion that death had taken place where the body was found, in Lawson's woods. I do not believe he was cross-examined on that. That was his stated, clear opinion, that death had taken place in Lawson's woods. He gave the cause of death as strangulation by the blouse knotted around the neck. And, Gentlemen, you will have among the Exhibits you take out to the Jury room, a picture, Exhibit forty-two, that will show you how that blouse was about the neck. That picture was taken at the funeral home.

Now, Doctor Penistan, after all these observations, gave the time of death, which is important. He gave the time of death as from seven p.m. to 7:45 p.m. on the date of Tuesday, June 9th. That is an hour and fifteen minutes, two hours after the last meal, and no one has raised, I suggest, a suggestion or doubt, serious doubt but what she finished her last meal – consumed her last food at a quarter to six, as described by her parents.

Now, on what did he base his observation? On what did he base his opinion? First he had the stomach, which he described as distended with about a pint of contents. These were put in a jar. The jar was taken to Toronto, to Mr. Brown. The evidence of Mr. Brown was he turned the jar and contents over to Mr. Funk of the laboratory. You heard my explanation, that I had run out of expert witnesses. I did not call Mr. Funk, but I made him available to the defence. You haven't heard from Mr. Funk. I only leave to you, Gentlemen, from the evidence of Doctor Penistan, what went into the jar, the amount that went into the jar, to draw your reasonable inference.

Now, he observed the limited degree of of digestion or change in these contents. The absence or near absence of anything in the intestine, the small intestine leading from the stomach. He observed the extent of decomposition, and he observed the extent of rigor mortis in the body, and from those three factors he arrived at the opinion he gave you of the time of death as being from 7:00 p.m. to 7:45 p.m.

Now, what doubt does the defence cast on that opinion of Doctor Penistan, on the time of death? Obviously the defence speaks to show you that it was later, that Doctor Penistan was wrong. And on what do they rely? I might have mentioned, incidentally, that Doctor Brooks was present during the autopsy and confirmed the observations that he and Doctor Penistan each made of the stomach contents, the extent of digestion and so on. But Doctor Brooks, probably, despite his high qualifications in the general field of medicine, did not give opinions or attempt to do so on the rigor mortis factor, because he acknowledged that to be the field of Doctor Penistan.

Now in advancing their theory that death was later. What does the defence put before you? They called Doctor Brown who never saw the stomach, who never was in the woods, never saw the body, never saw the quantity of food in the stomach when it was opened, the nature of the food, never noted the emptiness of the intestines. No chance to know anything about rigor mortis, the state of the body, its decomposition, but just from learning, just from learning. He gives a time of three and a half, four hours, for an average meal. He doesn't know how much the girl ate. Nobody has any actual record of that. He gave this estimate of three and a half to four hours for an average meal to leave – mind you, Gentlemen, to empty out of the stomach. But this stomach, as described by Doctor Penistan when he removed it and looked at it, was distended with food. It wasn't an empty stomach. It was, largely, a full stomach.

So I suggest, with all respect to Doctor Brown and his qualifications, that he just hasn't any basis for giving a counter estimate on the time of death at all. I don't know whether, if you followed through on his opinion, when an average meal leaves a stomach in three and a half hours, and you found a half empty stomach, whether that means the food has been there one hour and a half, or one hour and three-quarters, I don't know how he would enlarge that. But he simply based everything on an empty stomach, which wasn't here. And again, Gentlemen, he didn't have any of those other aids, rigor mortis, decomposition and the other things to go on with at all. So I say, with all respect, there is nothing, absolutely nothing, for Doctor Brown to give you, or Doctor Brown did give you, to interfere with Doctor Penistan's opinion.

Now, Doctor Brown was quoted yesterday as saying that the examination of the stomach, as a means of indicating time of death, was an unreliable test. I did not so regard his evidence. I suggest to you, Gentlemen, that what he said was acknowledging it was used, that he said it was and it has to be used with caution.

Well, you heard Doctor Penistan during his considerable time in the box, and I suggest from your observations of Doctor Penistan, his person, manner of giving testimony and his responsible official position and years of experience, you can safely assume he would be cautious in a case like this, and everything considered, taking the three bases for his opinion, that you can take it with safety that this girl was killed, that she died from 7:00 p.m. to 7:45 p.m. on Tuesday, June 9th. I don't know whether the doctor – I think they made it clear, but the stomach ceases to function on death and that is the basis for this test. Nothing more gets out of the stomach once death takes place.

Now, we come to apply that opinion of time of death and I suggest to you Gentlemen, it is awfully important when this girl died. Now, who was with her during this time? What person or persons had the opportunity to kill her from 7:00 p.m. to 7:45 p.m.? I suggest that a review of the facts narrows those facts like a vice on Steven Truscott and no one else.

The trial judge dealt with the medical evidence as to the time of death as follows:

Doctor Penistan said, having regard to the food that he found in her stomach, and the fact that in his opinion the stomach empties itself after a meal within two hours, that she had died within two hours after having her supper.

The evidence was that she had left home at a quarter to six, that she had finished her supper, I should say, at a quarter to six in the evening, so Doctor Penistan concluded that she had died before a quarter to eight.

Later he said:

According to Doctor Penistan, and to the medical evidence, she died at a time which is not altogether, in any view, inconsistent with her having finished her dinner at about a quarter to six. Doctor Brown says, and I must draw it to your attention, that it takes three and a half to four hours to empty the stomach and it is on the basis of that that the defence asks you to say that she could not have been killed before Steve returned at 8:00 p.m. You have Doctor Brown's testimony. It is unfortunate always, that medical men should disagree on what is more or less a scientific point. Doctor Brown says three and a half hours to four hours.

Now, the stomach, of course, was not empty. Doctor Penistan said there was still a pint of food in the stomach and he removed that pint. It is true there is not a pint of food in the bottle now, and it is for you Gentlemen to accept or reject Doctor Penistan's evidence that he took a pint out, but Doctor Brooks was there and saw the pint. Don't forget that the bottle went to the Attorney-General's Laboratories, for tests and we don't know exactly what happened to it there except it was handed to some man whom we have not seen. It will be for you to say whether you accept Doctor Penistan's theory, an Attorney-General's Pathologist of many years' standing, or do you accept Doctor Brown's evidence.

In his objections after the conclusion of the judge's charge, counsel for the defence said:

And, My Lord, it is the theory of the Defence that Doctor Penistan was in error when he said that the time required to empty the stomach after a normal meal was one to two hours. You did tell them that Doctor Brown said that this time was three and a half to four and a half hours, but it is the theory of the Defence if Doctor Penistan was incorrect and Doctor Brown was right, then that would throw out Doctor Penistan's calculations as to the time of death. With respect, My Lord, I would submit Doctor Brown's evidence was dismissed very summarily by Your Lordship. This is a man of very considerable prominence, and should carry a considerable amount of weight, My Lord.

In the course of a re-charge of the jury the trial judge dealt with this as follows:

I am asked to point out to you that the theory of the Defence is that Doctor Penistan is in error when he says it only takes an hour or two hours to empty the stomach and you can accept the evidence of Doctor Brown, or at least, Doctor Brown's evidence should raise a doubt in your mind. You can understand the point is that his theory is that food took three and a half hours from a quarter to six to leave the stomach, that she must have died at a time later than the time that Steven was at the river, that she must have died after Steven came home, and therefore, it couldn't be Steven who killed her. That is what the theory of the Defence is. I am not going to go over all the evidence again.

Dr. Penistan's evidence in chief as to the time of death as shown by the quantity and condition of the stomach contents was as follows:

Q. Yes, that is my next question, Doctor.
A. The stomach, under normal conditions, proceeds with the digestion of food and as it is digested the stomach empties through the duodenum into the small intestines. This process is normally completed within two hours. I have to bear in mind here that the food in the stomach, as I said, appeared to have been very poorly chewed, appeared to have been bolted, and swallowed without proper chewing, which would tend to slow down the digestion and the emptying of the stomach. I think, therefore, that while – if I found a normal meal, normally chewed, well-chewed meal in the stomach, digested to the slight extent this food was digested, I would conclude that it had not been there for more than an hour. I would, however, make some allowance for the fact of the poor chewing of the food and give as my opinion that the food had not been in the stomach for more than two hours.

Q. Could it have been for a lesser time?
A. It could certainly, sir have been for a lesser time.

Q. To what?
A. I would estimate between one and two hours.

Q. You were in the Courtroom when Mrs. Harper testified this girl finished her meal at a quarter to six?
A. I was, sir.

Q. On that basis, sir, you would put her time of death at ...

A. As prior to a quarter to eight.

Q. As early as ...
A. Probably between seven and a quarter to eight.

As to fixing the time of death from post-mortem changes he said in chief:

> Q. Apart from the stomach, these contents, Doctor, is there any other observations that would assist in determining the cause of death or the time of death?
>
> A. Yes, sir. I referred in my description of the body to the post-mortem changes which were beginning to occur in the fat underneath the skin and in the lungs and indeed, in most of the organs of the body. I refer also to the fact that rigor mortis was still, although only just, demonstrable. Having regard to the environment and the atmospheric conditions about that time, which as I recollect clearly the weather was hot and the environment was damp, conditions under which changes tend to take place rather more rapidly than usual, I felt that these – the state of the body suggested that death had occurred some two days previously.
>
> Q. I take it, Doctor that is supplementary to your stomach observations?
>
> A. That is divorced from the observations on the stomach. Should I add it was my view that the changes were entirely compatible with the time of death as shows from the stomach contents and the other evidence?

In cross-examination, the question of the accuracy of an estimate made from observing post-mortem changes was dealt with as follows:

> Q. Doctor, you told us about the post-mortem changes in this body?
> A. Yes, sir.
>
> A. And there were many factors that could contribute to the variation of time that it would take for those changes to occur, would it not?
> A. Yes, sir.
>
> Q. And that is not a very accurate way of estimating the time of death. It would be difficult to tie it down within five or six hours of those changes, wouldn't it?
> A. Yes, sir.

The cross-examination of Dr. Penistan was directed to showing the unreliability of an estimate of the time of death based on an examination of the contents of the stomach. It showed:

i) that the examination of the stomach contents was visual and by the naked eye;

ii) that there were differences between the description of the contents as given by Dr. Penistan at the trial and (a) at the preliminary hearing and (b) as recorded in his notes made at the time of the autopsy;

iii) that there are many factors which may slow down or speed up digestive processes;

iv) that unchewed peas, of which there were many, are not digested in the stomach at all because they are covered by cellulose;

v) that the doctor made no test of the hydrochloric acid contained in the stomach contents.

Dr. Brooks described the removal and visual examination of the stomach contents. He was not asked to give an opinion as to the time of death.

Dr. Brown's evidence may be summarized as follows:

He said, in chief, the normal emptying time of the stomach after a mixed meal containing starch, protein and fat would be three and one-half to four hours; that one hour should be added if the meal was poorly masticated; that any estimate of time of death from stomach contents must be made with caution as there are so many factors which can cause great variations; and that in cases of accidents requiring an emergency operation it is thought dangerous to operate if the patient has eaten within the past six or eight hours because he may vomit and cause suffocation.

In cross-examination he said that in the normal case the stomach would be empty at the end of three and one-half to four hours and counsel for the Crown stressed that the stomach of the deceased was by no means empty. Dr. Brown agreed that Dr. Penistan had a better opportunity of forming an opinion than he himself had because Dr. Penistan had actually seen the contents of the stomach. He said he had never before been called into court to testify as to the time of death of a deceased person.

(b) *Summary of medical evidence at trial and on the reference relating to the condition of Truscott's penis.*

At the trial, evidence was given by Doctors Addison and Brooks, who medically examined Truscott on the night of June 12 at the R.C.A.F. guardhouse at Clinton. The only other evidence by an actual observer of his condition was given by Truscott himself on the reference.

The medical examination was conducted in the presence of Truscott's father. Dr. Addison, a medical doctor at Clinton, who had practised for 20 years, described his observations as follows:

The penis, on first examination, appeared swollen and slightly reddened on the distal end ... By stretching the skin, pulling it upwards towards the body, there were two large raw sores – they were like a brush burn. They were raw and there was serum oozing from the sores. They were located just behind the groove on the lateral side of the penis on either side. Roughly about the size of the ball of my thumb. The diameter, circumference involved would be roughly that of a quarter – a twenty-five cent piece – each one.

I have never seen one as sore as that at any time – of that nature. I have seen one a few months ago that had a cancer of the penis that looked an awful lot sorer... It (Truscott's) was sorer than any I have ever seen other than those two I have mentioned.

Dealing with the cause of these injuries he said:

There would have to be friction in an oval shaped orifice. An oval shaped knot hole or something like that. Something of an oval shape and sufficiently rough to cause a friction or wear of the outer surface of the skin.

He expressed the opinion that these abrasions could have been caused by a boy of this size and age trying to make entry into a girl of twelve. Truscott was sexually developed, the same as any man, and trying to make entry could cause the sores on his penis.

There was no scab on these lesions, there was a serous discharge.

Dr. Brooks was the senior medical officer at the R.C.A.F. station at Clinton. He described Truscott as a sexually well developed adult. He found on each side of the shaft of Truscott's penis, a lesion just bigger than a twenty-five cent piece. There was no bleeding. There was oozing and by the time of the examination, the oozing was stagnant. He estimated the duration of the lesions at between 60 and 80 hours before. He stated that this was the worst lesion of this nature that he had ever seen. Since he started medical school he had done 20 years of medicine and he had never seen one as bad as this.

In his opinion the lesions were caused by pushing the erect organ into a very narrow orifice. They could have resulted from penetration or attempted penetration of the private parts of a young girl such as Lynne Harper. There was no injury to the glans of the penis.

Evidence was given at the trial on behalf of the defence by Dr. Brown, of London Ontario, who was in the Canadian Army for five years, and who subsequently did post-graduate work in internal medicine, with emphasis on diseases of the digestive system.

The facts stated by Doctors Addison and Brooks were recited to him. He stated he had seen very similar types of lesions. He said a lesion of the size of a twenty-five cent piece is a large size. He had seen lesions of at least a ten-cent size.

As to the cause of such a lesion, he said it would be highly unlikely that penetration would produce a lesion of this sort. The penis is rarely injured in rape. When injured, it is usually a tearing injury confined to the head of the penis, which has a larger circumference. When the hymen is ruptured by the head there may be a pulling that will tear the urinary opening and the fold of skin (frenum) leading from that opening to the foreskin.

Truscott testified for the first time at the Reference. He said that the description of the lesions given by Doctors Addison and Brooks at the trial did not fit the condition that existed on the night the examination was made. The sores were a lot smaller than they had been described. There was a sore on each side, well on the way to healing. There was no oozing whatsoever. They had been in that condition for two weeks.

When he first noticed anything unusual, it was about six weeks prior to his arrest. There were little blisters. They continued to worsen until the time he was "picked up". One blister would break and it just seemed that more would appear. He did not know what caused them to break.

He did not tell his father about them because he was embarrassed. The first persons whom he told about the condition as he first noticed it were his counsel on the Reference when they interviewed him at the penitentiary. He was then asked by Counsel what it looked like when he first noticed it.

The condition had never existed before. A similar condition did develop subsequently on his back and side of the neck. The condition of his penis cleared up while he was at Guelph. It just seemed to heal and went away. It did not hurt.

On the Reference, evidence was given relating to this point by a number of doctors.

Dr. Marcinowsky described an inflamed cyst of the dorsum of Truscott's penis, at Guelph, in May 1962.

Dr. Danby, a specialist in dermatology, practising in Kingston, gave evidence as to his treatments of Truscott for dermatitis at Kingston on different occasions in respect of his face, shoulders, upper arms and ears. Dealing with the condition described by Dr. Addison, he expressed the opinion that if there were an injury which had occurred two or three days before, there would have been bleeding visible in and around the lesions.

He disagreed with Dr. Addison's opinion as to the possible cause of the lesions, i.e., attempting to have intercourse with a young girl. He had never, in his experience, seen lesions of the kind described attributed to forceful intercourse. He had never seen lesions on the side of a penis attributed to force in intercourse. He was not aware of any medical literature, describing such lesions, attributing them to force in intercourse.

If the condition originated in a number of blisters, that condition could have resulted in lesions of the kind described, apart from intercourse. The condition could have begun as a case of herpes simplex. The area is one where sweating, contact of skin surfaces, secondary bacterial infection and irritation could combine to produce lesions.

Dr. Wrong, of Toronto, a specialist in dermatology, was questioned as to his opinion of the view expressed by Dr. Addison concerning the possible cause of the lesions. He said that such lesions are seen in many dermatological conditions, not just following injury. They are seen with many diseases in which blisters appear on the skin.

> I would say these lesions are not diagnostic of any one specific thing and I personally, if I had examined him, with the descriptions read, would not have been able to say definitely these could not have been caused by such alone.

He said it is extremely unlikely to have such an injury caused by intercourse or attempted intercourse, but he would not say it was impossible. He had not found anything comparable to this in the standard textbooks.

It would be unusual for simple herpes to affect two sides of the penis at the same time, but not impossible. Simple herpes of itself would not produce erosions. Secondary infection could do so, i.e., simple herpes plus infection, or irritation from sweating, and the skin surfaces rubbing together.

Dr. Petty, of Baltimore, is the assistant medical examiner for the State of Maryland. He had never seen lesions on either side of the shaft of the penis allegedly as a result of intercourse of any type. He had never read of penial lesions following intercourse. It was highly improbable that they could have been caused in that way.

Dr. Camps, of London, professor of forensic medicine at the University of London, when asked about the opinion of Doctors Addison and Brooks respecting the cause of the lesions, said:

From a mechanical point of view and from my experience I don't think that this is the sort of injury which could occur from sexual intercourse. It is the wrong part of the organ for one thing. The commonest injury occurring in this type of forced intercourse is a tear of the prepuce, which mechanically is one place that is vulnerable and which can be pulled on, or when push and force is exerted it is pulled in that way.

Asked regarding medical literature on the subject, he had not found anything indicating a lesion of that sort.

However, so little interest is paid in textbooks to this type of injury that in many textbooks it is barely mentioned.

Dr. Simpson, of London, Head of the Department of Forensic Medicine at Guy's Hospital, called by the Crown, gave the following evidence:

Q. Finally, Dr. Simpson, I think you have read and you have heard read in this Court the evidence of a Dr. Addison and a Dr. Brooks relating to penile injuries to the accused Steven Truscott, and I think, sir, I know you were aware, in addition to that evidence, the evidence of Mr. Truscott himself relating to these injuries. Have you any comments regarding those, sir?

A. Yes, sir, when I first read the description of these I had not seen a picture of them and, of course, I did not see them, but when I first read a description of them I found them perplexing, for I would agree with the evidence I heard, they are not the ordinary kind of injury one sees in forcible or difficult sexual intercourse. But having heard the evidence of Steven Truscott that he – if I understood it correctly – already had some condition of soreness on his penis, this seems to me to give a clue to the rather curious nature of these two patches.

Q. In what way, Dr. Simpson?

A. Well, I think that if Truscott was right and he had patches there, there are two possibilities. One is that these patches – I think they were described as quarter size or thereabouts, patches on each side of the penis, and the other is that these patches were rubbed in some way which caused them to become more sore or to weep or crust, and I would regard that as being consistent with the penis being thrust into or being held, to be pushed into or being held in some way in a sexual gesture as a part of a sexual assault.

(c) *Summary of Medical Evidence given on the Reference witness by witness*

Henry John Funk is an analyst in the biological field with the Attorney General's Department. On June 12, 1959, he received the jar containing the stomach contents. On a visual examination he described it as being made up of pieces and chunks. Its general consistency reminded him of a thick stew. His examination was made between June 12 and August 31. He found pineapple, celery, pickled cucumber, cauliflower, peas, onion, potatoes, and what appeared to be two types of meat. It seemed to be consistent with ham and some type of fowl. Many of the foods that were supposed to have been eaten by Lynn Harper he found in the mixture. The total volume of the mixture was 250 cubic centimetres – eight to nine ounces.

Dr. Noble Sharpe. He has been the Medical Director of the Attorney General's Department since 1951 and is now about to retire. From 1923 to 1950 he did hospital pathology. He received the jar from Funk on June 12. For his examination he removed between 50 and 60 cubic centimetres. He saw undigested food mixed with some that was partially digested. He recognized certain vegetables but remembers only peas, some of which had been swallowed without chewing and were whole. He made no further examination of the recognizable parts because Mr. Funk was going to make the detailed examination.

The stomach contents were strongly acid. He concluded that gastric juices had been secreted and it was not just a recently chewed and swallowed meal. His rough estimate of the time needed to develop that amount of acid was about one hour. It was quite a good amount. He saw some muscle fibres, striated muscle fibres, and knew that meat had been eaten but had no idea what kind of meat. He described the contents as resembling a thick, lumpy stew. There was little or no fluid in it. Based on the thick consistency and the fact that the acid was present, he considered that the stomach contents had not been long enough in the stomach to be suitable for passing out into the duodenum. It was not in the condition of chyme, at which stage the contents are ready to pass into the duodenum.

It is known that after an ordinary meal the contents are ready to leave the stomach at the end of two hours and that they go out in small amounts, about three cubic centimetres at a time, for the next two hours so that by the end of the fourth hour after the food has been taken, the stomach is usually nearly empty. In his opinion the stomach contents had been in the stomach for one to two hours after eating. He admitted that there are many conditions that cause variation – likes and dislikes, preparation of the food, proper cooking, whether or not the food is fatty as fatty food takes longer to digest, the state of hunger of the person concerned, whether he had been exercising before eating or taking it easy, emotions, anatomical position of the stomach, and many others.

He agreed with what he wrote some time ago in an article "Rate of Cooling as an Index of Time of Death". It is as follows:

> For a long time I had felt that pathologists are placed in an awkward position by the emphasis in courts on estimation of the time of death from the rate of cooling, rigor mortis, decomposition and stomach contents. These four bases for estimation depend on variable factors. The pathologist is usually asked by the investigating officer to give them a rough starting time for investigation or the period in which particularly to focus. This may get into the report and is later mentioned in court.
>
> Both prosecution and defence are prone to emphasize those points which are of benefit to their particular view of the case. The time based on one or more of these four examinations is at most an approximation, an inspired or educated guess. It is more likely only a probability or a hunch. It is of use to the investigator but of much less value to the court.

Dr. Cedrick Keith Simpson is head of the Department of Forensic Medicine, Guy's Hospital, London; Professor of Forensic Medicine, University of London; Lecturer in Forensic Medicine, University of Oxford; Home Office Consultant since 1935, and has done work with the Forensic Science Group of Scotland Yard since that date. The summary of his opinion is contained in the following extract:

> A. I would say that, my lord, it appears to me in this case most creditable that Dr. Penistan paid particular attention to this matter. In my own experience this is not always so. I would say that his conclusion, based, as I see it, on the presence in the stomach of something approaching a pint of relatively dry food, that is to say, without a measureable quantity of fluid which could be separated from it, from the fact that it was of a kind and quality which he observed and had confirmed in the laboratory, from the fact that this whole amount, with the exception of a little material

which had passed on to the small bowel, still lay in the stomach, I would say that unless he took into consideration some unusual or extraordinary conditions, that he was right to conclude that it was likely that death had taken place somewhere up to two hours after eating that meal.

There was a fragment of food in the bronchial air passage, which is common in asphyxial deaths. The cause of death was strangulation by a ligature. There was injury to one of the voice box bones, discoloration of the face and the characteristic asphyxial hemorrhage in the lungs and thymus gland.

On an examination of the photographs taken at the scene where the body was found, there was nothing inconsistent with death having taken place where the girl was found and photographed. He agrees with Dr. Penistan that the twigs on the ground would cause the type of puncture wound found on the body.

As to lividity, looking at two photographs taken in the mortuary, he agreed that the chin and left cheek and region over and above the left eyebrow and the nose showed pallor against the general colour of the face, the colour he takes to be that described as lividity engorgement. The discoloration was consequent on strangulation. His explanation was that two other photographs taken where the body was found show the body turned on its left side and lying partly on some sheeting or covering. So long as the blood was fluid when this took place, it would be natural for the pressure to give these areas just where they appear to have developed. He was asked how long blood remains fluid in a dead body and he could not give any definite answer. Sometimes it never appears to clot; sometimes it clots in a short period and becomes dissolved again. The variations are so vast that no figure can be given. As to the absence of acid phosphatase on the twigs and dandelion leaves which were preserved for sampling and taken at the scene of the crime, he said:

A. Well, I have seen many cases of both sexual intercourse against resistance as shown by injuries and other marks about the body, and I would say that in some of them one does see seminal fluid not only in the vagina but at the orifice and extending from it on to the thighs or down between the crotch, but by no means always, and I would certainly not regard the absence of spermatozoic fluid on the ground between the crotch area as giving any evidence that sexual intercourse of some kind did not take place where the body lay.

As to rigor mortis, one of the witnesses said that an arched back and the fingers indicated that this was present in the mortuary. Dr. Penistan had said that rigor mortis had almost passed away. Dr. Simpson said that he was surprised to hear the witness refer to the arched back as an indication of the degree of rigor. He said that was the natural shape of the body and that dead or alive, it would preserve its shape. He says that one sees that every day. It is a matter of common sense and personal observation.

As to the suggestion of rigor mortis in the fingers by Dr. Petty, he said that two of the fingers were being held by the assistant to hold the hand in a certain position for the taking of photographs.

His estimate of the emptying of the stomach and the time of death as indicated by it is contained in the following extract:

> Q. Doctor, if I may turn for a moment, sir, to a general discussion of the stomach contents – and again in this matter I am making the assumption and premise that you have heard read the evidence of Dr. Penistan regarding the stomach content, you have heard the evidence of Mr. John Funk and you heard the evidence of Dr. Noble Sharpe – based on that premise, what do you say, doctor, as to setting of a time or approximate time of death from stomach contents?
>
> A. Well, sir, I would say that based upon my own experience of those cases in which the time of the last meal is known, and based upon the relatively few quotations that can be listed from the textbooks in forensic medicine – I refer to Sidney Smith and Polson, in particular, and based upon the enormous – I think no other word could be used to describe it – enormous literature from the physiologists on the emptying process of the stomach, it would seem to me there is general consensus of view that the process of emptying is a gradual one which appears to be best described in terms of a half life, that is to say, during a period of time which seems to be within thirty minutes and an hour, around about forty-five minutes, perhaps, the stomach half empties itself, and then in a similar period half empties itself again, and again, and again. So that it is described as a half life. I would say that if these observations are correct – and there is an overwhelmingly large literature in support of this – that one might have expected, as Sidney Smith and Polson and my own experience, of course, one might have expected the bulk of the meal to have left the stomach inside two hours. This seems to me a generalization which experience and experiment support.
>
> Q. Based on what you have read from the original trial transcript and what you have heard in this court, what conclusion and opinion would you have come to in this matter?
>
> A. As I say, I think – certainly earlier in my evidence, sir – I think that based on the amount of food in the stomach as compared with the little, the very little, I think it was described, that had started to pass into the small bowel, based on its character and the relatively little indeed which appears to be an unmeasurable quantity of food which was present, that this girl's death must, if the stomach be taken as an indication of it – and I

think it is the one useful indication in this case – must have taken place within two hours of her taking that meal.

Q. Doctor, are there, as has been described in this Court, variables that do in fact affect the digestion, such as emotion?

A. Yes, sir, I think that if that view is looked at more critically, I think one has to be prepared if there is some evidence to qualify it in some way. If there is some evidence about outside conditions that – such as emergency, for instance – that may affect the stomach, then one must be prepared to qualify it, but in the absence of such evidence I would say that Dr. Penistan was quite right to give as an indication and estimation a period which is about usual, about normal, which would be likely, and the last thing I would say, sir, about that, is that there are of course upper and lower limits to this. Some stomachs, some stomach contents empty a little earlier and some a little later.

Q. Doctor, I just have two further questions, one dealing, sir, with the evidence that was given in this Court relating, Dr. Simpson, to changes in the decomposition of this body, and very generally, and paraphrasing again, they were referred to as swelling, bloating and lack of venous patterning and other decomposition changes. What value, if any, sir, based on your experience, do you attach to decomposition changes such as I have just mentioned to you?

A. I would say, sir, that those words, described as stated decomposition which is becoming well marked, and they did not appear to be present in this case, that the earliest of changes is commonly, usually I think, a discolouration in the flanks of the body or in the veins rising up out of the trunk, and this is likely to be seen from about forty-eight hours, but it varies according to temperature.

Q. Were you suprised to read and to hear and not to find here swelling and bloating and a venous pattern?

A. No, sir, no, these I would not expect to be likely to become evident until about the second to third, to fourth day, or later on, that depending on the outside conditions.

Q. There was also a reference very briefly to the lack of greenish discolouration in the flanks of the body. What is your comment, if any, sir, regarding that?

A. Well, sir, this is the earliest of the signs. As I say, it would be likely to appear somewhere about the second day, the forty-eighth hour, but it need not be present. Indeed it need not appear at all.

Dr. Milton Helpern has been chief Medical Examiner for the City of New York since 1954 and is visiting Professor of Pathology, Cornell University; Professor and Chairman of the Department of Forensic Medicine, New York University School of Medicine. Cause of death was strangulation. The food of microscopic size in the bronchials was one incident in the process of dying by strangulation. The place of death was where the body was found. He disagreed with Dr. Petty that twigs would not cause the puncture wounds. He agreed with Dr. Simpson that apparent blanching and whitening shown in the photographs to which he referred was attributable to the body having been turned on its side and that the only valid evidence on this subject was to be found in a photograph of the body before it was disturbed or turned and which showed no blanching. He disagreed with Dr. Petty that there was any evidence of rigor mortis in the arched back or the fingers.

His opinion as to stomach contents is contained in the following extract:

> Q. Now, based on your experience that goes back many years, sir, based on those, the factors developed and shown by that testimony, what if any opinion would you have as to how long that stomach content had been in that particular stomach of this young girl?
> A. In my opinion, from the amount of food in the stomach and from the fact that this was a healthy body, the body of a healthy young girl, and from the fact that death was rapid, I think it is reasonable to conclude that the time it took this person to die was rather short, and from all these factors I would conclude that this food had been ingested no more than two hours after – that is, that death had occurred, I'm sorry, gentlemen – that death had occurred no more than two hours after the food was ingested. I think that is the rule in these cases.
> Q. That is from your experience in these matters, sir?
> A. Yes, I have been particularly interested in recent years in the emptying time of the stomach, and we have had enough cases in which we could find a large amount of recently ingested food, that is, easily recognizable food in large amounts and in which we were able to determine the time the food was ingested, and in those cases the food was ingested less than two hours prior to death.
>
> I might explain, in discussing this I don't want to be – to appear to be just arbitrary about this thing. There are conditions which do slow up the emptying of the stomach, and the most common condition that does this is coma. In other words, this opinion could not be common in a man who was knocked down by an automobile and then died as a result of brain injury, having lain in a coma for several days. I have seen food in the stomach in cases like that which has been in the stomach for over a week, but in a person who is healthy, who dies suddenly or rapidly, I would say that this amount of food and the condition it was in is indicative of a time of death, about two hours or within two hours of the ingestion of the food. Now, this is the rule.

Dr. Samuel Robert Gerber has been the Coroner, since 1937, of Cuyahoga County, Ohio, which includes the City of Cleveland.

Without going into his evidence in detail, he agreed with Dr. Simpson and Dr. Helpern as to the cause of death, the place of death and cause of the signs of blanching.

He agreed with the others and Dr. Penistan that the arched

back and the fingers were no indication of rigor mortis.

His opinion was that the food had been in the stomach less than two hours after ingestion.

Dr. Charles Sutherland Petty is now Assistant Medical Examiner for the State of Maryland. He was Chief Resident in Pathology at various hospitals from 1952 to 1955 and a Teaching Fellow at Harvard Medical School in the Department of Pathology from 1952 to 1955; Instructor and Assistant Professor of Pathology, Louisiana State School of Medicine 1955 to 1958; Associate Professor of Forensic Pathology, University of the State of Maryland and Associate in Public Health Administration, Johns Hopkins University.

Dr. Penistan's report was put before him and he was asked for his conclusion as to the time of death. His opinion was that the time of death could only be stated within very broad limits. These broad limits are stated to be:

> A. These broad limits lie anywhere between several minutes to several hours; thirty minutes to perhaps eight hours. The missing factors here: Dr. Penistan mentioned the bolting of the food or the rapidity evidently with which the food was eaten. The fact it had not been well chewed is a factor which caused him to advance the time from one hour to perhaps two hours after eating, the interval between eating and death. But I do not see that he has taken into consideration any of the many other factors which might change the emptying time of the stomach or change the amount of food that one would see in the stomach at the time of the autopsy.
>
> Q. What are, in a general way – Would you describe the factors which must be – which cause a variation in the rate of digestion and the rate of the emptying of the stomach?
>
> A. Well, there are many. We do not know, for example, whether this girl was taking drugs; we do not know whether this individual, in fact was emotionally disturbed; we do not know whether there was loss of the stomach contents significantly, that is, into the duodenum or, indeed, further into the small and large intestine; and, as a matter of fact, we do not know how much, if any, of the food was lost through either opening into the stomach. There are two, the top opening from the esophagus and the bottom opening into the duodenum. We do not know even, for example, whether or not there was loss of food through the esophagus either during the act of dying or after the death occurred.

On a consideration of Dr. Brooks' evidence given at the trial as to the contents of the stomach, he repeated his opinion that the estimate would vary from minutes to hours.

The evidence of Mr. Funk, the analyst, and Dr. Noble Sharpe

was then put before him and he was asked to assume the correctness of the description of the contents given by these witnesses. His answer was:

> Q. Now, again assuming the correctness of the description of the contents given by Mr. Funk and Dr. Sharpe, does that affect the opinion that you have expressed?
>
> A. No, sir, it does not, because we do not know what factors were present between the time the meal was eaten and the time that death occurred.

Again returning to Dr. Penistan's evidence as between one and two hours, or prior to a quarter to eight, and probably between seven and a quarter to eight, his answer was:

> Q. The question I want to now ask you, what is your opinion as to whether the time of death can be put within such narrow limits, based on the stomach contents and the state to which digestion had proceeded, assuming the evidence of Dr. Penistan as to his observations is correct, and assuming the evidence of Mr. Funk and Dr. Sharpe, as to their observations, is correct?
>
> A. Based on the appearance of the stomach contents, the amount of the stomach contents, the degree to which the stomach contents had apparently been digested, I would find myself completely unable to pinpoint any time, a figure such as seven o'clock to seven forty-five, or a quarter to seven to a quarter to eight.

On being questioned about Dr. Penistan's finding that very little had passed through the duodenum into the small intestine, he replied:

> Q. Just taking the information as you have it, the facts I have given to you by themselves, if you were in possession of those facts and that description, what would be the limits either way in which you would place the time of death?
>
> A. Again, sir, several minutes, 20, 30, 40 minutes, perhaps five days, possibly as long as eight hours.

(NOTE: It says five days in the record. We assume that the witness must have intended to say five hours.)

He then went on to deal with rigor mortis and what is sometimes called post-mortem lividity or hypostasis. He found evidence of rigor mortis from the arched back and the position of the fingers and the position of the leg on the mortuary table "provided the leg has not been placed there deliberately or accidentally".

His conclusion was that the onset of rigor mortis is rapid in a warm environment (and the weather was very warm on June 9, June 10 and June 11). He also says that rigor mortis disappears more rapidly in a warm environment and his conclusion was that this body had been where it was found "perhaps less time than has been indicated in some of the evidence I have read". His conclusion was that death occurred later than 7:45 p.m. on June 9.

From the photographs and the rigor mortis alone I would be unable to say precisely when death occurred but that from this amount of rigor mortis I would be inclined to put it on the light side of two days. The light side or the short side of two days, rather than forty-eight hours.

He noted the absence of bloating and venous patterning and skin slippage. He would expect to see this sort of thing in a body dead forty-eight hours in the temperatures which were given in evidence.

Then, by way of summary:

Q. Then, Doctor, I now, having taken you over Dr. Penistan's evidence with respect to the stomach contents and his evidence with respect to the existence of rigor, his evidence with respect to the beginnings of putrefaction and having referred you to the photographs of the – Taking the total picture into consideration, the amount of fluid, the evidence of postmortem changes as described and shown in the pictures, can you come to any opinion as to the time of death?

A. Well, the best opinion I can come to on the time of death is this: It is my opinion that the body has been dead in the neighbourhood of thirty, thirty-six hours, possibly forty hours and I am taking my time now from the autopsy time, not from the time of sighting of the body; but I cannot narrow the limits to less, perhaps, than twelve hours. I clearly have the impression from examination of these photographs, and with particular reference to those things that I have pointed out already to this Court, that the body has been dead not an inconsiderable time short of forty-eight hours; but, I cannot pinpoint that in time, less perhaps. A range perhaps of less perhaps than eight or ten or twelve hours.

Q. In your opinion is it possible for anyone, on the basis of the facts that have been disclosed with relation to the stomach contents, post-mortem changes, to place that period of death within the narrow limits of 7:00 p.m. and 7:45 p.m. on June the 9th?

A. Of course not. Not unless we know precisely what happened between the time that the child was last seen and the time when death occurred; and, of course, if we knew that we would know the time of death.

The time of the autopsy was approximately 48 hours after the girl was last seen.

He next went on to deal with the place of death. Dr. Penistan's report as to what he found when he arrived at the scene was put to him in detail. First, he did not think that the puncture wounds had been caused by twigs. He referred to the puncture wound under the left shoulder, a scratch mark on the front of the left thigh extending over the left kneecap and down to the top of the left foot, and small "interruptions" of the skin's surface on the buttock. He thought the scratch marks on the leg indicated a dragging of the body in a limp condition. He disagreed with any theory of the causation of the marks by twigs. He thought the twigs would be pressed down and would not penetrate. He demonstrated by the use of fountain pens scattered on the desk before him.

He would have expected some spots of semen, acid phosphates to be present at the crotch or very close to it or on the leaves or twigs or whatever was immediately beneath that point of the body.

As to the presence of vegetable matter in the bronchi, he thought it was in a microscopic amount. He called it a remarkable finding in view of the presence of the ligature about the neck. All the other experts thought it was a normal incident of death by strangulation.

Q. What inference did you draw or what is your conclusion from the presence of vegetable matter in the bronchi?

A. I call this a very remarkable finding in view of the presence of a ligature about the neck. The blouse or the ligature about the neck would certainly compress the neck organs and would certainly tend to cause the esophagus, or the tube leading from the mouth down to the stomach, to be collapsed; and I would find it difficult to explain how this food material, this vegetable material found its way into the lung passages that have not a route to go out of the stomach, through the esophagus, to be aspirated and drawn into the air tubes themselves. I think it is quite remarkable in view of the ligature or restricting band about the neck.

Q. What would that indicate to you about the time the vegetable matter got into the bronchi?

A. Inhalation of apparently vomited stomach contents is not an unusual thing during death. I would, therefore, believe this occured during the act of dying, possibly slightly before, during the act of attack, whatever that may have been; and, therefore, I believe this related to the death, if that is an answer to your question, sir.

Q. Are you able to form any opinion as to whether aspiration of the vegetable matter into the bronchi occurred before or after the application of the ligature?

A. As I have already indicated, I think that this occurred before the application of the ligature.

He next examined the photographic exhibits at some length leading up to the conclusion that the body was on its left side shortly after death. It is expressed in the following extract:

Q. What in your opinion caused that?

A. I believe this body laid on its left side for a period of time after death and was moved at a later time.

Q. And why do you reach that conclusion?

A. Because of the pattern of the wrinkles present and the depression on the outer aspect of the left upper arm and the blanch or relatively white areas involved in the left breast and probably also the left side of the face. I believe this is the pattern of a post-mortem lividity which develops shortly after death when the body was on that side so that the blood drained down into that side, that the hypostasis became, as forensic pathologists put it, fixed or partially fixed so that when the body was again placed on its back that the markings of its previous position were left and did not vanish because all of the blood had been drained out of that area into what was now the bottom and down side of the body. So, in this photograph, if taken in conjunction with the other photograph which we have seen, it is my opinion that the body was first on its left side and then was turned at a later time and put on its back in the position in which it was found.

Q. And what would cause – You say, for instance, on the left breast there is an area that is whiter?

A. Yes.

Q. What would create the whitening or lighter colour?

A. This is where the breast itself was pressing against whatever the body was lying on and prevented the blood from flowing into that area.

Q. How soon after death would the body have to lie in that position to develop this pattern?

A. This is not subjected as rigor mortis and stomach contents to any specific or definitive answers. The blood begins to settle in the body immediately following death. The point really is at what point was the body moved after death. If the body remained on its left side for a period of time after death until some of the blood was fixed, that is, there was some clotting, perhaps, of the small blood vessels, possibly some passage of red blood cells out into the surrounding tissue, then the point at which this occurred to a significant degree, but the main majority of the blood was still fluid so that when the body was shifted again now onto its back the ordinary hypostasis pattern developed. I could not say precisely, but I would say possibly the inner limit of an hour, an hour and a half, the inner limit of several hours. I do not know, four, six hours, somewhere within this period of time.

Q. How long would the body have to lie in that position?

A. I would say the body would probably have to lie there for a period of certainly an hour or two, in this region.

As to the lesions on the penis, he said that he had never seen lesions on either side of the shaft of the penis allegedly as a result of intercourse of any type. Nor did he know of any reference to this possibility in the literature. He thought it highly improbable that these lesions would be caused by intercourse.

Dr. Frederick Albert Jaffe is presently lecturing in Pathology at the University of Toronto and is an Assistant Pathologist, Toronto Western Hospital. He has been a Regional Pathologist for the Province of Ontario since 1951. He is soon to assume the duty of Medical Director of the Forensic Section in succession to Dr. Noble Sharpe.

He considered that the stomach contents and the state to which digestion has proceeded after the last known meal a most unreliable guide as to the time of death. He had read the evidence of Dr. Penistan as to the stomach contents; also that of Dr. Brooks, and heard the evidence of Dr. Sharpe and Mr. Funk. On the assumption that the girl started her dinner at 5.30 p.m. and finished at 5.45 p.m., he would not place the time of death within the period 7.00 to 7.45 o'clock with any reasonable degree of certainty.

His opinion of the time of death, as indicated by the post-mortem changes, is contained in the following extract:

> Q. Now, dealing – passing from the stomach contents to the postmortem changes which were observed, again assuming you heard read the evidence of Dr. Penistan as to the post-mortem changes he observed, that is, the very slight rigor that was present, the infestation of the body by maggots, and assuming the correctness of all Dr. Penistan's observations and also his statement that autolysis was present but the body had not yet begun to putrefy or had not reached a stage of putrefaction, do those facts enable you to form an opinion as to when death occurred?
> A. Only within very wide limits. I believe on the basis of Dr. Penistan's description and the photographs which I was able to see, that death has occurred no less than twenty-four hours before the discovery of the body.
> Q. Could you go any farther than that?
> A. To me the really outstanding feature of the body, both basing my view upon the autopsy protocol and Dr. Petty's description of the photographs, is the absence of those changes of decomposition which one would expect to find in a body which had allegedly lain two days in an environment which was certainly very hot and humid. This to me is one of the outstanding characteristics of this body. I would place the time perhaps half way between twenty-four and forty-eight hours.

He agreed with Dr. Petty as to the cause of the blanching.

Dr. Francis Edward Camps is a lecturer in Forensic Medicine at the London Hospital Medical College, Royal Free Hospital Medical College and the Middlesex Hospital Medical School and a professor of Forensic Medicine at the University of London.

His opinion of the significance of the contents of the stomach is contained in the following extracts:

> Q. First of all, Dr. Camps, what is your opinion as to whether the contents of the stomach and the state to which digestion has proceeded in relation to the last known meal consumed by the deceased, is a reliable guide to the time of death?
>
> A. It is so variable that this generally has been described as being of no value in assessing the time of death within a limited period. That is to say, what you can say is, first of all, that the contents indicate the nature of the last meal that the person has had. In other words, it enables you to say they have had nothing else to eat since the last meal. And, secondly, that death has occurred within a number of hours. It is possible, by taking other matters into consideration, to place perhaps within that number of hours a distance in one or other direction; but other than that, it is quite impossible.

* * *

> Q. Assuming the correctness of the observations of Dr. Penistan and Dr. Brooks and Dr. Sharpe and Mr. Funk, what is your opinion as to whether on this – on that basis you could, with any reasonable degree of certainty, state that the time of death of the deceased was between the hours of 7:00 p.m. and 7:45 p.m., having regard the fact that she finished her last known meal at 5:45?
>
> A. I would say it is quite impossible and, in fact, I would say it could be dangerously misleading to the investigating officers.

As to rigor mortis, he disagrees with Dr. Penistan's finding in the following extract:

> Q. Does the evidence with respect to the existence of rigor mortis and its extent enable you to express any opinion with respect to the time when death occurred?
>
> A. No. I think, once again, there is so much variation in rigor mortis that, at the best of times, you cannot express an answer except within a reasonably broad limit. In this particular case I think it was a pity that the examination for rigor mortis was not done at 1:45 but waited until 7:15. But, on the basis of the appearance of the body, of the fact that the appearance is, to some extent, and I can say no more than that, present again only at the scene of the crime but also on the autopsy table, I think one must assume that rigor mortis was pretty established still, certainly a little earlier in the evening.

On this point he is in direct conflict with Doctors Penistan, Simpson, Helpern and Gerber. As to post-mortem changes, his opinion is expressed in the following extract:

> Q. You have also heard the evidence read of Dr. Penistan with respect to the other post mortem changes – that is, the presence of autolysis, the infestation of certain parts of the body by maggots, and assuming again the correctness of those observations, does that enable you to determine the time of death?
>
> A. No. I would like to make it quite clear, if I may, I am in no way criticizing Dr. Penistan's observations. The only thing here is, first of all, that the

autolysis I find supremely surprising for forty-eight hours, to be so little in the temperature and under these conditions.

In the temperatures established during the 48-hour period, he would have expected to find more post-mortem changes than were found on this body. The implication of this is contained in the following extract:

Q. Does he not refer to autolysis in paragraph 4?
A. Yes, that is right. Yes, I would repeat what I said, that the temperature, even putting it at its lowest, for forty-eight hours I would expect to find more post mortem changes than were found in this body. The implication of that, had I been there, would have been, having found the stomach contents in the condition which could be to indicate death at the end of one hour or up to nine or ten hours, would make me put my time of the death closer to the ten than to the one. That is the only observation I can make. I find, also, it is very remarkable from this point of view that there is no green discolouration of the abdomen on the right side, which we normally reckon to appear somewhere about forty-eitht hours. So that would also tend to put it back.

He explained the blanching in the same way as Dr. Petty, i.e., that the body had lain on its side. He thought an hour might be reasonable. It might have been much less than that.

He expressed some doubt whether the puncture marks described by Dr. Penistan would have been caused by twigs. He thought they would more likely cause scratch marks, not a straight hole. He thought that some sort of sharp thing that might have caused the scratch mark down the leg might have caused the puncture marks.

Because of the absence of acid phosphatase, he expressed the opinion that where the body was found was not the place where the rape occurred. He thought that if it had occurred here, there would have been more injury on the back.

As to the injury to Truscott's penis, he did not think it was the kind of injury that could occur from sexual intercourse. The commonest injury is a tear of the prepuce. "However, so little interest is paid in textbooks to this type of injury that in many textbooks it is barely mentioned."

Another body of medical evidence had to do with dermatology.

Dr. Emilian Marcinkovsky is a physician at the Ontario Reformatory at Guelph. On March 3, 1961, he treated Truscott for an infected burn of the right internal ear. He treated him with compresses and chloromycetin. He found that Truscott was sensitive to this drug and he was kept in hospital. On June 28, 1961, there was further treatment.

On December 27, 1962, Truscott was suffering from dermatitis in the armpits. The doctor thought it was the result of chemicals, the detergent in the washing. He called it contact dermatitis.

On May 15, 1962, he treated him for an inflamed cyst of the dorsum of the penis. On May 24, he marked the medical card "Cyst now not inflamed. Excision will be indicated if frequently inflamed."

Dr. Norman McKinnon Wrong. He graduated in 1927 from the University of Toronto and has been on the teaching staff since 1932. From 1954 to 1962 he was Associate Professor of Medicine in charge of Dermatology at the University of Toronto. His opinion on the cause of the lesions on the penis is:

Q. What is your opinion as to whether the lesions – the lesions as described, could be caused in that way?

A. The lesions described, or what we call erosions of the skin, such erosions are seen in many dermatological conditions, not just following injury, superficial injury of the skin, and we see them with many diseases in which blisters appear on the skin, so that I would say these lesions are not diagnostic of any one specific thing, and I personally, if I had examined him, with the descriptions read, would not have been able to say definitely these could not have been caused by such alone.

Q. Have you any opinion as to the likelihood of an injury such as that being able to be caused by intercourse or attempted intercourse?

A. I would think it rather unlikely or extremely unlikely. I would not say impossible, but I would say extremely unlikely that a lesion on the side of the shaft of the penis would be caused by intercourse.

Q. Are you familiar with any medical literature attributing lesions of that kind on the sides of the penis to trauma or injury involved in or received during forcible or violent intercourse?

A. I have not gone over the medical literature exhaustively, but I have not found anything comparable to this in the standard textbooks.

He also was of the opinion that it was most unlikely that the abrasion on the right labia of the deceased about the size of a finger-nail, was caused by a penis. He thought that the condition of the penis described by Dr. Brooks and Dr. Addison indicated simple herpes.

As to the precise conditions observed by Dr. Addison and Dr. Brooks, he explained them as follows:

A. I think simple herpes plus infection or plus irritation from sweating and the skin surfaces rubbing together. I don't think that simple herpes in itself usually produces erosion, but secondary infection could very well produce these erosions.

He had never seen any lesions on the shaft of the penis which had been attributable to forcible intercourse or trauma. He had seen injury about the meatus and around the frenum, but never traumatic lesions on the shaft of the penis as a result of intercourse.

Dr. Charles William Elliott Danby is an Assistant Professor of Medicine at Queen's University, and the Consultant in Dermatology for the three federal penitentiaries at Kingston, Collins Bay and Joyceville.

He treated Steven Truscott on January 30, 1964, for infected dermatitis of the left side of his face extending from the level of his eyelid down to below the mouth, with an oozing, scaling and crusty condition. His opinion was that this was secondarily infected dermatitis due to some agent that had irritated his skin. Truscott told him that it had been present for a year. The doctor saw him on five subsequent occasions, the last time being April 24. There was good improvement up to March 1st. Then, on April 15th, he had a patchy nummular type of eczema involving the back part of his shoulders, upper arms and his face and ears. On his last visit, April 24, he had improved.

Counsel then put to him the description of Truscott's condition that was given by Dr. Addison and Dr. Brooks at the trial.

Q. This was the view expressed by Dr. Addison, a brush burn of two or three days' duration, was his description. But that is part of the description. Assuming the size, the description of the raw sore, oozing, having the appearance of a brush burn of two or three days' duration; from that description would you be able to reach any conclusion as to the nature and cause of these injuries?
A. I would think that in the area where these lesions have been described, if it were an injury that had occurred three days before, or two days before, there would have been haemorrhage or bleeding visible in and around these lesions. Now, one must remember that in this area the skin is very thin. I would think a good comparison would be the thickness of the skin of your eyelid. If we remember that the skin is made up of two parts, the epidermis and dermis. For convenience, the epidermis is the outer layer of the skin, below which there are blood vessels ready to bleed and is not thicker than six one hundredths of a millimetre. It is tissue paper thin. I would think that if this had been due to injury there would have been haemorrhage.

Q. Would you be able to give any information as to the extent or the degree of the bleeding or haemorrhaging that would occur from injury of that kind?

A. I have in the past, and I still do occasionally, perform an operation called dermo-abrasion of the skin in which we abrade the skin in order to improve the appearance of scars. Now, we do not have to abrade it very deeply to get copious bleeding.

He went on to say that he did not think that these lesions could have happened by the penetration or attempted penetration of the organ into the private parts of a young girl. He had seen six or seven cases of a tearing of the praeputium. He was not aware of any medical literature on this subject.

Next, he dealt with the injury to the labium majus. This was testified to by Dr. Penistan and Dr. Brooks. He thought it was unlikely, if not impossible, that this could occur from an attempted penetration.

He thought that the condition described by Dr. Brooks and Dr. Addison was herpes simplex (cold sores).

There was, in addition evidence given by psychiatrists called by the Crown and the Defence. We do not consider that this evidence assists us in coming to our conclusion.

Conclusions

After all the evidence given on the Reference, the issues are still the same as those which faced the jury – who raped and killed this girl. The evidence both as to fact and opinion has to be considered as a whole. We begin with Truscott's oral evidence on the Reference. It differs from the evidence given by all those witnesses who saw him on the road before 7 p.m. and described his movements. These movements give an impression of aimless loitering of no particular significance to him. This may account for his failure to remember whom he had met and who had seen him. On the other hand, although as a boy of 14½ years, he had heard all these witnesses give evidence at the trial. The evidence had some connection with that of Jocelyne Goddette and to the jury could have indicated that he was waiting for someone and that the person for whom he was waiting was Jocelyne Goddette, who by her subsequent actions indicated that she was looking for him and did not find him.

The evidence of the time of departure from the school grounds is of decisive importance in this case. According to Mrs. Nickerson and Mrs. Bohonus, it was not later than 7.15 p.m. and Truscott had appeared about 7 p.m. On the Reference Truscott for the first time gave his time of departure as within a minute of 7.30 p.m. By 7.30 Richard Gellatly and even Philip Burns on foot were back at home. But Truscott had told the police that he did remember meeting Gellatly. Gellatly remembered meeting Truscott and he was not cross-examined. One of the certainties in this case is that this meeting did happen. We find it impossible to accept Truscott's evidence given before us that he and the girl left at 7.30 p.m. and that they did not meet Gellatly.

Further, Jocelyne Goddette, according to Mr. Lawson's evidence, left Lawson's barn at 7.25 p.m. If Truscott's time is taken, she would have been on the road ahead of him. So would Arnold George, for she and George were on the road near the bush at approximately the same time. Jocelyne Goddette and Arnold George could not have failed to see Truscott and the girl if they had left the school grounds at 7.30 p.m. The case for the prosecution, as put to the jury, was that Truscott and Lynne were ahead of Jocelyne Goddette and Arnold George and were not seen after passing Gellatly.

Our conclusion is that Truscott's evidence on the Reference does not and cannot disturb the finding implicit in the jury's verdict, that after passing Gellatly, Truscott and Lynne went into Lawson's bush.

It is also implicit in the jury's verdict that the girl died where she was found in Lawson's bush and that she was not picked up at the intersection and subsequently brought back dead or alive by someone other than Truscott. We do not think that this conclusion could be disturbed by anything to be found in the evidence given at the trial or on this Reference.

We have described the conditions found by Dr. Penistan when he went to the scene. Dr. Petty and Dr. Camps said that they would have expected to find spermatozoic fluid at the crotch or in the blood at the crotch or on the leaves and twigs in the immediate area of the crotch if intercourse had taken place where the body was found. Dr. Simpson said that he "would certainly not regard the absence of spermatozoic fluid on the ground between the crotch area as giving any evidence that sexual intercourse of some kind did not take place where the body lay". Dr. Penistan said that the intercourse took place "while the child was dying, when the heart had stopped or had almost stopped beating". His reason for this conclusion was that although the injuries to the parts were severe, the bleeding from them was extremely small.

Dr. Petty developed a theory based upon an examination of the photographs that the body must have lain on its left side for an hour or two following death. We have quoted at length from his evidence and that of others on this subject. He found signs of blanching on the left side of the face, the left breast and the left arm from certain photographs taken after the body had been moved both at the scene and after transportation to the mortuary. These signs are not apparent from the photograph of the body lying on its back, taken at the scene before the body was turned on its side. Dr. Simpson, Dr. Helpern and Dr. Gerber all said that if the photographs did indicate some blanching, the simple explanation was to be found in the movement of the body at the scene and afterwards. The descriptions given by Dr. Penistan and Dr. Brooks of the condition of the body at the autopsy were inconsistent with the existence of any blanched areas on the face capable of demonstrating hypostasis. They were the only ones who saw the body. The others were testifying from their observation of photographs.

Dr. Penistan said that the face was dusky in colour as far down as the ligature and that this dusky colour was caused by strangulation and not by post mortem changes. This colouring was absent from the rest of the body except perhaps for the arm, where some post mortem lividity had occurred. He pointed out that this was a dependent part whereas the front of the face was not. The colour of the face was due to the fact that the blood could not escape past the ligature and not due to hypostasis, that is, a condition caused by settling of blood in the dependent parts of an organ.

Our conclusion on the evidence relating to blanching is that whatever traces suggesting this condition were observable from the photographs are to be attributed to the movement of the body in the bush, movement to the mortuary and movement in the mortuary. This evidence does not disturb our conclusion that the place of death was where the body was found.

On the subject of rigor mortis, we think that the man who actually saw the condition had an overwhelming advantage over those who were testifying from photographs. He says that the condition had almost passed off. Yet Dr. Petty testified to rigor mortis from what others described as the natural arching of the back and a natural position of the fingers which were being held by the assistant in order that a photograph could be taken. We are of the opinion that Dr. Penistan's evidence on rigor mortis must be accepted and that defence evidence on this subject tending to put the time of death at a later hour must be rejected.

On the question of the contents of the stomach and the state of digestion as indicating the time of death, there was diversity of opinion. Doctors Sharpe, Simpson, Helpern and Gerber supported Dr. Penistan's opinion that death occurred prior to 7.45 p.m. Dr. Petty, Dr. Jaffe and Dr. Camps rejected any possibility of such precise definition. We have already set out their opinions in detail earlier in these reasons. There is no need of repetition. We do, however, wish to explain that with each medical expert we chose the opinion which he expressed in his own words in examination-in-chief. We think it is better done this way because we could not see that on cross-examination any expert retracted or seriously modified what he said in chief.

We think that the evidence indicates that this was the same meal that the girl had finished eating at 5.45 p.m. We know the time of the meal. This was a normal healthy girl of 12 years and 9 months who had eaten a normal meal. There is no evidence of any complicating factor apart from an expression of annoyance because she could not go swimming.

Dr. Petty spoke of factors which might change the emptying rate of the stomach – drugs (which seems to be out of the question in this case), loss into the duodenum, loss through the esophagus during the act of dying or after death occurred. We have the definite evidence of Dr. Penistan on loss into the duodenum. He says there was very little. It is difficult to think of loss through the esophagus when one considers how this girl died. There were microscopic particles of food in the bronchii, a common occurrence in death by strangulation.

Again we say that this opinion evidence must be related to all the other evidence. We have the known facts of the meal, the time when she finished, that she was in the school grounds engaged in normal activity after the meal and before she started down the road. We have the time when she started down the road and it was not later than 7.15 p.m., not 7.30 as Truscott said. She was found 42 hours later in a bush off the road at 1.45 p.m. on Thursday, June 11, 1959. The jury's verdict must have rejected Dr. Brown's time of three or four hours after the meal because it contained no possibility of accuracy in relation to this case if they came to the conclusion that Truscott did not take the girl to the intersection.

We are faced with the same problem. No new issues were raised before us but there was a great volume of new evidence. The weight of the new evidence supports Dr. Penistan's opinion. But the decisive point in this case is still the one put to the jury by the trial judge and decided against the accused.

The Court heard 467 pages of new oral evidence on this Reference. According to firmly established rules, none of this would have been admissible had these proceedings been by way of appeal. But in view of the terms of the Order of Reference the Court decided to hear everything and did hear everything that the parties thought relevant.

Another aspect of the medical evidence related to the condition of Truscott's penis. Truscott, in his evidence before us, introduced an explanation of the condition of his penis, as described by Dr. Addison and Dr. Brooks following their examination on Friday evening, June 12, 1959, three days after the girl's disappearance. They saw the condition and described it in detail. Their opinion was that it was consistent with forcible intercourse with a girl of the age of Lynne Harper. Truscott's father was present when this examination was made. Truscott and his counsel were present in court when the evidence of the two doctors was given. There is no indication in any of the evidence that was before the jury that these injuries were the result of a pre-existing condition. On the reference, Truscott said that there was a pre-existing condition which started about six weeks before he was picked up. This is his evidence:

> A. It was about six weeks before I was picked up. And it started off, what appeared to be little blisters, and continued to worsen from there until it was in the state it was when I was picked up.
> Q. What caused it to worsen? How did its appearance change?
> A. Well, one blister would break and it just seemed that more would appear.
> Q. Do you know what caused them to break?
> A. No I don't.
> Q. Now, when you first noticed this condition that you described did you tell your father about it?
> A. No, I didn't.
> Q. Was there any reason why you didn't.
> A. I was too embarrassed.
> Q. Do you recall the first person to whom you described this condition when you first noticed it?
> A. Yes, I do.
> Q. Who was it?
> A. It was yourself and Mr. Jolliffe.
> Q. Myself and Mr. Jolliffe. And where did you describe that to us?
> A. Collin's Bay penitentiary.

We find it impossible to accept Truscott's statement that he had never described the condition of his penis, as it existed prior to June 9, 1959, to anyone before he described it at the penitentiary to his counsel on the Reference. It may be that, on his first discovering the condition he was too embarrassed to tell his father about it. But when the condition existing on June 12 was discovered by Dr. Addison and Dr. Brooks on their medical examination of him, in the presence of his father, and when those two doctors described the condition which they found at the trial, and drew inferences from it, it is incredible that no disclosure was made by him to his father and to his then counsel as to the condition which he says had existed for six weeks before he was picked up.

If the condition which Truscott described did exist for some time prior to June 9, we have the evidence of Dr. Simpson that the patches could have been rubbed, causing them to be more sore, and that this is consistent with a sexual assault. Dr. Danby and Dr. Wrong, the two expert dermatologists called by the defence on the Reference, who testified on this matter, both recognized the possible impact of irritation in activating the condition described by Truscott.

Our conclusion is that there was a pre-existing condition and that it was disclosed by him prior to his trial, although no evidence about it was given before the jury. The serious condition found and described by Dr. Addison and Dr. Brooks was consistent with the aggravation of a pre-existing condition resulting from a sexual assault upon Lynne Harper.

When the case went to the jury, they had before them the evidence given at the trial which we have summarized above. It was all circumstantial. Their verdict read in the light of the charge of the trial judge makes it clear that they were satisfied beyond a reasonable doubt that the facts, which they found to be established by the evidence which they accepted, were not only consistent with the guilt of the accused but were inconsistent with any rational conclusion other than that he was the guilty person. On a review of all the evidence given at the trial we are of opinion that, on the record as it then stood, the verdict could not be set aside on the ground that it was unreasonable or could not be supported by the evidence. Indeed, it being implicit in their verdict that the jury completely rejected the evidence of those witnesses who said that they had seen Truscott pass over the bridge with Lynne Harper, and Truscott's statements as to having seen Lynne Harper enter a motor car, we are of opinion that the verdict was in accordance with the evidence.

We are also of opinion that the judgment at trial could not have been set aside on the ground of any wrong decision on a question of law or on the ground that there was a miscarriage of justice. It follows that, in our opinion, the judgment of the Court of Appeal for Ontario dismissing the appeal made to it was right.

On this Reference we heard the additional evidence summarized above. It disclosed differences of opinion amongst the expert medical witnesses who testified. As has already been pointed out, none of this fresh evidence would have been allowed if the case had come before us on an appeal in the ordinary way under s. 597A of the *Criminal Code*. Because of the terms of the Order-in-Council referring the matter to us, we decided to receive this evidence and it becomes our duty to weigh it with a view to determining whether it causes us to doubt the correctness of the judgment at the trial. We have come to the conclusion that it does not.

There were many incredibilities inherent in the evidence given by Truscott before us and we do not believe his testimony. The effect of the sum total of the testimony of the expert witnesses is, in our opinion, to add strength to the opinion expressed by Dr. Penistan at the trial that the murdered girl was dead by 7.45 p.m. We have dealt above with the evidence which we heard as to what observation of a car at the junction of Highway No. 8 and the county road could be made from the bridge 1,300 feet to the south.

We have already stated our conclusion that the verdict of the jury reached on the record at the trial ought not to be disturbed. The effect of the fresh evidence which we heard on the Reference, considered in its entirety, is to strengthen that view.

We turn now to certain legal objections taken by counsel for the defence on the Reference. He argued that the learned trial judge should have declared a mistrial because Crown counsel, in his opening address to the jury on September 16, said in part:

> I might say then that in sequence that on Friday night – I should say the Friday a statement was taken from the accused by Inspector Graham and the other Police, one of the other Policemen, signed that night by him...

At this point he was stopped by the trial judge.

The Court of Appeal for Ontario rejected this submission on the ground that in his opening address read as a whole Crown counsel had made it clear to the jury that the statements made by Truscott to the police which he intended to introduce were not in the nature of "confessions at all or anything like that".

In our opinion there is another ground on which the submission should be rejected. In the discussion had in the absence of the jury after the learned trial judge had stopped Crown counsel from making any further reference to the statement he made it plain that if the statement, when tendered, was ruled inadmissible he would be prepared to declare a mistrial. On the afternoon of September 18, the statement was ruled inadmissible but counsel for the accused did not then or at any subsequent point in the trial ask that a mistrial be declared. We think it clear that defence counsel elected to proceed with the trial and that the verdict cannot be impugned on this ground.

Defence counsel also submitted that the trial judge erred in permitting Jocelyne Goddette and Arnold George to be sworn. The determination of this question depends on the interpretation to be placed on s. 16 of the *Canada Evidence Act* which was considered in this Court by Anglin C.J.C., in *Sankey v. The King*, where he said:

> Now it is quite as much the duty of the presiding judge to ascertain by appropriate methods whether or not a child offered as a witness does, or does not, understand the nature of an oath, as it is to satisfy himself of the intelligence of such child and his appreciation of the duty of speaking the truth. On both points alike he is required by the statute to form an opinion; as to both he is entrusted with discretion, to be exercised judicially and upon reasonable grounds. The term "child of tender years" is not defined. Of no ordinary child over seven years of age can it be safely predicted, from his mere appearance, that he does not understand the nature of an oath. Such a child may be convicted of crime. *Crim. Code,* section 17-18. A very brief inquiry may suffice to satisfy the judge on this point. But some inquiry would seem to be indispensable.

We are of opinion that the learned trial judge properly exercised the discretion entrusted to him and that there were reasonable grounds for his concluding that both Jocelyne Goddette and Arnold George understood the moral obligation of telling the truth.

The reasons of our brother Hall indicate that he would have ordered a new trial on a number of grounds. Since we feel obliged to differ from the opinion he has expressed, we think it necessary to state our view on each of the grounds dealt with in his reasons.

1. *Truscott's admonition to Jocelyne Goddette to keep the appointment secret.*

The judge's ruling on this point was favourable to Truscott. He limited the effect which the jury could give to Jocelyne Goddette's evidence on the appointment to an explanation of why she was on the road looking for Truscott.

We think the evidence had a wider relevancy. According to many witnesses, Truscott was moving about the road between 6.30 and 7 p.m. The suggested inference from this is that he was looking for Jocelyne Goddette. Then he turned up at the school grounds at 7 p.m. and talked to Lynne Harper. His explanation of the conversation was that she was looking for a ride to the intersection.

It is said that this was uncontradicted. It could not be otherwise with an unheard conversation between two persons, one of whom was dead at the time of the trial.

The conversation between Truscott and the girl is open to another interpretation. It took place only a few minutes after Truscott had been on the road looking for Jocelyne Goddette according to the Crown's submission. It was open to the Crown to put it to the jury that he was taking Lynne Harper when Jocelyne Goddette failed to appear, and taking her on the same errand.

The admonition to Jocelyne Goddette to keep the matter secret is no more a reflection on Truscott's character than the invitation itself. It is part and parcel of the same conversation and one part cannot be separated from the other. The jury was entitled to know what the whole conversation was and the witness when testifying to such a conversation should not be compelled to stop at a certain point. This was early in the trial. The girl's credibility was involved. No one knew at this stage whether Truscott would give evidence at the trial. If she had only been permitted to tell one part of the conversation, it is impossible to tell how counsel for the defence would have used that.

We do not think that any of this conversation between Truscott and Jocelyne Goddette was any reflection on Truscott's character. To put it at its worst for Truscott, it means no more than this: that he had a tentative date arranged with Jocelyne Goddette. He wanted a date with a girl that night and he took Lynne Harper when Jocelyne Goddette was not available. We have already mentioned that this has some bearing on the submission of the prosecution that his story of the ride, the sole purpose of which was to take her to the intersection, may not have been true. It does not amount to trying to prove bad character or a disposition to murder and rape.

Counsel at the trial was satisfied with this instruction given by the trial judge. He had no reason to object and there is no ground for saying that on this point there should be a new trial. Counsel on the reference did not take this objection.

Maxwell v. The Director of Public Prosecutions is no authority for the rejection of the evidence in question here. In that case, a person was charged with manslaughter as a result of the performance of an abortion. He gave evidence of his good character. He was cross-examined about a previous trial for manslaughter involving another alleged abortion. He had been acquitted at that trial. The cross-examination was held to be bad on two grounds – as not being relevant to the issue before the jury and because it did not tend to impair the credibility of the accused as a witness.

2. *The bicycle tracks.*

This has to do with the bicycle tire marks which were found in the field north of Lawson's bush. Corporal Erskine gave evidence about these tire marks which he had photographed. Defence counsel did object to the admissibility of the evidence from the photographs. The tire marks were similar to the marks that would be made by Truscott's bicycle.

Defence counsel emphasized that these tire marks were of little or no significance in the case. He dealt with the matter in the following extract:

> Then there was evidence about marks along the roadway at the north side of the bush, and Exhibits twelve, thirteen and fourteen were taken by Corporal Erskine and filed here. These exhibits showed the dried mud along the north edge of the bush in this little laneway or driveway. Now, these were taken, according to the note on the back, on the 13th of June. We heard the evidence of the Sergeant from the R.C.A.F. Station as to the rainfall. In June there had been a trace of rain on the 1st. No rain from then until either the 10th or the 11th, when it was .24 or .27 inches, about a quarter of an inch. .24, I think he said. He said if it was .25, it would be a quarter. However, it makes no difference because it was after the 9th of June, which is the important date. But we had no rain in June prior to the 9th, except a trace, and you heard Sergeant Calvert say a few drops or a little sprinkle you would walk out in without putting a coat on.
> Now I suggest to you that it is quite clear from all these pictures that these tracks were made when the mud was soft. You can see where the mud squeezed

up between the little irregularities in the tire. It must have been soft to make that mark. It couldn't possibly happen if this dirt was in the hard-packed condition that we find it in these conditions. That dirt must have been baked hard long before the 9th of June. We have the temperatures in the eighties, high temperatures, hot weather. My friend may say to you that May was a rainy month. You heard Sergeant Calvert go over the rainfall for the last sixteen days of May, and .25 or .2, so and so of rain. Very light rain. The total rain in sixteen days, something over three inches. Many of you men are farmers. You know the effect of these pictures much better than I do. You can use your own good judgment as to how long it took for that land to become parched like that, how many days before the pictures were taken the last rainfall had occurred and these tracks made there.

Immediately afterwards he pointed out that the evidence showed that Truscott had been along the tractor trail at least three times, the last one of which was about a week before the 9th of June. He and his friend were building a tree fort in the bush. Crown counsel dealt with that in the following way:

The bicycle marks, Gentlemen, I am not going to linger over. Corporal Erskine's evidence that he found tire marks, combinations of the two wheels, but they are in as Exhibits. You will have them with you. That he made comparison and that he found those marks in the laneway and you will remember the distance down. I, frankly, don't. That they compare. That they are a combination. Now, it is true there could be similar tires, certainly, but where you get radically different tires – you look at them and you will find them in combination, it would seem to be fairly strong evidence that that bicycle was down there.

But gentlemen, as I said about a circumstantial evidence case, that is the beauty – there is nothing beautiful about this at all – but that is one of the strong facts about it. You have a pile of facts and if there is one or two that are not conclusive you still, you still have the conclusive proof of the facts that are there.

A defence witness was called to say that Steven and he had a tree house or fort or something, and that Steven was in with his bicycle. I wouldn't waste your time by arguing that isn't a possibility, but I just put this forward for what it may seem to be worth for you, that that is more evidence that Steven was down that lane with that bicycle. By no means conclusive it was that night he was down. The Defence went to great efforts to counteract those marks.

That soil – or that weather expert, Calvert, Sergeant Calvert, about the dryness. Now we all know this about farms, if you get an area near a bush and there are lots of trees in that lane, and that area will stay a longer time damp. Other things might be quite dry, adjacent portions, even if you don't get any rain. There was plenty of rain in May and none in June, but there could be dampness, I suggest to you what is elementary, enough to make those marks, but that is only one of the great stack of facts that are amassing for your assistance.

The trial judge dealt with them as follows:

Nothing belonging to the accused boy was found in the locality, in the neighbourhood of the body, as you will recall. There was a tire mark in the field about seventeen feet north of the fence that ran along this lane, and Constable Erskine, who testified, said that the marks of the tire were similar, I think that is as high as he put it, were similar to the tires that were put in evidence of the bicycle belonging to the accused boy, and you are asked to find that those marks were made by this bicycle. That is what the Crown asks you to find. The bicycle is not a common one.

If the trial judge's remarks are taken in conjunction with the address of Crown counsel and the defence, there could be no doubt here that the issues were squarely before the jury, and defence counsel did not see fit to object to the charge on this point.

We cannot agree that it was conclusively shown that the tire marks must have been made many days preceding June 9th, nor that the learned trial judge should have directed the jury in the light of the evidence of the meterorologist Calvert to exclude from their consideration the evidence relating to the tire marks. It was for the jury to weigh the evidence of the tire marks in the light of the evidence given as to the weather conditions. We do not think that anyone took this evidence as a salient feature of the case. The salient feature of the case is Truscott's disappearance from the road after the meeting with Gellatly.

3. *The locket*

This was worn by Lynne Harper on the evening of June 9th. It was not found on her body but hanging on the wire fence that ran along the west side of Lawson's bush. The inference is open that whoever murdered Lynne Harper removed the locket from her neck. To do so he had to unclasp it. It was found unclasped and suspended on the wire fence. Truscott had described the locket in some detail. The evidence was properly admissible and the question was one of weight for the jury.

The matter of the locket and its significance to the jury was raised in the address to the jury of counsel for the defence. His suggestion to the jury was that the place where the locket was found was the place where the girl was taken into the bush either alive or dead. This suggestion is contained in the following extract from his address:

Now the evidence would indicate that if Lynne Harper were dragged in there, through that wire fence, that she was dragged in at a point on the County Road about three hundred feet south of the north edge of the bush. And the reason for saying that is this, that that is the point where Corporal Sayeau says the locket was found.

Now, we have this locket. Do you remember a locket was put in as an Exhibit? A locket and chain, and that the chain was delivered to Mrs. Archibald by Sandra. You remember the little girl, Sandra Archibald. When Sandra gave the locket to her mother, the mother said the chain was open, and Sandra told you how she found the locket and chain suspended partly over one wire. Part of it may have been on the ground and part of it was suspended over the wire on the fence, with the chain on the outside and the locket on the inside, or vice versa. Probably you will remember that better than I do. But that appears to be where – the point where this girl was brought, or her body entered that area. Now, I suggest if Truscott took Miss Harper in at that point, somebody would have seen it. The fence there was in much better condition than the fence on the north side. It is most unlikely that he would drag the bicycle in. If he had dragged it in there would be, in all likelihood, some mark on the bicycle.

The Crown was entitled to answer this proposition and we do not regard that answer as theorizing "without one iota of evidence", "inflammatory" or a "fanciful theory".

4. *Car bearing Licence No. 981-666*

When Truscott was asked by the police what he had seen on the road when he took Lynne Harper to the intersection as he said, he mentioned Richard Gellatly and he also said that he had seen on the road an old model Dodge or Plymouth car bearing licence No. 981-666 but that the first three digits may have been in a different order. He also said that there was a man and a woman in this car. There was such a car with licence No. 891-666 belonging to a Mr. Pigun, who was then stationed at Clinton. A number of people, including Mr. Pigun, who owned cars with licences bearing some resemblance to the number given, were called to testify and all said that they were not on the county road on the evening of June 9th. Hall J. is of opinion that the Crown was not entitled to call these witnesses because this was a collateral matter and Truscott could not be contradicted on it.

In our view, this was not a collateral matter. It was strictly relevant to the fact in issue – whether Truscott was on the road when he said he was. In effect, he said that from leaving the school grounds with Lynne Harper and until his return, that he was never off the road and that he saw a car bearing a certain licence number. The owners of all these possible cars say that they were not on the road.

The inference that the jury was asked to draw in part from this evidence and from all the other evidence is that Truscott did not see and could not have seen the car that he described; that if he had actually been on the road all the time he would not have made such a statement because he would have known better and that, in consequence, he was not where he said he was at the material time. Facts relevant to this issue are not collateral facts.

5. *The Judges' Instruction*

It will be for you to say whether you accept Doctor Penistan's theory, an Attorney-General's Pathologist of many years' standing, or do you accept Doctor Brown's evidence.

The criticism made is that the extract above quoted was a misdirection and that the jury should have been told that as between Dr. Penistan and Dr. Brown, if the evidence of Dr. Brown left a reasonable doubt in their minds as to the time of death, they must acquit. We disagree with this proposition. The choice was not simply between Dr. Brown and Dr. Penistan. That evidence had to be considered in relation to the whole of the evidence, and a reading of the trial judge's instructions in full to the jury makes it plain that that is what they were told to do.

These are the instructions that he gave to the jury, in summary, at the very end of his charge:

Now, Gentlemen, in order to arrive at a verdict in this case – before I mention that, I wish to say to you this. You will have to ask yourselves, about each branch of the evidence. Is it consistent with the boy's guilt? And is it inconsistent with any other rational conclusion? But you just can't separate one piece of evidence from the other from the rest of the evidence. You will have to ask yourselves on the whole evidence which you accept, on the whole evidence that you accept, is this evidence susceptible of any other conclusion than that this boy is the killer of Lynne Harper? But if you think any other rational conclusion possible on this evidence, you will acquit him, and if the evidence raises a doubt in your mind, you will acquit him. When I say raises a doubt in your mind, I mean a reasonable doubt. Not a foolish doubt or a doubt because you are hesitant about doing your duty, and I am sure I need not say to a Jury of the County of Huron that I know you will accept your responsibilities in this matter, come what may, and that you will bring in a verdict according to your conscience. It must not be a doubt that is raised by fear, prejudice or caprice, but an honest doubt of a Juryman endeavouring to do his duty.

In order to bring in a verdict you must all agree upon it. If you do not agree you cannot bring in a verdict – you disagree. There is no obligation on any of you to agree. If, after you have discussed it fully, and considered it dispassionately among yourselves, you should disagree with your fellows, it is your duty to

277

express your disagreement. Do not forget what I said about the onus of proof. The onus of proof is entirely on the Crown. It never shifts. There is no obligation whatever or any duty on the prisoner to prove his innocence. It is for the Crown to prove his guilt and the Crown must prove that guilt beyond a reasonable doubt. You must feel sure about it.

Now, Gentlemen, as I see this case you may bring in a verdict of course, of not guilty. The jury is always able to do that if the Crown has not proved its case or you have even a reasonable doubt about it. You may bring in a verdict of not guilty or you may bring in a verdict of guilty as charged. There is no other verdict open to you in this case on this evidence.

6. *Dr. Brooks should not have been permitted to give his opinion that the sores on Truscott's penis and the condition of the body at the scene indicated a very inexpert attempt at penetration.*

Dr. Brooks graduated in medicine in England in 1943. He was registered to practise in England in 1946. He is a member of the College of General Practitioners in Canada. He was the Senior Medical Officer at the R.C.A.F. Station at Clinton, Ontario.

He saw these penial lesions. He had an opinion as to their cause. He thought they were about three days old. He also had an opinion about the injuries to the girl which he had seen in the bush and in the mortuary.

We are of the view that a general practitioner with this experience is entitled to give his opinion to the jury as to the cause of the conditions that he found, whether it is a physical cause or any other cause. This kind of evidence is not limited to specialists. *Regina v. Kuzmack* does not state any such rule.

In *Regina v. Kuzmack,* the accused was convicted of murder. It was alleged that he had stabbed a woman and severed her jugular vein. His defence was that the death was an accident. He said that the woman attacked him with a butcher knife and that she was killed accidentally when he was trying to take the knife away from her. The woman also had cuts on the fingers of the right hand. The doctor who testified as to the cause of death also said that when the right hand was put up to the neck, the wounds on the fingers were in the same direction as the wound on the neck. His conclusion was that the hand was on the neck when the knife was put into the neck. His conclusion was rejected by the Appellate Division as "a mere guess which anyone might have made".

278

Whether or not this was a correct ruling in the particular case is of no concern now. But the ruling is not authority for rejecting the opinion of a general practitioner as to the cause of lesions which he had personally observed and described.

7. *Admissibility of the underpants as evidence.*

These were the garments that Truscott was wearing at the time of his arrest and were taken from him then. They were very dirty and showed traces of blood and male sperm. It was open to the jury to infer that these were the underpants that Truscott was wearing on June 9 and to decide whether the traces of blood and male sperm had any significance in the case. The trial judge cannot withdraw consideration of such evidence from the jury.

8. *Extracts from the instructions given to the jury in relation to the evidence of Philip Burns.*

It is said that the trial judge gave contradictory instructions regarding the evidence of Philip Burns, and the following extracts are cited in support of this conclusion:

Now the first is that Philip Burns was, of course, not sworn, and he said he didn't see Lynne and Steve on the road as he went north, and no one corroborates him in that respect, so that his evidence is worthless so far as you can use it in convicting the accused boy.

* * *

Then you, of course, won't forget Philip Burns' evidence that he left the river around between seven to seven-ten or thereabouts, seven-fifteen, and walked up the road and saw nothing of Steve and Lynne as he went up the road. That evidence was given, as I told you before, without Philip Burns being sworn.

We do not interpret the first extract, when read in context, as being a direction to the jury that Burns' evidence was worthless. The jury had been recalled as a result of objections raised by counsel to the charge, and in the first sentence of that extract the trial judge is only stating what that objection was, and not his own ruling upon it. This is made clear by the next three following sentences:

But you could hardly corroborate a statement that I didn't see somebody. You may corroborate that he wasn't on the road, and I expect that is what Philip meant, that Steve and Lynne weren't on the road as he passed along it.

Now, of course, he met Jocelyne and he met Arnold George as he went along that road, and they were sworn, and they said that they didn't see Lynne or Steve on that highway, so in that respect their evidence is capable of corroborating Philip's.

In our opinion this instruction was correct.

9. *Direction regarding the evidence of Douglas Oats and Gordon Logan.*

The learned trial judge dealt with the effect of the evidence of these two boys in the following passage from his charge:

Now then, it is the theory of the Defence, and they brought evidence to show that, as I say, this little Douglas Oats saw them going across the bridge and then, in a few minutes, according to the boy by the name of Gordon Logan – Gordon Logan also says he saw them going north on the bridge and in about five minutes he says he saw Steven return alone. Well, as regards Gordon Logan, it will be for you Gentlemen to say whether you believe his evidence, and it is very important, Gentlemen, because if you believe the Defence theory of this matter and believe Steven's statement to the Police and to other people, that the girl was driven to Number Eight Highway and entered an automobile which went east; it is my view that you must acquit the boy if you believe that story.

In other words, I will put it this way. In order to convict this boy, you have to completely reject that story as having no truth in it, as not being true. You have to completely reject that story.

In our opinion this was a clear-cut, positive direction to the jury as to the impact of the evidence of Oats and Logan, if accepted by the jury, and there is a positive direction to acquit if Truscott's story, supported as it was by that evidence, were believed. The jury is not directed that they could only acquit if they believed that story, but that, if they believed it, they must acquit. The continuing onus upon the Crown to prove its case beyond reasonable doubt, and the absence of any obligation upon the accused to prove his innocence was clearly stated on more than one occasion, as shown in the extract from the charge previously quoted.

What this particular passage does, and quite properly does, is to make clear to the jury the vital importance of the evidence of Oats and Logan, and to stress that they could not convict Truscott unless his account of what happened was completely rejected as having no truth in it.

10. *Reference as to the possibility of Truscott having returned with Lynne Harper from No. 8 Highway.*

In charging the jury the trial judge had two undisputed facts from which to start. First, that Truscott had ridden Lynne Harper on his bicycle north on the country road toward No. 8 Highway. Second, that her raped and dead body was found in Lawson's bush, and that, in consequence of that, someone had brought her there, alive or dead. The Crown's case was that Truscott had taken her there, and that he had never taken her to No. 8 Highway. The case for the defence was that Truscott had left her at that highway, and had returned alone, she having been picked up in a car at the highway, and that some unknown person had brought her back to Lawson's bush. The trial judge apparently felt obligated to discuss all possibilities and suggested the possibility of her having been brought back from No. 8 Highway by Truscott.

In our opinion this was unnecessary, but when he finally dealt with the matter, in answer to a request by the jury for further direction of evidence, corroborated or otherwise, of Lynne Harper and Steven Truscott having been seen together on the bridge on the night of June 9, he made it abundantly clear that there was no witness who said that he had returned to the bridge with her, and that there were two witnesses, Allan Oats and Logan, who said he was on the bridge alone.

We cannot agree that the effect of the judge's direction on this point withdrew from the jury the most vital issue in Truscott's case. It was quite clear from the charge that the jury could not convict Truscott if they accepted Logan's evidence.

11. *Reference to Truscott's "calmness and apathy".*

In his charge the trial judge put the question "You will ask yourselves and you will ask yourselves the reason if this boy is guilty, why he has shown such calmness and apathy."

Counsel for the defence had urged that Truscott's demeanour and attitude, when he returned to the school yard and was seen there by a number of children, was completely inconsistent with guilt, and in putting this question to the jury the trial judge sought to raise this issue in their minds.

What he meant is clearly illustrated in his original charge, when he said "It is pointed out by the Defence, and very properly so,

281

and it is something you must consider, and that is his demeanour when he returned, that he seemed to be natural."

He then cited the evidence of three children who had seen him at the school yard, who described his appearance as "normal."

From time to time in the course of these reasons we have mentioned the fact that defence counsel took no objection to certain rulings made by the trial judge, certain evidence that was introduced to which objection is now taken and certain comments of the trial judge and Crown counsel made in the course of the proceedings. It should be clearly understood that it is not suggested that the failure of defence counsel to object to the admissibility of evidence or to any part of the trial judge's charge or to any comments by the judge or counsel in the course of the proceedings constitutes an answer to any valid objections now made to the conduct of the trial. The failure of defence counsel to make such objections is only mentioned in these reasons for the purpose of indicating that counsel who acted on Truscott's behalf do not appear to have attached any importance or validity to the objections in question.

Answer to the question submitted on the Reference

For all of the foregoing reasons our answer to the question submitted is that had an appeal by Steven Murray Truscott been made to the Supreme Court of Canada, as is now permitted by section 597A of the *Criminal Code* of Canada, on the existing record and the further evidence this Court would have dismissed such an appeal.

HALL J. (*dissenting*): – Steven Murray Truscott, then age 14½ years, was tried before the Honorouble Mr. Justice Ferguson and a jury at Goderich in September 1959 on an indictment as follows:

> The Jurors for Our Lady The Queen present that Steven Murray Truscott on or about the 9th day of June, 1959, at the Township of Tuckersmith, in the County of Huron, did unlawfully murder Lynne Harper, contrary to The Criminal Code of Canada.

On the 30th day of September 1959 the jury returned a verdict of guilty with a recommendation for mercy. An appeal to the Court of Appeal for Ontario by Steven Murray Truscott against

SUPREME COURT OF CANADA

his conviction was dismissed on the 21st day of January 1960. By Order-in-Council P.C., 1960-87, dated the 21st day of January 1960, the sentence of death passed upon Steven Murray Truscott upon his conviction on the indictment aforesaid was commuted to a term of life imprisonment in the Kingston Penitentiary. Application for leave to appeal to this Court from the judgment of the Court of Appeal for Ontario was refused on the 24th day of February 1960.

Section 597A of the *Criminal Code* was enacted in 1961, providing as follows:

597A. Notwithstanding any other provision of this Act, a person

(*a*) who has been sentenced to death and whose conviction is affirmed by the court of appeal, or

(*b*) who is acquitted of an offence punishable by death and whose acquittal is set aside by the court of appeal,

may appeal to the Supreme Court of Canada on any ground of law or fact or mixed law and fact. 1960-61, c. 44, s. 11.

By Order-in-Council P.C. 1966-760, dated the 26th day of April 1966, pursuant to s. 55 of the *Supreme Court Act*, His Excellency The Governor General referred to the Supreme Court of Canada for hearing and consideration the following question:

Had an Appeal by Steven Murray Truscott been made to the Supreme Court of Canada, as is now permitted by section 597A of the Criminal Code of Canada, what disposition would the Court have made of such an Appeal on a consideration of the existing Record and such further evidence as the Court, in its discretion, may receive and consider?

When the application was made in February 1960 for leave to appeal to this Court from the Court of Appeal of Ontario, s. 597A had not yet been enacted. The application so made was under s. 597(1)(*b*) which provided that an appeal lay by leave to the Supreme Court on a question of law alone. The application then made was restricted to the following grounds:

1. Was there any evidence of such a character that the inference of guilt of the Appellant might, and could, legally and properly be drawn therefrom by the jury?

2. Was the Appellant deprived of a trial according to law by the remarks made by Crown Counsel in his opening to the jury?

3. Did the learned trial Judge err in allowing the Crown witnesses, Jocelyne Goddette, Anold George, and Tom Gillette to be sworn?

4. Did the learned trial Judge err in failing to properly define corroboration for the jury?

5. Did the learned trial Judge err in instructing the jury that certain unsworn witnesses were in fact corroborated?

6. Did the learned trial Judge err in his charge to the jury in regard to the doctrine of reasonable doubt?

On the reference in this Court, the substantial grounds upon which the trial and conviction were challenged were materially different from the foregoing although there were included some elements of the same grounds, but essentially this is a completely new procedure and the Court must now deal with law and fact and with questions of mixed law and fact. Much new evidence was heard in these proceedings under the authority of the Order-in-Council and the accused himself testified for the first time. He maintained his innocence as he had done since his conviction in 1959.

Having considered the case fully, I believe that the conviction should be quashed and a new trial directed. I take the view that the trial was not conducted according to law. Even the guiltiest criminal must be tried according to law. That does not mean that I consider Truscott guilty or innocent. The determination of guilt or innocence was a matter for the jury and for the jury alone as its dominant function following a trial conducted according to law.

The case against Truscott was predominantly but not exclusively one of circumstantial evidence. I recognize fully that guilt can be brought home to an accused by circumstantial evidence; that there are cases where the circumstances can be said to point inexorably to guilt more reliably than direct evidence; that direct evidence is subject to the everyday hazards of imperfect recognition or of imperfect memory or both. The circumstantial evidence case is built piece by piece until the final evidentiary structure completely entraps the prisoner in a situation from which he cannot escape. There may be missing from the structure a piece here and there and certain imperfections may be discernible, but the entrapping mesh taken as a whole must be continuous and consistent. The law does not require that the guilt of an accused be established to a demonstration but is satisfied when the evidence presented to the jury points conclusively to the accused as the perpetrator of the crime and excludes any reasonable hypothesis of innocence. The rules of evidence apply with equal force to proof by circumstantial evidence as to proof by direct evidence. The evidence in both instances must be equally credible, admissible and relevant.

Applying the foregoing to the trial under review, I find that there were grave errors in the trial brought about principally by Crown Counsel's method in trying to establish guilt and by the learned Trial Judge's failure to appreciate that the course being followed by the Crown would necessarily involve the jury being led away from an objective appraisal of the evidence for and against the prisoner. The Crown approached the prosecution on the theory or hypothesis that young Truscott had planned to take Jocelyne Goddette into Lawson's bush to have some improper relations with her and when she failed to show he was so intent on taking some girl to Lawson's bush that evening that when Lynne Harper came to him in the school yard he seized upon this accidental meeting to persuade her to go with him and to her death. This approach is borne out (1) by Crown Counsel's statement in his opening address to the jury as follows:

> I should deal with the accused, who is in the same grade, although older than the deceased girl, and at the same school. He was, at the time, and still is, the son of a Warrant Officer who also lives in the Married Quarters on the Station. Now, in considering the movements of this accused relative to the crime, you will hear from one, who may be a very important witness in your estimation, Jocelyne Goddette. She is a girl from the same grade, and she will tell you of arrangements she made with Steven Truscott at school on the Monday and the Tuesday before, in or near this same bush where this body was found, to look for a certain purpose she will outline. You will hear that better from her lips as to their arrangement together to go to this bush, and that was at, let us say in the area of six o'clock, roughly. *You will hear better the times from her and certain things said by way of caution of bringing anyone or telling anyone.*

(The italics are mine.)

and (2) by the questions put to Jocelyne Goddette which stressed the secrecy of the original arrangement with Jocelyne for the two to meet at about six o'clock on the county road near the bush area. The evidence given by Jocelyne Goddette as to her arrangement to meet with Truscott was as follows:

> Q. And on Monday, June 8th, Jocelyne, did you have a conversation with Steven Truscott?
> A. Yes, sir.
> Q. Will you tell what that conversation was, please?
> A. Well, on Sunday, I had gone to Bob Lawson's barn and I had seen a calf

there. I mentioned that to Steve on Monday, and he asked me if I wanted to see two more newborn calves... And I said: "Yes". And he asked me if I could make it on Monday and I said: "No", because I had to go to Guides.

MR. HAYS:

Q. Make what?
A. If I could go with him to see the calves and I said: "No".

Q. Where were you to go with him?
A. Well, he didn't tell me on Monday.

Q. Well, go ahead?
A. And then he asked me if I could make it on Tuesday and I said I would try. And then on Tuesday, he told me if I could go and I just told him I didn't know, and he said to meet him, if I could go, on the right-hand side of the County Road, just outside of the fence by the woods, *and he kept on telling me not to tell anybody because Bob didn't like a whole bunch of kids on his property.*

(The italics are mine.)

Q. Now, that is on Tuesday, June 9th, is it, that that conversation is, Jocelyne?
A. Yes, sir.

Q. And when were you to go?
A. Well, at six o'clock.

Q. On Tuesday?
A. Yes, sir.

Q. And where – did you see Steven later after school?
A. Yes, sir. He came to my house at ten before six and I didn't answer the door, my brother did, and Steven asked me if we had any homework and I said we had English for our English test on Wednesday, and when he was just getting on his bike to go away, I told him I didn't think I would be able to make it because we were just starting supper, but that I would try.

This evidence was admissible and relevant to establish why Jocelyne said she was looking for Truscott that evening excepting possibly the words I have put in italics, but reading as it does the phrase was rather innocuous because it gives the reason for keeping quiet, and with nothing more the learned judge could have told the jury to ignore it. Even a failure to do this would not have been serious. However, after some intervening questions and answers the subject was deliberately reopened and the following question was put to Jocelyne by Crown Counsel and an answer solicited which emphasized the secret aspect of the proposed meeting of these two teen-agers:

Q. Was there any more conversation between you then, on Tuesday?

286

A. Well, he just kept on telling me to "don't tell anybody to come with you", and that is all.

and this was magnified by the learned judge who, following this question and answer, said:

HIS LORDSHIP:

Q. Say that again. He just kept on telling me what?
A. Not to tell anybody.

This was when the damage was done. These last two answers were wholly inadmissible. In dealing with this particular item, the majority opinion says:

The admonition to Jocelyne Goddette to keep the matter secret is no more a reflection on Truscott's character than the invitation itself. It is part and parcel of the same conversation and one part cannot be separated from the other. The jury is entitled to know what the whole conversation was and the witness when testifying to such a conversation should not be compelled to stop at a certain point.

That observation is only partly correct in that it is incomplete. It expresses the ordinary rule but that rule is subject to a number of exceptions. It is often the duty of counsel to forewarn a witness not to volunteer or blurt out as part of the narrative in an answer evidence that while part of that narrative is inadmissible as, for instance, references to confessions or admissions made by an accused or evidence of bad character and many others. It is not a case of volunteering or blurting out that is being dealt with here but a conscious and deliberate drawing from the witness evidence that was bound to be prejudicial and as an integral part of establishing the Crown's theory that Truscott was planning harm to Jocelyne Goddette.

The evidence had no probative value to prove Truscott murdered Lynne Harper and should have been rejected when tendered by the rule which excludes evidence of similar acts which Viscount Sankey said in *Maxwell v. Director of Public Prosecutions* was "one of the most deeply rooted and jealously guarded principles of our Criminal Law". Having thus laid this foundation, Crown Counsel elaborated the theory and put it forward as proof of Truscott's guilt in his summation to the jury saying:

Now, there is substantial support for Jocelyne's evidence that she went looking for Steven, and support for her evidence of these conversations. She went on

287

to tell how she couldn't go with him on Monday night. Well then, there was a tentative date for six o'clock on the Tuesday night. And that he, Steven, came to the house and called for her. He called there at ten minutes to six but she was having her supper, *and I suggest to you, Gentlemen, that if they were late having their supper, it was a God's blessing to that girl.*

(The italics are mine.)

* * *

Here is the relevancy of that, Gentlemen. He missed his first prospect and what more logical and likely person to accept his proposal to go with him on short notice than a girl he knows is fond of him, soft on him, whatever you will, and likely to take up his invitation?

Now, we are told–again we come back to Mrs. Nickerson and Mrs. Bohonus. They talked and she sat on the bicycle tire and they went–I suggest that they then went down to the bush. I suggest that is a reasonable inference, that Steven gave Lynne the new-born calf invitation that he had previously extended to Jocelyne, and that he gave her that, either at the school or as they rode–walked or rode, and if it wouldn't sound like a good proposition to an adult or to some girls, older girls, other girls, we must remember, it was coming from a boy that she liked. She was fond of. That she would want to be with. And, unfortunately, that may have removed what would otherwise be a little caution. And also, there was evidence that Lynne was interested in ponies, at least, and had gone to this house on the highway, to see ponies. I don't think, Gentlemen, I am asking you to make too much of a deduction but what she would be very likely to fall for the lure of the new-born calves coming from Steven, *and that she went with him to the bush and to her doom.*

(The italics are mine.)

There was no evidence of the conversation between Truscott and Lynne in the school yard or as they left together excepting Truscott's statement to the police that Lynne had asked him for a ride to No. 8 Highway which from the nature of things was uncontradicted. There was no suggestion in the evidence of those who saw Truscott and Lynne together in the school yard from which it could be inferred that Truscott was trying to induce or persuade Lynne to go anywhere with him. Mrs. Bohonus said it was Lynne who appeared to her to be doing the talking.

The learned judge in his charge to the jury recognized the impropriety of this prejudicial and inflammatory appeal but too late to undo the harm as I shall discuss later. Notwithstanding what the learned judge said in this regard, it is significant to note that at pp. 54 and 55 of the Crown's factum on this reference is to be found:

It is submitted that the following inference may be properly drawn from the evidence adduced at the trial and from that evidence supplemented by the evidence on the Reference:

> (1) *Truscott was bent on taking a girl into Lawson's Wood on June 9th.* His expressed purpose was to look for new-born calves, but this was coloured by his desire for secrecy;

(The italics are mine.)

The majority opinion also says:

> We do not think that any of this conversation between Truscott and Jocelyne Goddette was any reflection on Truscott's character. To put it at its worst for Truscott it means no more than this: that he had a tentative date arranged with Jocelyne Goddette. He wanted a date with a girl that night and he took Lynne Harper when Jocelyne Goddette was not available. We have already mentioned that this has some bearing on the submission of the prosecution that his story of the ride, the sole purpose of which was to take her to the intersection, may not have been true. It does not amount to trying to prove bad character or a disposition to murder and rape.

This appears to ignore the reality of the situation when considered in the actual setting as it was being developed at the trial by Crown Counsel and entirely repugnant to what Crown Counsel said in the extracts from his summation to the jury quoted above when he said, referring to Truscott having called for Jocelyne Goddette *"and I suggest to you, Gentlemen, that if they were late having their supper, it was a God's blessing to that girl"*, and when he followed that with his reference to Lynne Harper and said that Truscott gave Lynne the new-born calf invitation and *"that she went with him to the bush and to her doom"*.

The majority opinion rightly points out that the facts in *Maxwell v. Director of Public Prosecutions* differ materially from those of the case at bar. It was not the factual situation that Viscount Sankey was dealing with in the extract that I have quoted. He was stating a long established principle applicable to many factual situations. *Maxwell's* case was an obvious if not a flagrant violation of the principle. Violations can and do occur in less obvious instances. The present case is one of those. Crown Counsel was pursuing a planned course of action that included the subtle perverting of the jury to the idea that Truscott was sex hungry that Tuesday evening and determined to have a girl in Lawson's bush to satisfy his desires, if not Jocelyne, then Lynne.

It was inevitable that this horrible crime would arouse the indignation of the whole community. It was inevitable too that suspicion should fall on Truscott, the last person known to have been seen with Lynne in the general vicinity of the place where her body was found. The law has formulated certain principles and safeguards to be applied in the trial of a person accused of a crime and has throughout the centuries insisted on these principles and safeguards being observed. In the great majority of cases adherence to these fundamentals is not difficult but in a case like the present one, when passions are aroused and the Court is dealing with a crime which cries out for vengeance, then comes the time of testing. It is especially at such a time that the judicial machinery must function objectively, devoid of inflammatory appeals, with the scales of justice held in balance.

This standard was not lived up to in the trial under review in a number of instances which one by one were damaging to Truscott and taken collectively vitiated the trial. Nothing that transpired on the hearing in this Court or any evidence tendered here can be used to give validity to what was an invalid trial. A bad trial remains a bad trial. The only remedy for a bad trial is a new trial. Accordingly, the validity of the trial is, in my view, the dominant issue. With deference to contrary opinion, I see no purpose in erecting a massive and detailed structure of evidence, inference and argument confirming a verdict that has no lawful foundation upon which to rest.

It was the Crown's theory at the trial that Truscott took Lynne into Lawson's bush by way of the tractor trail, having carried her on the handle bar of his bicycle to a point on the tractor trail some 350 feet east of the county road and then induced her to enter the bush through the fence, concealing his bicycle nearby. It must be observed in passing that at the hearing in this Court Mr. Bowman, of Counsel for the Crown, advanced the theory that Truscott took Lynne into the bush from the county road at or near the point where the locket was later found hanging on the fence. Crown Counsel at the trial had an altogether different theory which he put forward concerning this locket – but I shall revert to this later.

At the trial the Crown led evidence to show that Truscott entered the tractor trail with Lynne. This was evidence by Corpo-

*

290

ral Erskine, the very first witness called by the Crown, that on the 13th day of June (two days after Lynne's body was found) he observed and photographed certain bicycle tire marks which corresponded with the tread on the tires of Truscott's bicycle. Defence Council objected to the photograph (Exhibit 13) being received, but was overruled by the learned judge who said regarding the photograph:

> Mr. Hays seems to think it has something to do with the case. I don't think I can rule it out on the grounds you put forward.

This Exhibit 13 shows conclusively that the tire marks photographed by Corporal Erskine must have been made many days preceding June 9th. The marks were made when the soil in which they were imprinted was wet and there had been no rain in the area, with the exception of a trace in the night of May 31st-June 1st and that throughout the period June 1st to June 9th the temperature had been in the high 80's and low 90's. Perhaps the best way to illustrate the impossibility of these tire marks having been made on June 9th is to reproduce Exhibit 13 showing the parched terrain with the wide cracks in the surface. Here is a reproduction of Exhibit 13:

Notwithstanding that the evidence completely negatived the use of these tire marks as evidence implicating Truscott on June 9th, Crown Counsel argued to the jury in his summation as follows:

> The bicycle marks, Gentlemen, I am not going to linger over. Corporal Erskine's evidence that he found tire marks, combinations of the two wheels, but they are in as Exhibits. You will have them with you. That he made comparison and that he found those marks in the laneway and you will remember the distance down. I, frankly, don't. That they compare. That they are a combination. Now it is true there could be similar tires, certainly, but where you get radically different tires – you look at them and you will find them in combination, it would seem to be fairly strong evidence that that bicycle was down there.
>
> But, Gentlemen, as I said about a circumstantial evidence case, that is the beauty – there is nothing beautiful about this at all, but that is one of the strong facts about it. You have a pile of facts and if there is one or two that are not conclusive you still, you still have the conclusive proof of the facts that are there.

The learned judge should have charged the jury in the light of the evidence of the meteorologist Calvert and with Exhibit 13 before him that they must exclude from their consideration the evidence relating to these bicycle tire marks. This he failed to do, but instead, and in my opinion wrongly, left the jury to understand that they could use that evidence as part of the proof against Truscott that he had ridden Lynne along that tractor trail the night she disappeared. He said:

> Nothing belonging to the accused boy was found in the locality, in the neighbourhood of the body, as you will recall. There was a tire mark in the field about seventeen feet north of the fence that ran along this lane, and Constable Erskine, who testified, said that the marks of the tire were similar, I think that is as high as he put it, were similar to the tires that were put in evidence of the bicycle belonging to the accused boy, and you are asked to find that those marks were made by this bicycle. That is what the Crown asks you to find. *The bicycle is not a common one.*

(The italics are mine.)

That was misdirection on a salient feature of the evidence for it was part and parcel of the Crown's case at the trial that Truscott took Lynne into the bush from the tractor trail and that he had hidden his bicycle so well that it was not seen by Jocelyne Goddette when, as she says, she went along the tractor trail looking for Truscott and calling his name. This presupposes that Truscott had the foresight to anticipate that Jocelyne would come along the tractor trail looking for him and to conceal his bicycle against that eventuality; a theory that attributed to Truscott a carefully planned design to harm Lynne and escape detection.

The majority opinion, in dealing with the matter of the bicycle tire marks, says: "We do not think that anyone took this evidence (the tire marks) as a salient feature of the case." I find it difficult to see how this statement can be substantiated. Who knows what the jury considered salient? This evidence was regarded as sufficiently important by Crown Counsel as to insist that it be received.

I referred earlier to Mr. Bowman's theory that Truscott took Lynne into the bush from the county road at or near the place where Lynne's locket was found on the fence. In his argument to this Court, Mr. Bowman said:

> My submission was, my lord, that they disappeared from the county road, and my submission was that it might be reasonably inferred that they went into the wood, and that they got into the wood through the barbed wire along the county road. It was broken down in two or three places, and the locket was found there, which could have some significance. They could have gone in anywhere, my lord, but I submit that there is one possible way. Whether or not that is what the jury accepted I cannot say.

However, at the trial, in dealing with this locket, Crown Counsel put forward a more sinister theory which, if accepted by the jury as Crown Counsel intended it should be, made the 14½ year old Truscott out to be a cunning criminal who, having taken the locket from Lynne when he strangled her, *later and before he was taken into custody planted the locket where it was found to mislead the police* and to lay the foundation for a defence to be used later if necessary that Lynne was murdered elsewhere and then brought to where she was found. He said to the jury:

> Now, the Defence has raised the matter of a locket. And do you recall Steven's statement to Constable Hobbs and Corporal Wheelhouse – maybe it is Sergeant Wheelhouse on Thursday. He was interviewed by Hobbs and another officer, Johnson, I believe on Wednesday. And then when Hobbs went back on the Thursday, he said: "Have you anything to add?" "Yes, she was wearing a necklace like a gold chain and heart, possibly plastic." I am not sure whether one or the other officer put in the word "Plastic".
> "With an Air Force Crest embedded in it." Mark you, not on it, but in it, and sure enough, it is in it, not on it, but in it.
> Now, I ask you, Gentlemen, is that not an awful lot of details for this boy to have observed about this locket, if it is Lynne's, as he would ride along the road with her. Would he be able to give such a minute description of it as that, if that is all the chance he had to observe it? Now, Gentlemen, the Defence introduced this matter of the locket on the basis that it was found on the west – on a wire of the fence on the west side of the bush along the County Road. And the theory is,

I take it, from what my learned friend said yesterday, that in some way she was murdered elsewhere, brought back and dragged through the fence and this pulled off and stuck on the fence.

* * *

I have a theory, Gentlemen, to put forward only for your consideration, and that is this: that her attacker removed that locket, undid the fastener when the girl was dead, and he couldn't have got it off any other way, it is just too small to go over her head. And he took it off and took it with him and studied the detail after that he could never have studied in the interval of time that she was on the bicycle, to have found that that crest was embedded in the locket. It is only theory, Gentlemen. Reason it out for yourselves. And then if you deduce it that way, ask yourselves the possible identity of anyone who would take a souvenir away from a body like this. Who would want to take it away? Would it be someone rather young? Would an older man ever be bothered with it? You may have difficulty reasoning out the "why". But ask yourselves this, if it were taken, studied out so that these details could be given, *could it have been taken back and planted, so to speak, where it was found?* And what is the point of that? Remember, there is Wednesday, Thursday, Friday, before the accused is arrested, but the investigation is on.

(The italics are mine.)

The learned judge permitted Crown Counsel to so theorize to the jury without one iota of evidence to support the theory that Truscott under suspicion as he then was had the cunning to *plant* the locket where it was found – a theory that was prejudicial and inflammatory. This was error in a material aspect.

Now, what was the evidence regarding this locket? First, it was not actually identified as the one Lynne was wearing on June 9th. Lynne's father, F/O L. B. Harper, refused to say the locket produced in Court was Lynne's, saying only that Lynne had one similar to it. Mrs. Harper said she did not know whether Lynne was wearing her locket or not that evening and when shown the locket she said, "I couldn't say certainly. It looks like it. It was very similar." The locket produced in evidence was said to have been found by a ten year old girl, Sandra Archibald. Her unsworn evidence was as follows:

Q. Sandra, when you were out picking berries, did you find something valuable?
A. Yes.
Q. Where did you find it, Sandra?
A. I found it near the woods where Lynne was found.
Q. Could you say just where it was?
A. I can't remember.
Q. What did you find, Sandra?

A. I found a locket, like a necklace.

Q. Pardon?

A. I found a heart-shaped necklace.

Q. A heart-shaped necklace?

A. Yes.

Q. Could you describe it? Tell us about it a little more?

A. It was whitish and had this Air Force thing inside, and when I found it, it was open.

Q. What was open, Sandra?

A. The chain that you put around your neck.

Q. And where was it, Sandra?

A. Well, the chain, it was hanging on the fence and it was inside, in some grass and the heart was outside.

Her evidence as to finding the locket was not corroborated. Having found it, she said she took it home and gave it to her mother the same day. The mother, Mrs. Aida Archibald, testified as follows:

Q. Are you the mother of Sandra Archibald, who testified here yesterday, Mrs. Archibald?

A. Yes sir.

Q. And I produce to you a locket which is Exhibit twenty-three in this matter. Would you look at it, Mrs. Archibald. Did that come into your possession at any time?

A. Yes sir.

Q. At what time?

A. Around ten to five on June the 19th.

Q. From what source?

A. From my daughter. She picked it up.

Q. That is Sandra, who testified?

A. Yes sir.

Q. And what did you do with it?

A. Well, at the time I didn't know what to do.

Q. What did you do?

A. And some of the kids...

Q. Never mind what anybody said. What did you do?

A. I turned it over to two S.P.'s.

Q. Who was that?

A. Sergeant Johnson and Mr. Wheelhouse.

Q. At the time your girl gave it to you, was the clasp open or closed?

A. It was open, sir.

Q. When you turned it over it was in the way you got it?

A. I put it in a Kleenex, sir.

Truscott had told Constable Hobbs on June 11th that Lynne was wearing a gold chain necklace with an R.C.A.F. crest in it when giving the ride to Lynne on his bicycle. It was from this evidence that Crown Counsel was permitted to dramatize the locket incident into a formal submission that it was *planted* where it was found by Truscott to mislead the police.

It was not the only fanciful theory put forward by the Crown to the jury to prejudice Truscott without any supporting evidence. Evidence was led that Truscott told police officers Wheelhouse and Hobbs on the Thursday that he had seen an old model Dodge or Plymouth car somewhere on the county road on the evening of June 9th bearing Licence No. 981,666. The Crown called a witness from the Department of Transport, one Saunders, to show that Licence No. 981,666 was registered to one Thompson of Brampton. Thomson, on being called, said he was not near Clinton at all that evening. Saunders testified that Licence No. 189,666 was registered to one Vasil of Toronto and was for a 1957 Pontiac four door; that Licence No. 198,666 was issued to one Mika of Scarborough for a 1955 Buick; No. 819,666 was in the name of McLaren of Drumbo and was for a 1957 Oldsmobile hard top. Then as to No. 918,666 registered to a Miss Wilkins of Kitchener for a 1949 Plymouth. Miss Wilkins was called and said her car was never out of the Kitchener area; finally as to No. 891,666, a Mr. Pigun then on the R.C.A.F. Station at Clinton was called to establish that his car, a 1949 Chevrolet Sedan, was not on the county road on the evening of June 10th. Now all this evidence was, in my opinion, inadmissible. Truscott had not volunteered having seen a car with Licence No. 981,666 in proof of having taken Lynne to No. Eight Highway. He does not suggest that he met that car north of the tractor trail. His statement in this regard as given by Constable Hobbs is as follows:

Q. What was the next you saw of Steven Truscott?
A. I next saw Steven Truscott at the school at the R.C.A.F. Station, Clinton. It was the following morning. Thursday, June the 11th, 1959. I was accompanied by Sergeant Wheelhouse of the R.C.A.F. Police. We went into the school and inquired of Mr. Trott, the teacher, if we could have a room in which to question various children regarding the missing girl, with hopes of finding some information as to where she might be. I started off by having Steven brought into the room and I asked him if there was anything further he could add to our conversation of the date previous. He said: "Yes, she was wearing a gold chain necklace that had a heart with an R.C.A.F. crest in it." I asked him if he had seen anyone else while he was giving the ride to Lynne on his bicycle. *He replied that he*

had seen Richard Gellatly. I asked him if he saw any other vehicles, motorcycles or motorcars during this ride. He replied that he had seen an old grey Plymouth or Dodge. I asked him if he could remember the occupants. He said: "A man and a lady." I said: "By any chance, Steven, can you remember the licence number of the car?" He said: "Yes, it was 8..." pardon me. "It was 981,666." I asked him if he saw anyone else. He replied that on the way down he had waved to Arnold George, who was swimming in the river. I asked him again to repeat the licence of this old grey Plymouth or Dodge and he did, without hesitation. He said: "981,666." I asked him what he did after watching the others swimming at the river. He replied that he cycled back up the County Road. I asked him a third time to repeat the number of this motorcar, this old grey Plymouth or Dodge, and without hesitation again, he gave me the number 981,666. Our conversation ended and I went to a telephone to get a registration check on this licence number.

(The italics are mine.)

The majority opinion says in connection with this item: "In our view, this was not a collateral matter. It was strictly relevant to the fact in issue – whether Truscott was on the road (the County road) when he said he was." The fact is Truscott never suggested that he was not on the County road. He told police he carried Lynne northward on that road and on the Crown's theory he carried her 3,366 feet before he reached the tractor trail – well over half a mile. It was at this time that he met Richard Gellatly and on being further questioned told of having seen the car with Licence No. 981666. No suggestion here that he was saying he saw that car north of the tractor trail. If there is one fact upon which Crown and Defence and all Counsel were in agreement it is that Truscott carried Lynne on his bicycle from the south end of the County road to a point at least as far north as Lawson's bush. The statement regarding this car was accordingly a collateral matter. Evidence in contradiction of it was therefore inadmissible; it was tendered as Crown Counsel said:

Now, this is only on the question of credibility. There is nothing in the main theory of this case that bears on that car, as far as I know. But again, if a man, or a young man, is telling falsehoods, *I put it forward as indicative of a guilty state of mind.*

But even more improperly it was argued by Crown Counsel that it was additional evidence of Truscott's cunning. He put it to the jury this way:

891,666 a 1949 grey Chevrolet registered to Mr. Pigeon. Now, we called Mr. Pigeon. He is with the R.C.A.F. Station at Clinton. We called him and he testified how on the night in question he went down from his garden on Number Four Highway, south to Brucefield going out, not by the east side – not by the County Road at all, but down through what is described as the main gate. I don't say he used that expression. You will be able to figure it out from the map. He never was near where Truscott put him, *and I suggest, Gentlemen, with respect, that Steven Truscott had seen that car around in the interval between the Tuesday and the Police coming to him, and he was getting some ammunition ready and he snapped out a number on the gamble that that car might have been on the County Road.* He got one digit off on the number. He got a shade off on the make. It is a Chev. against a Plymouth or Dodge. He had the grey right. But it misfired because we were able to bring before you Mr. Pigeon, and he never was on the County Road that night, and he related his movements.

(The italics are mine.)

The learned judge admitted this evidence and this was error. The error was compounded and the real damage done when he permitted Crown Counsel to make the charge of fabricating evidence without stopping him then and there. Without this unsupported suggestion, the calling of seven witnesses on this aspect of the case alone would have been nothing more than a waste of time, but all this time was used so Crown Counsel could put to the jury the idea that Truscott had fabricated the story in preparation for his defence. One may question in this connection why the evidence was limited to a transposition of the first three ciphers only. If one of the 6's be transposed with the figure 1 the number of possibilities is greatly increased.

The learned judge showed that he was well aware that the case was one where the jury might be influenced by the nature of the crime for he warned them at the beginning of his charge as follows:

There is another matter I should like to mention to you. The circumstances of the killing of this little girl are shocking. As I said, they are revolting in the extreme, and one would think that only a monster could be guilty of such a killing. The accused is charged with this monstrous crime and he is just a lad of little more than fourteen years, fourteen and a half. Now, you must not permit the fact of his youth in any way to prevent you from bringing in a verdict in accordance with your conscience. Nor, on the other hand ought you to allow the revolting nature of the facts surrounding this case in any way influence you to bring in a verdict which is, in any way, shape or form, contrary to the evidence, or based on anything but the evidence. You must not be prejudiced in any way.

But that warning came too late. It was nullified in advance by the manner in which the Crown had elected to build its case and by the judge's failure to exclude the evidence with which I have dealt and by his failure to stop Crown Counsel when in his speech to the jury he advanced subtly worded inflammatory arguments which should have been repudiated on the spot. Only in respect of the reference to Jocelyne Goddette did the judge tell the jury to disregard what Mr. Hays had said and in this particular instance the warning came much too late. It was not possible in my opinion to undo the damage done by this belated direction. There are instances where a trial judge may, by directing the jury to purge from their minds evidence which should not have been heard or to completely ignore erroneous statements or arguments made to them, enable a Court of Appeal to say under s. 592(b)(iii) that no substantial wrong or miscarriage of justice has occurred, but the present case is not one of those. The errors and inflammatory arguments were too numerous and too integrated into the whole of the case as to be capable of coming within the exception provided for by that section.

The evidence was as conclusive as evidence can be that Lynne was strangled and raped. It was argued on behalf of Truscott both at the trial and before this Court that Lynne was not murdered where her body was found. I do not find it necessary to go into this phase of the case in detail because, in my view, the evidence was such that the jury, if the issue had been properly left to them, could find that she was murdered at the place where her body was found. I will deal later with this aspect of the charge.

More important, however, in so far as Truscott is concerned is the submission that the evidence failed to establish that her death occurred prior to 7.45 p.m. on June 9th. If she was murdered later than this time, Truscott could not be the guilty person. It is as simple as that.

The argument that death was later than 7.45 p.m. June 9th was stressed by Defence Counsel at the trial. Both the Crown and the Defence went fully into the medical aspects of this issue before the jury.

In summary, at the trial Dr. Penistan the pathologist had testified that in his judgment death had occurred in the period between 5.45 and 7.45 p.m. June 9th, basing his opinion on the fact that Lynne had finished her supper at a quarter to six and that when the autopsy was performed, it was found that the stomach had not emptied as it would normally have done within two hours. Another medical man, Dr. Berkley Brown, a specialist in internal medicine on the staff of the University of Western Ontario, called on behalf of Truscott, testified that the stomach would not empty for a matter of three and a half to four hours. Here was a conflict on a decisive aspect of the case which the jury would have to resolve. The learned judge charged the jury as follows:

> According to Doctor Penistan, and to the medical evidence, she died at a time which is not altogether, in any view, inconsistent with her having finished her dinner at about a quarter to six. Doctor Brown says, and I must draw it to your attention, that it takes three and a half to four hours to empty the stomach and it is on the basis of that that the defence asks you to say that she could not have been killed before Steven returned at 8:00 p.m. You have Doctor Brown's testimony. It is unfortunate always, that medical men should disagree on what is more or less a scientific point. Doctor Brown says three and a half hours to four hours.
>
> Now, the stomach, of course, was not empty. Doctor Penistan said there was still a pint of food in the stomach and he removed that pint. It is true there is not a pint of food in the bottle now, and it is for you Gentlemen to accept or reject Doctor Penistan's evidence that he took a pint out, but Doctor Brooks was there and saw the pint. Don't forget that the bottle went to the Attorney-General's Laboratories, for tests and we don't know exactly what happened to it there except it was handed to some man whom we have not seen. *It will be for you to say whether you accept Doctor Penistan's theory, and Attorney-General's Pathologist of many years' standing, or do you accept Doctor Brown's evidence.*

(The italics are mine.)

The last sentence was clearly a misdirection to the jury. The jury should have been told that as between Dr. Penistan and Dr. Brown, if the evidence of Dr. Brown left a reasonable doubt in their minds as to the time of death, they must acquit. No jury can be told that they have to accept the evidence of one witness or that of another. The burden is on the Crown to satisfy the jury on every material aspect of the case beyond a reasonable doubt. I do not find it necessary to go in detail into the medical evidence given on the reference in this Court. This has been done in the majority opinion and is seen to be contradictory in the extreme. This much must, however, be said that it tends strongly to increase the doubt a juryman may honestly have had as to the time of death, if properly charged.

The medical evidence tendered in this Court and not heard by the jury cannot be used to nullify the damage done by this misdirection. The jury should have been properly charged. This Court cannot substitute its view of the medical evidence for that of the jury.

There is, however, one aspect in particular of the medical evidence heard in this Court that has an important bearing on the case. It is the evidence relating to the penile lesions. At the trial the Crown, on the evidence then before the Court, argued that the sores on Truscott's penis as described by Drs. Addison and Brooks had been caused by rape or forced intercourse. That was the theory of the Crown and the case went to the jury on this hypothesis. As such, it was, I think, the most damaging piece of evidence at the trial connecting Truscott with Lynne's death. The point was stressed by Crown Counsel. He said in part:

> Now, Gentlemen, Doctor Addison is a General Practitioner in the Town of Clinton, and has been for many years. You heard his background, his qualifications, and I suggest to you, one and all, that Doctor Addison comes into this case with no axe to grind and is worthy of credence. That Doctor Addison was an impressive witness, that is for you, Gentlemen. You saw him and heard him. Now, Doctor Addison would know all about, from his years and years of general practising, know all about the shape and nature and so on, of the private parts, both of a man and of a twelve-year old girl. And Doctor Brooks would know the same thing, and both those men pledged their opinion in that box, that the injuries to the accused's private parts were such as could have been caused by penetration of a young twelve-year old girl's private parts, and they went further, that observing these wounds, they would give their opinion they were from two to three days old.
>
> * * *
>
> Gentlemen, that is right in Doctor Addison's line and right in Doctor Brooks' line, and they gave that time as being two, three, four days, which would bring it right to the indecent assault on this girl, within latitudes, but you didn't get any help from Doctor Brown. To my best recollection of his evidence, he never talked about that at all. He couldn't. He didn't see them. If you received his evidence differently, use it. But I just submit, in short, that Doctor Brown's evidence in the abstract, we might call it, no matter how well intentioned, just can't, I respectfully suggest, throw any shadow of doubt on the opinions of Doctor Addison and Doctor Brooks as to cause and time that I have gone over.

The medical evidence given in this Court greatly negatived this theory although it was said that having sores of the kind described, they could be aggravated or rubbed by intercourse or by some other cause. There is a great difference in the two positions. The possibility of aggravation of an existing condition by one of two or more causes is altogether different from the assertion that the sores were initially caused by raping the girl. This becomes of greater significance when the admissibility of Dr.

301

Brooks' evidence at the trial is considered.

Particular stress was placed on Dr. Brooks' evidence that in his opinion the sores on Truscott's penis indicated "a very inexpert attempt at penetration". Dr. Brooks' evidence on this point was inadmissible. He was testifying as an expert as to a matter that was not in his special knowledge and the evidence was prejudicial to the prisoner. The majority opinion deals generally with the admissibility of Dr. Brooks' evidence. The only part which I consider inadmissible is the phrase just quoted.

In *Regina v. Kuzmack*, the right of a medical witness to testify as an expert, was dealt with by Porter J.A. as follows:

> When the doctor gave his evidence before the jury he was called as an expert to give his opinion as to the cause of death. Such an opinion is admissible when, but only when, the subject on which the witness is testifying is one upon which competency to form an opinion can only be acquired by a course of special study or experience. It is upon such a subject and such a subject only that the testimony is admissible. In the testimony of the doctor in this case, having described the wound in the neck, he went on to discuss two small cuts on the hand of the deceased, stating that they had been caused by a sharp instrument and could have been caused by the knife.
>
> "Q. Those cuts on the right hand, on the fingers, did they have any particular significance to you? A. The only thing I can say is to point out that when the hand was put up to the neck the wounds in the fingers were in the same direction as the wound in the neck. Q. And what is your conclusion from that? A. I would say that they could have occurred at the same time. Q. In what manner? A. I should think that the hand was at the base of the neck when the knife was put into the neck."
>
> The latter conclusion was quite incompetent for the doctor to give as an expert because it was merely conjecture and not on a subject requiring any special study or experience. It was a mere guess which anyone might have made. Yet it was given to a body of laymen by a doctor with the weight that ordinarily attaches to an opinion expressed by a professional man, and a doctor in particular.

There were references to another piece of evidence which, in my judgment, were very prejudicial to the prisoner. They are the references to the male sperm said to have been found on the underpants Truscott was wearing on the Friday night when he was arrested. Crown Counsel invited the jury to speculate from the dirty appearance of the garment that the undershorts in question were those Truscott had been wearing when he assaulted Lynne. Here is how he put it:

> My suggestion to you, Gentlemen, is that these are the underwear he was wearing, whether he took them off temporarily or not at the time of the indecent assault on the girl, and he did get this sperm at that time. You are just as capable

as I on reasoning that out, and I would be less than fair to you if I said or left you with the impression that you had nothing to go on. I tell you what I think you can go on. You can forget the evidence of bowel movement. You can overlook that when you get the garment out, and you can look at the rest of the under-wear, and you can figure, as I suggest to you, that it was worn a long time, and that is about all I can be of assistance to you, in this respect. Forget the fecal matter and just look at the other, and I think you will arrive at the conclusion – I suggest you will arrive at the conclusion he had it on for a good many days, and that you may be able to make the deduction that that is what he was wearing. As I say, whether he had it off temporarily, or not, at the time of the actual attack, and that the sperm is from the attack on the girl.

In his charge to the jury, the learned judge said:

It is said that the soiled underpants are consistent with innocence. You will recall the underpants that were taken off the boy at the jail were fouled as well as soiled. You need not pay any attention to the fouling. Mr. Brown, who exam-ined them in the laboratory, said that they showed evidence of blood inside and out. Inside and out. There were minute quantities, but particularly around the fly.

After the judge had finished his charge, Crown Counsel, amongst other things, in discussing objections to the charge, said:

And the other thing, My Lord, in your reference to the shorts at the jail, the Crown does attach great significance to the finding of male sperm on those shorts. Your Lordship mentioned blood. Your Lordship did not make refer-ence...

and on recalling the jury, the learned judge said in part:

Then, of course, the Crown relies very much on the fact that male sperm was found on the dirty underpants. That is consistent with an act of sexual interc-ourse, but of course, it is by no means conclusive that it is the result of sexual intercourse at all or sexual intercourse with this girl. It could be the result of other things, you know, but it is a circumstance which is not inconsistent. *It is consistent with an attack on this girl.*

(The italics are mine.)

All this might have been unobjectionable if there had been evi-dence upon which the jury could have found that the underpants in question had been those actually worn by Truscott on the eve-ning of June 9th. But there was no evidence to that effect. The point was conceded in the argument before this Court. That being so, the references by Crown Counsel and particularly what the learned judge said were prejudicial in the extreme based as they were on something that was not in evidence at all. Those underpants should never have been marked as an exhibit or shown to the jury. In any event, if reference could have been made to these underpants, then it was incumbent upon the

303

learned judge to put to the jury the defence which had been urged by Truscott's counsel that the medical evidence established that male sperm had a very short life. That sperm ejected on the Tuesday would have been dead and not identifiable as such long before Friday night in the circumstances of the heat and filthy condition as testified to. This he did not do.

A great deal of discussion took place regarding the evidence of the children who testified at the trial, some under oath, some not. I do not find any error in this regard. The learned judge exercised the discretion he had and in my view that discretion ought not to be interfered with. He charged the jury correctly that the unsworn testimony had to be corroborated before it could be acted upon. His charge on the subject of corroboration was correct. I must, however, refer specifically to the manner in which he dealt with the evidence of Philip Burns who had not been sworn. In instructing the jury, he referred to this witness and said correctly:

> Now the first is that Philip Burns was, of course, not sworn, and he said he didn't see Lynne and Steve on the road as he went north, and no one corroborates him in that respect, so that his evidence is worthless so far as you can use it in convicting the accused boy.

However, when the jury was recalled a few minutes later for more instructions, he said concerning this same witness:

> Then you, of course, won't forget Philip Burns' evidence that he left the river around between seven to seven-ten or thereabouts, seven-fifteen, and walked up the road and saw nothing of Steve and Lynne as he went up the road. That evidence was given, as I told you before, without Philip Burns being sworn.

How can one evaluate the effect on the jury of this contradictory instruction?

Nor was this the only instance of contradictory and confusing instructions. The conflict between the evidence for the Crown on the one hand pointing to Truscott having taken Lynne into the bush by way of the tractor trail and the evidence for the Defence that he had continued northward across the bridge with Lynne on the handlebar of his bicycle was, as stated in the majority opinion, the most vital issue in the case and it was one entirely for the jury. The learned judge in his charge put the issue to the jury as follows:

> Now then, it is the theory of the Defence, and they brought evidence to

show that, as I say, this little Douglas Oats saw them going across the bridge and then, in a few minutes, according to the boy by the name of Gordon Logan – Gordon Logan also says he saw them going north on the bridge and in about five minutes he says he saw Steven return alone. Well, as regards Gordon Logan, it will be for you Gentlemen to say whether you believe his evidence, and it is very important, Gentlemen, because if you believe the Defence theory of this matter and believe Steven's statement to the Police and to other people, that the girl was driven to Number Eight Highway and entered an automobile which went east; it is my view that you must acquit the boy if you believe that story.

In other words, I will put it this way. In order to convict this boy, you have to completely reject that story as having no truth in it, as not being true. You have to completely reject that story.

The concluding sentence of the first paragraph of the above was clearly misdirection. The second paragraph was a proper charge and put the accused's case favourably to the jury, but what did it convey to the jury when he equated the error with the correction by introducing the latter with *"In other words"?* A judge may state a proposition incorrectly and effectively correct the mistake but he does not do it by equating two divergent propositions.

Additionally, real and irreparable harm was done to the accused on this vital issue when the jury, having asked for a redirection as follows:

FOREMAN OF THE JURY:

A redirection of evidence, corroborated or otherwise, of Lynne Harper and Steven Truscott being seen together on the bridge on the night of June the 9th.

the learned judge, after reviewing the evidence in some detail, said:

That is the evidence with respect to him being on the bridge, the two of them being on the bridge together, the only evidence. They were there in the neighbourhood of seven twenty-five or seven-thirty, but as I pointed out to you, you must reject the story that he went to Number Eight and the girl got in a car there, you must reject that story to convict him. If you find that although he went to Number Eight Highway with the girl and he brought her back again – and she was back, somebody brought her back – you will have to find he did bring her back again – then the going back and forth across the bridge is of very little importance – very little importance, because the question is, did he kill her? That is the point in this case. If there is any other help I can give you, don't hesitate to ask me, Gentlemen, but that is all I can say about it now.

and still later when the jury was recalled a fourth time:

HIS LORDSHIP:
Bring the Jury back, please.
...Jury returned.

I dislike having to bring you back so often and interrupt your deliberations, but I do it only at the request of Counsel.

I told you when you were last out here, that if Steve brought Lynne back across the bridge, if he brought her back across the bridge, it doesn't make much difference whether he went over the bridge or not, but there is, of course, no eye witness that says that he did. No eye witness said that Steve and Lynne came back from Number Eight Highway, across the bridge, although there is Allan Oats and Logan who say that they saw Steve on the bridge alone. Logan saying five minutes after he went north he came back alone. Somebody brought her back some time. Somebody brought her back some time.

This introduction of the idea or theory that Truscott may in fact have taken Lynne to Number Eight Highway and brought her back to the bush had not the slightest foundation in the evidence or in any inference which could be drawn from the evidence. It came wholly out of thin air. The Crown's case was that Truscott had not taken Lynne to Number Eight Highway at all.

These redirections, particularly in view of the Foreman's question as quoted above, must on any objective reading of what was said, compel acceptance of the argument that the most vital issue in Truscott's case was actually withdrawn from the jury's consideration at this late time in the trial when they were told:

I told you when you were last out here, that if Steve brought Lynne back across the bridge, if he brought her back across the bridge, it doesn't make much difference whether he went over the bridge or not, but there is, of course, no eye witness that says that he did.

and coming as it did after the learned judge had said in his charge:

Now you see, if the accused boy drove or rode Lynne Harper to Number Eight Highway, then you must ask yourselves who brought her back, because somebody brought her back. Somebody brought her back. Is it possible that the accused brought her back? You will ask yourselves and you will ask yourselves the reason, if this boy is guilty, why he has shown such calmness and apathy. Is it because there is an element of truth in his story that he took her to Number Eight Highway, because somebody brought her back. Did he bring her back, if he took her?

The reference to 'apathy' in this passage by the learned judge was purely gratuitous. The word itself or a condition or conduct so describing Truscott does not appear in the evidence. It had been urged that his appearance and conduct were normal. The learned judge wrongly transposed 'normal' into 'apathy'. The dictionary definition of 'apathy' is 'insensibility to suffering or feeling'. 'Apathy' in relation to the crime in question here was a description highly damaging to the accused.

As previously mentioned, it was urged as a defence that Lynne had not been killed where her body was found. I have already expressed my view on this branch of the case. I think the jury was entitled on the evidence before them to find against this contention. But it was a defence open to the accused on the evidence and which had to be left to the jury. Here again, in my view, the learned judge withdrew that defence from the jury when in his charge he said:

> The Defence theory, what the Defence asks you to believe, is that she was attacked elsewhere and brought back dead. That she was attacked elsewhere, killed some place else. That theory, of course, is contrary to the medical evidence which says she bled at the place where she was found dead. She bled there and she could not have bled there if she were dead. If she was dead there would be no bleeding.

When Truscott returned to the school yard about 8:00 p.m. on June 9th, he was asked by Warren Hatherall, "What did you do to Lynne Harper – throw her to the fish" to which he replied, "No I just let her off at the highway like she asked." The following morning Lynne's father came to the Truscott home at 7:30 a.m. to inquire if the Truscott boys had seen Lynne. The older boy Kenneth said "No". Then Steven said "Yes, I took her to the corner on my bicycle and she hitched a ride on number eight highway". Later that same morning at 9:30 a.m., Truscott was interviewed by the police and he told the police that he had picked Lynne up outside the school the evening before between seven and seven-thirty; that Lynne told him she may go to see the people in the little white house on the highway and that she had to be home at eight or eight-thirty. He also said that having left Lynne off at number eight highway he cycled back to the bridge and while there looked back and saw her getting into a late model Chevrolet, which had a lot of chrome and could have been a BelAir model. He also said it appeared to have a yellow licence plate. He was interviewed several times in the next few days and told the same story, adding some details as he was questioned more closely.

The Crown took the position that Truscott was lying as to his movements after he reached the Lawson bush area on the county road. Accordingly, a great volume of evidence was tendered and received to convince the jury that Truscott was lying and that he had not gone any further north on the county road than the tractor trail at the north limit of Lawson's bush. No objection can be taken to this procedure because the Crown had the burden of establishing beyond a reasonable doubt that Truscott had taken Lynne into the bush and there murdered her, in other words to translate Truscott from the situation that he had had the opportunity to commit the crime into the certainty that he was the only one who could, in the circumstances, have done so.

It was for the jury to weigh that evidence. In the evidence so to be weighed was the vital question whether in fact Truscott could have seen and recognized a Chevrolet BelAir car with a yellow licence plate. Truscott insisted to the police that he had. The police evidence at the trial supported by photographs was that licence plates could not be seen from the bridge where Truscott said he was when he said he saw Lynne get into the car. On the evidence which the jury then had, the jury could reasonably have believed that Truscott was lying in saying that he saw a yellow licence plate. However, in referring to this important point, the learned judge confused the statement by Truscott to the police that he had seen a yellow licence plate with the statement made in respect of the old car with Licence No. 981,666. In his charge to the jury dealing with being able to see a car on number eight highway from the bridge, he said:

> The boy was asked by the Police, naturally, what happened, and he told the Police that he took her down to Number Eight Highway. He repeatedly told the Police that, and she got in a car. The Police took him down to the bridge and he pointed the spot where he was standing on the bridge, and the bridge is thirteen hundred feet south of Number Eight Highway, and they conducted certain experiments there to demonstrate that not only was it not possible, according to the police testimony, to see the numbers on a licence plate, but that you couldn't distinguish the licence plate at thirteen hundred feet. You heard the officers testify that that couldn't be seen.
>
> Now, you have to regard, of course, for the differences in ages and the possibility that a man at age forty has not as good eyesight as a boy aged fourteen. The Crown asks you to say that the story is a fabrication because you couldn't see the licence plate, much less could you read the numbers at that distance. And if he brought her back, if it was he who brought her back, it doesn't matter much. It doesn't matter much

and later said:

> The Crown submits the story about going away in a car is a complete false-hood because you couldn't read the licence plate from the distance that Steve says you could read it,...

When Defence Counsel drew the error to the learned judge's attention, he recalled the jury and said in part:

> I made an error in telling you that the number Steve gave of the car, was the car on Number Eight Highway. This was a car on the County Road, but it was not the car on Number Eight Highway.

That would have corrected the error effectively, but having so corrected the mistake, he continued:

> You will recall the Police went down and took photographs of the car, took photographs of the road with a car at the end of the road, and a car at Number Eight Highway, and they ask you to find from that and from the evidence of the Police officers, themselves, that it would have been impossible to have seen the licence plate of the car from the bridge and therefore, the story told by the accused is a fabrication.

neutralizing the correction he had made by inviting the jury to conclude from the photographs and the police evidence that no one could have seen the licence plate at that distance and in consequence Truscott's story was a fabrication.

On the reference in this Court it was shown that a yellow licence plate on an automobile at the intersection of number eight highway could be seen from the bridge if the car was in a certain position at the intersection. The Crown did not attempt to controvert this evidence. I am bound to say that had the evidence given on the reference regarding what could be seen from the bridge and concerning the unreliability of the photographs used by the Crown on this point been before the jury in the first instance, the jury could reasonably have taken an entirely different view of Truscott's story as put in evidence by the police *and of his credibility.*

At the trial the Defence stressed that Truscott could not have raped and murdered Lynne in the forty-five minute time interval that he was away from the school yard because if he had done so his clothes and person must necessarily have shown evidence of a struggle and he would have been blood stained and his appearance abnormal. The evidence was all one way that on his return to the school yard at about 8:00 p.m. he was normal without any blood on his clothes or on his person and that he chatted with some school mates before continuing on home to babysit as he had been asked to do by his mother. The mother too testified that there was no blood on the clothing and that the boy was normal as usual.

The learned judge dealt with this aspect of the defence as follows:

> At about eight o'clock the accused boy appeared back at the school. Ask yourselves, on this evidence, is there any explanation, on any construction of it, of the whereabouts of the boy between around seven-thirty and the time he appeared back at the school. John Carew saw him around eight o'clock and Lyn Johnson saw him and Lorraine Wood saw him come back and he stopped and talked to his brother, Kenneth. They heard some conversation about the trading of wheels and about the shoes he was wearing. Oddly enough, the older brother, Kenneth, has not appeared in this case. It is pointed out by the Defence, and very properly so, and it is something you must consider, and that is his demeanour when he returned, that he seemed to be natural. William Wilkes, who is age fifteen, who was called by the Defence – bring William Wilkes in, if he is here. He is in grade Nine at the Clinton Collegiate Institute.
>
> He says that they sat on the ground for ten or fifteen minutes and he talked to Steve, who appeared perfectly normal, and there were no marks on him or anything of that kind. Lyn Johnson says that he appeared to be normal. Lorraine Woods says he appeared to be normal, but I point out, Gentlemen, there are two sides to that meeting. There was a group of boys and girls playing around in this locality. They were all acquaintances. Perhaps I shouldn't say all. Lyn Johnson and Lorraine Wood were acquaintances of this boy. There was a group of children. Truscott didn't go over to them. He didn't go over to them, didn't spend any time with them. He talked to his brother and that is all, and then he went directly home. He may have been normal, but did he do what you would think a boy of that age would do, meeting his girl friends and boy friends when he came back on to the grounds. He was asked by Warren Hatherall, who had seen him go away, he was asked: "What did you do with Harper, feed her to the fishes?" Hatherall wasn't sure whether he answered or not. He didn't give an answer that Hatherall could give us, anyway.
>
> Stewart Westey corroborates Hatherall in part in that respect, because he says that when Hatherall asked the question, Truscott said: "I let her off at the highway like she asked."
>
> And William McKay, he wasn't sworn, a child age ten, said he saw Steve leave with Lynne and return alone and he asked Steve where Lynne was. Of course, his evidence unsworn testimony, age ten, is corroborated by Westey and by Hatherall. As I pointed out, Truscott didn't stop and talk to these boys, he went directly home. Miss Johnson and Lorraine Wood were not closer to him than fifteen feet. It is for you to say whether *at that hour of the night* they were in a good position to observe his demeanour and the looks of his clothes.

(The italics are mine.)

The jury who heard this direction could not but be influenced into believing that Truscott somehow kept away from anyone who might have sensed abnormality in his conduct or observed blood on his clothes or person. Any fair reading of the evidence given by those who were in the school yard when Truscott returned at 8.00 o'clock must convince one that Truscott did not keep away from anyone there, but on the contrary acted very normally while staying on the school premises for some ten to fifteen minutes. The reference to 'that hour of the night' would imply that the evidence indicated a condition of poor visibility. It was actually about 8:00 p.m. daylight saving time nearing mid-June when according to all the evidence on the point it was still broad daylight. Lyn Johnson, a witness for the Crown, who was, as the learned judge says, not closer than fifteen feet (she said about twenty-five feet) was able to describe how Truscott was dressed. She said in answer to Crown Counsel:

Q. How was Steven dressed?
A. He had a red pair of jeans on and a whitish shirt and brown canvas boots with thick rubber soles, and red socks.

A trial judge has the right to express his own opinion or opinions in the course of his charge to the jury, but he has the *duty* to put the defence of the accused fairly to the jury. This he did not do on this branch of the case.

For all of these reasons, as stated at the beginning, I would quash the conviction and direct a new trial.

Because I take the position that there should be a new trial, I have refrained from commenting on many aspects of the evidence such as the evidence of Jocelyne Goddette for the prosecution and that of Gordon Logan for the accused and that of many other witnesses and factors, the weight and value of which will be for the new jury if there is one. However, it should, I think, be said that if Jocelyne Goddette's evidence is accepted as sworn to by her it was about 6:30 p.m. and not at 7:30 p.m. that she was along the county road and the tractor trail looking for Truscott. In this connection the majority opinion says, "There is something very wrong with Jocelyne Goddette's times". She could be mistaken as to the time but it must cast doubt on her testimony that Truscott came to the Goddette home at about ten minutes to six. The interval between the two events was very short. That Truscott went to the Goddette residence shortly before six was an important and integral part of the Crown case. Jocelyne Goddette was the Crown's key witness in disproof of Truscott's story that he had taken Lynne further north than the tractor trail.

In several places throughout the majority opinion the point is made that as to such and such evidence or ruling or absence of ruling no objection was taken at the trial by Defence Counsel.

I could cite a score of decisions of this Court which say categorically that failure of counsel to object to the admissibility of certain evidence or to a trial judge's rulings in the course of the trial or to his charge to the jury, is not an answer to the objection or objections when advanced even for the first time in this Court. There are situations when the failure to object in the first instance will preclude counsel from being allowed to change his position, instances exist where the failure to object was intentional or not exercised and held in reserve to be raised on appeal and so on. In all of these, of course, the Court frowns upon the objection being raised for the first time on appeal. No such situation exists here. The consequences of Defence Counsel's failure to object at the trial do not fall upon counsel, but upon the client, in this case a 14½ year old boy on trial for his life.

I appreciate that after nearly eight years many difficulties will be met with if a new trial is held both on the part of the Crown and on the part of the accused, but these difficulties are relatively insignificant when compared to Truscott's fundamental right to be tried according to law.